W9-COW-678

XENOPHON

The Shorter Socratic Writings

XENOPHON

The Shorter Socratic Writings

Apology of Socrates to the Jury, Oeconomicus, and *Symposium*

TRANSLATIONS, WITH INTERPRETIVE ESSAYS AND NOTES

Edited by

ROBERT C. BARTLETT

CORNELL UNIVERSITY PRESS

ITHACA AND LONDON

First published 1996 by Cornell University

Printed in the United States of America

Library of Congress Cataloging-in-Publication Data

Xenophon
The shorter Socratic writings : Apology of Socrates to the jury, Oeconomicus, and Symposium / Xenophon : Robert C. Bartlett, editor.
p. cm.
Includes bibliographical references and index.
ISBN 0-8014-3214-6 (alk. paper)
1. Socrates. 2. Philosophers—Greece—Biography. 3. Philosophy, Ancient. I. Bartlett, Robert C., 1964– . II. Title.
B316.X5B37 1996
183'.2—dc20 95-37619

♾ The paper in this book meets the minimum requirements of the American National Standard for Information Sciences—Permanence of Paper for Printed Library Materials, ANSI Z39.48–1984.

Contents

Acknowledgments

I express my gratitude to the Social Sciences and Humanities Research Council of Canada and to the Andrew W. Mellon Foundation for postdoctoral fellowships that supported me during a part of the time I devoted to the preparation of this book. I am grateful also to Carnes Lord for graciously permitting me to reprint, in slightly revised form, his translation of the *Oeconomicus* that originally appeared in Leo Strauss, *Xenophon's Socratic Discourse: An Interpretation of the* Oeconomicus. Two anonymous reviewers read the manuscript with great care, and I am very much indebted to them both for their suggestions. Finally, I acknowledge the help in thinking about Xenophon that I have received from Professor Christopher Bruell. Whatever merits my contributions to this volume may have are due to his guidance.

R. C. B.

XENOPHON

The Shorter Socratic Writings

Editor's Introduction

After a century and a half of neglect, stemming from indifference or outright contempt, the writings of Xenophon are once again attracting serious scholarly study. This rehabilitation of Xenophon is clearest in the case of his political writings—the *Hellenica* and *Cyropaedia* in particular—and to a lesser degree his short treatises. Xenophon's four Socratic writings, however, have for the most part not received the attention they deserve, perhaps because those most likely to study them, the students of philosophy and political theory, have yet to shake off the view inherited from the preceding generation of scholars, according to which Xenophon was a far better soldier than Socratic.[1] The present volume is intended to rectify this deficiency, in the first place by presenting Xenophon as a competent and authentic Socratic who understood the core of Socrates' life and whose writings therefore reward careful study; and second by facilitating such study through the provision of new translations of the

[1] The most important exception is Leo Strauss, *Xenophon's Socratic Discourse: An Interpretation of the Oeconomicus* (Ithaca: Cornell University Press, 1970), and *Xenophon's Socrates* (Ithaca: Cornell University Press, 1972). Both are philosophic works in their own right, written with a concision that makes considerable demands on the reader: compare J. K. Anderson, *Classical World* 65 (March 1972): 240 with Christopher Bruell, "Strauss on Xenophon's Socrates," *Political Science Reviewer* 14 (1984): 263–318. See also Karl Joël, *Der echte und der Xenophontische Sokrates* (Berlin: R. Gaertner, 1893–1901); Sarah B. Pomeroy, *Xenophon's Oeconomicus: A Social and Historical Commentary* (Oxford: Clarendon Press, 1994); and Paul A. Vander Waerdt, ed., *The Socratic Movement* (Ithaca: Cornell University Press, 1994). A very helpful contribution is Donald R. Morrison's *Bibliography of Editions, Translations, and Commentaries on Xenophon's Socratic Writings, 1600–present* (Pittsburgh: Mathesis, 1988).

Apology of Socrates to the Jury, Oeconomicus, and *Symposium,*[2] translations that are aimed to be as literal as English usage permits.

The low estimation of Xenophon seems to have arisen first in Germany in the early-to-mid-nineteenth century and made its way from there to Britain and points west.[3] Its precise causes are difficult to determine, but reservations concerning Xenophon's moral character, his patriotism in particular, appear to have done him some damage. According to Theodor Gomperz, for example, Xenophon was marked by "arrogance and self-complacency" and engaged in "the most obtrusive self-glorification"; the way he "silenced [his] scruples" concerning the proposed expedition with the younger Cyrus "reveals to us a not very pleasing side of his character"—in general, an "unedifying versatility foreshadowed in his intellectual endowment as well as in his moral qualities, namely, in the excessive suppleness of his mind and tastes, in that lack of a solid centre of resistance which is as characteristic of the thinking and expressing as of the willing and acting personality."[4] B. G. Niebuhr is even harsher: "Verily a more degenerate son was never cast out by any state than this Xenophon! Plato too was not a good citizen . . . but yet how totally different is he from this old driveller, with his mawkish *stōmulmata* [chatter], and the lisping naïveté of a little

[2] For the fourth, see Xenophon, *Memorabilia,* ed. and trans. Amy Bonnette (Ithaca: Cornell University Press, 1994). That the three dialogues included here are meant to form a kind of whole apart from the *Memorabilia* results from the fact that, according to Xenophon, the activities characteristic of human beings fall into three categories, namely, speeches, deeds, and contemplation or silent deliberation (*Mem.* 1.1.19; *Anabasis* 5.6.28): the *Oeconomicus* is devoted to Socrates' speech, the *Symposium* to certain deeds, and the *Apology* to his deliberations, as is made explicit at the beginning of each dialogue.

[3] Some of the most important stages in the modern estimation of Xenophon can be seen in, G. W. F. Hegel, *Lectures on the History of Philosophy* (Atlantic Highlands, New Jersey: Humanities Press, 1983), 1:414; Friedrich Schleiermacher, "On the Worth of Socrates as a Philosopher," in *Xenophon's Memorabilia,* ed. Charles Anthon (New York: Harper and Bros., 1861); Eduard Zeller, *Die Philosophie der Griechen* (1844–52; rpt. Hildesheim: Georg Olms, 1990), 2/1:181–86 = *Socrates and the Socratic Schools,* trans. Oswald J. Reichel (New York: Russell and Russell, 1962). The coup de grace to Xenophon's reputation in the twentieth century was delivered by John Burnet; see, e.g., his *Plato's Phaedo* (1911; rpt. Oxford: Clarendon Press, 1989), xxi, xxvi, and passim.

[4] Theodor Gomperz, *Griechische Denker* (1895; rpt. Berlin: Walter De Gruyter, 1973) = *Greek Thinkers,* trans. G. G. Barry (London: John Murray, 1964); quotations are from 2:119–21 and 126 of the English translation. The episode Gomperz refers to is related at *Anabasis* 3.1.4–7.

girl!"[5] It is not possible to weigh here and now the merits of Xenophon's decision to aid Cyrus. Let it suffice to indicate that such moral qualms concerning Xenophon are by no means unanimous: Edward Gibbon, for example, states that "Cicero in Latin, and Xenophon in Greek, are indeed the two ancients whom I would first propose to a liberal scholar; not only for the merit of their style and sentiments, but for the admirable lessons, which may be applied almost to every situation of public and private life."[6]

What has probably done more harm to Xenophon's reputation today is the fact that scholars have lost sight of the need for, and hence have been unable to understand adequately, Xenophon's peculiar manner of writing, that is, his rhetoric. As one scholar has suggested, "It is reasonable to assume that the temporary eclipse of Xenophon . . . has been due to a decline in the understanding of the significance of rhetoric."[7] For according to the older view, to that of Cicero, Quintilian, and others, "the goddess of persuasion"[8] sat upon Xenophon's lips; Xenophon "the Attic Muse"[9] possessed, to an extraordinary degree, the art of persuasion or of rhetoric. Some of the manuscripts of Xenophon's works in fact go so far as to identify him as "Xenophon the Orator [*rhētor*]." To be sure, this identification must be understood in light of the fact that these same authorities, to say nothing of the man himself, considered Xenophon to be a Socratic. One may take as a working hypothesis, then, that the rhetoric of which Xenophon was a master is Socratic rhetoric.

Now Xenophon himself indicates something of Socrates' rhetorical strategy: if someone should contradict Socrates about something, but without having anything very clear to say, Socrates would bring the entire argument back to the hypothesis or presupposition and proceed through each point in the course of conversation, that is, "dialectically."

[5] B. G. Niebuhr, "On Xenophon's *Hellenica*," *Philological Museum* 1 (1832): 487 = "Über Xenophon's *Hellenika*," in *Kleine historische und philosophische Schriften* (Bonn, 1828), 1:467.

[6] Edward Gibbon, *Memoirs of My Life*, ed. Betty Radice (Harmondsworth: Penguin, 1984), 97, as well as 152. Consider also Strauss, *Xenophon's Socrates*, 179–80.

[7] Strauss, *On Tyranny*, ed. Victor Gourevitch and Michael S. Roth (New York: Free Press, 1991), 26.

[8] Cicero *Orator* 19.62 (also 9.32); Quintilian *Institutiones Orationae* 10.1.81–82, 1.33; Demetrius *De Elocutione* 37, 181; Tacitus *Dialogue on Oratory* 31.

[9] Diogenes Laertius *Lives of the Famous Philosophers* 2.57.

In this way, the truth became clear to his interlocutor, and perhaps clearer to Socrates himself. If, on the other hand, Socrates was permitted to go through an argument without challenge or interruption, he proceeded on the basis of mutual agreement or common opinion because he held this to be "safety in speech." In this latter procedure, Socrates took as his model the "safe" speech of Homer's wily Odysseus (*Mem.* 4.6.13–15; see *Iliad* 2.188–206). Thus Socrates possessed the capacity to speak differently to different audiences, to reach (mere) agreement with some on the basis of a reaffirmation of received opinion while attaining with others an agreement based on the recognition of the truth. The potential disparity between opinion and truth implied by this description of "safe speech" already indicates one reason for its use: to bring into question the truth of the most cherished opinions of one's interlocutor, opinions concerning justice, law, and the gods, for example, is to risk arousing his resentment and even anger.

That Xenophon himself possesses this capacity to speak safely or prudently is suggested by Dio Chrysostom in his remarks concerning the *Anabasis*:

> Should you be willing to read his work concerning the ascent [i.e., the *Anabasis*] very carefully, you shall discover no speech . . . which he has left out. . . . Should it be necessary to associate in a prudent way with the proud or conceited, and to avoid either suffering in some way at their hands when they are disgruntled, or enslaving one's thought to them in an unseemly way and doing what gratifies them in everything, these things too are present in [the book]. And in what way it is fitting to make use of secret speeches before generals in the absence of the multitude, and before the multitude in the same manner, and in what manner one should converse with kings, and to deceive one's enemies to their harm and one's friends to their advantage, and to speak the truth in a way that will not pain those who are needlessly disturbed by it and in a way that they will believe it . . . all these things the treatise competently supplies. (18.16–17)

Like his teacher, in others words, Xenophon is capable of saying different things to different people or of presenting the truth in such a way as to leave undisturbed those who might be troubled by it.

I suggest that when reading Xenophon one be alive to the *possibility* that the Socrates he presents makes use of the twofold rhetoric indicated. This amounts to nothing more than applying the guiding principle of Socratic rhetoric as stated by Xenophon to Xenophon's own Socratic writings. And through such effort, I submit, we begin to catch sight of a new, intriguing Xenophon, one characterized by "light-heartedness, grace, and flexibility"[10] who not only makes intelligible but indeed justifies the vivid and attractive portraits of him drawn by men of earlier times. Consider, for example, the remarks of William Barker, the first English translator, in 1567, of the *Cyropaedia*:

> Xenophon this philosopher hath not only travailed in the general knowledge of true reason to have right understanding [of] what is good and bad in life, and what is true and false in nature, but also travailed by experience to see the diversities of men's manners, and to acquaint himself with right order of civil government, and thereby hath attained to a great estimation of worthiness among the wise and learned, and judged a man most worthy, whose writings should be read with diligence, and travailed in for the fruits of wisdom. For he was Socrates' scholar.[11]

Especially intriguing—and beautiful—is the estimation of Xenophon, "that natural and simple genius of antiquity, comprehended by so few and so little relished by the vulgar," offered by Anthony Ashley Cooper, Third Earl of Shaftesbury, in his *Characteristics of Men, Manners, Opinions, and Times*: " 'Tis to the early banishment and long retirement of a heroic youth out of his native country that we owe an original system of works, the politest, wisest, usefullest, and (to those who can understand the divineness of a just simplicity) the most amiable and even the most elevating and exalting of all uninspired and merely human authors."[12]

The contemporary student or scholar may confess to feeling considerable puzzlement at this portrait of the philosophic Xenophon,

[10] Strauss, *Xenophon's Socrates*, 171.

[11] *The School of Cyrus: William Barker's 1567 Translation of Xenophon's Cyropaideia*, ed. James Tatum (New York: Garland, 1987), 3.

[12] Anthony Ashley Cooper, Third Earl of Shaftesbury, *Characteristics of Men, Manners, Opinions, and Times*, ed. John M. Robertson (1711; Indianapolis: Bobbs-Merrill, 1964), 2:309.

a "wise" and "most learned" man (Plutarch *Apophthegmata Laconica* §50; Polybius 6.45.1). What did earlier generations see that we for the most part do not? Might it be that Xenophon the Socratic has something to say after all concerning *the* Socratic question whose satisfactory resolution is, according to the Socrates of both Xenophon and Plato, the most serious concern for each of us—the question, namely, of the best way of life for a human being? The full rehabilitation of Xenophon depends in the first place on bringing this question to his writings, for only when we entertain the hope that the author may have something to teach us concerning a matter of this importance and even urgency will we be likely to apply ourselves with all the diligence we can muster; only this hope supplies the incentive needed to devote oneself to a careful examination of a text, its broad outlines as well as its details or nuances, its "form" (e.g., its dialogue form) as well as its "content." In so doing, one may come to doubt the merit of the contemporary criticisms of Xenophon and therefore also become open to the possibility, at least, that the earlier judgments in favor of him are correct. In order to test this possibility, the contemporary student or scholar would do well to approach the Socratic writings of Xenophon in a spirit of open-minded inquiry.

Even equipped with the motivation just sketched, however, most students today must rely on a translator to have access to a work written in a foreign language. Unfortunately, in the case of Xenophon, his English translators have not always carried out their office well. The translator of the *Memorabilia* and *Oeconomicus* in the Loeb Library edition, for example, states that Xenophon's mind "is a series of labeled pigeon-holes, each hole filled with a commonplace thought remorselessly analyzed. These elementary thoughts he produces again and again, for his reader's edification." And, "as with his thoughts, so with his words: he too often irritates the reader by incessant repetition of the same pattern of sentence, of the same formula, and even of the same word. . . . His mind moves in a narrow circle of ideas"—and this despite the fact that Xenophon is "a master of an extensive and multifarious vocabulary." Now from the "strange" fact that Xenophon "constantly uses the same word over and over again in the compass of a few lines," one might well conclude that Xenophon had good reason for doing so. The translator in question, however, convinced of Xenophon's dullness, can but shrug his shoulders: "A translator is often compelled to have recourse to synonyms."[13] To make Xenophon "better" than he is, to replace what Xenophon did say with what he "should" have said, is condescending not only to Xenophon but to the reader as well.

We have preferred to present Xenophon as clearly and precisely as possible and to let our readers judge for themselves. This means that we have followed Xenophon's Greek as closely as possible and have rendered a given Greek word by the same English equivalent whenever feasible, duly noting by means of a footnote the most important instances in which this has proved impossible. Although no translation can be simply literal and no translator simply free of the need to interpret, we have resisted the temptation to believe that we understand Xenophon better than he understood himself or that our minds moved in a larger "circle of ideas" than did Xenophon's. Such restraint on the part of the translator permits the reader to track the use of important terms—"justice," "the soul," "nature," "wisdom," "good," "noble," and so on—and to observe the varying contexts in which they are used. Whereas the translator of the Loeb edition felt obliged to render the word *aretē*, for example, as "moral benefit," "goodness," "excellence," and "virtue" (among others), we have consistently translated it by a single term, "virtue." To be sure, the precise meaning of *aretē* is a puzzle, but it is one that we believe Xenophon meant his audience to confront. And since readers can determine for themselves its various shades of meaning only by considering the different contexts in which it appears, the word must be allowed to appear. To conceal Xenophon's insistent use of a single term with a "multifarious" variety of terms is thus to deprive the reader of the opportunity of being puzzled by, and hence of learning from, Xenophon; it is to cover over his precision with a perhaps initially more pleasing but ultimately frustrating variety that is in any event foreign to him.

It should go without saying that literal translation brings with it some disadvantages, above all an occasional clumsiness of expression that is particularly regrettable in the case of "the sweetest and

[13] E. C. Marchant, *Xenophon in Seven Volumes* (Cambridge: Harvard University Press, 1923), 4:xxvi–xxvii.

most graceful Xenophon" (Athenaeus *The Deipnosophists* 504c). But unless or until one learns to read Greek oneself, this disadvantage is outweighed by the advantage of permitting the most direct access possible to what Xenophon actually wrote.

ONE

Apology of Socrates to the Jury

Translated by Andrew Patch

(1) And[1] regarding Socrates, it is in my opinion also worth recalling how, when he was summoned to court, he deliberated about his defense and the end of his life. Now about this others too have written, and all touched on his boastful manner of speaking[2]—a fact which shows that Socrates really did speak in that way. But they did not make quite clear that he already believed death to be preferable to life for himself, so that his boastful speech appears to be rather imprudent. (2) Hermogenes, the son of Hipponicus, however, was a comrade of his and reported about him such things as make it clear that his boastful speech fitted his purpose. For upon seeing Socrates conversing about everything rather than about the trial, this man said that he said: (3) " 'Shouldn't you also consider, Socrates, what you will say in your defense?' and that the other at first answered: 'Then don't I seem to you to have spent my life caring for my defense?' "

And [Hermogenes said[3] that] when he next asked, " 'How?'

I have used the text of François Ollier, *Banquet—Apologie de Socrate,* 2d ed. (Paris: Société d'Édition "Les Belles Lettres," 1972), by permission of Les Belles Lettres, Paris.

[1] The work begins with the copulative and/or adversative particle *de* as though in mid-argument (cf. J. D. Denniston, *Greek Particles,* 2d ed. [Oxford: Clarendon Press], s.v., C.2.ii [172]). Xenophon's *Oeconomicus* begins in the same way.

[2] The word here translated as "boastful manner of speaking" is *megalēgoria,* which means literally "talking big." It signifies arrogant or boastful speech.

[3] The words "Hermogenes said" do not occur in the Greek but must be supplied throughout Sections 3–9 and 11–27. Such ellipsis of verbs of saying is not unusual in Greek, especially, as here, in the context of a lengthy report. The name "Hermogenes" appears in the Greek only twice (§§2 and 9).

—'Since I have gone through life doing nothing unjust, which I believe to be the noblest[4] care for one's defense.' "

(4) And [Hermogenes said that] when he then responded, " 'Don't you see that the Athenian juries, when annoyed by a speech, often killed those who did nothing unjust, and often acquitted those who acted unjustly but whose speech moved them to pity or who spoke agreeably?' Socrates said: 'Yes certainly, by Zeus, and twice already I tried to consider my defense, but the *daimonion*[5] opposes me.' "

(5) And [Hermogenes said that] when he then said, " 'You say amazing things,' the other answered: 'Do you really believe it amazing if in the opinion of the god too it is better that I die now? Don't you know that up to this time I never conceded to anyone that he had lived better than I? For—a thing which is very pleasant—I knew that I had lived my whole life piously and justly, so that, while greatly admiring myself, I found that my associates recognized the same things about me. (6) But now, if my age will advance further, I know that it will be necessary to pay the dues of old age, to see and to hear less well and to learn with more difficulty and to be more forgetful of what I have learned. And if I perceive that I am becoming worse and I find fault with myself, how' " [Hermogenes said that] he said, " 'could I still live pleasantly?'

(7) " 'And perhaps,' " [Hermogenes said that] he then declared, " 'the god too, on account of his good will, is arranging for me that I end my life not only at an opportune age, but also in the easiest way. For it is clear that, if I am condemned now, it will be possible for me to avail myself of the death which has been judged by those in charge of this business[6] to be of all deaths the easiest, least troublesome to friends, and productive in them of the most regret.[7] For whenever someone leaves behind nothing unseemly or distressing

[4] Or, "most beautiful," "finest" (*kallistēn*).

[5] Socrates' famous "divine sign" or "voice." See, e.g., *Memorabilia* 1.1.2 ff., 4.8.1 ff.; Plato *Republic* 496c; *Apology of Socrates* 27c–e, 31d, 40a; *Theages* 128d1 f.

[6] Presumably the public executioners are meant.

[7] Reading *tōn teleutōn* with some of the mss. instead of *tōn teleutōntōn* with Ollier. The latter reading may be correct, however, for it supposes only a very minor as well as a common error in transcription (haplography), and it seems to yield less awkward Greek than the mss. It would alter the translation given in the text as follows: ". . . it will be possible for me to avail myself of the death which has been judged by the ones who are in charge of this business to be easiest, least troublesome to friends, and productive in them of the most regret for those who were dying."

in the thoughts of those near him, but passes away while having a healthy body and a soul able to show kindliness, how could he not be missed? (8) And the gods were correctly opposing the consideration of my defense speech,' " [Hermogenes said that] he declared, " 'at that time when it seemed that we must seek the means of acquittal in every way. For it is clear that, if I had accomplished this, instead of presently ending my life, I would have arranged to end it while being pained by sicknesses or by old age, where all the difficult and cheerless things converge.'

(9) " 'No by Zeus, Hermogenes,' " [he said that] Socrates said, " 'I will not eagerly promote these things; but as many noble things as I believe to have obtained both from gods and from human beings, and the opinion which I have of myself—if by displaying these things[8] I vex the jurors, then I will choose to die rather than to live longer by slavishly begging to gain a much worse life instead of death.' "

(10) And he affirmed that, since this was Socrates' view, when the plaintiffs accused him on the grounds that he did not believe in the gods in whom the city believes but brought in other strange *daimonia* and corrupted the young,[9] he came forward and said: (11) " 'But I, men, wonder at this in the first place about Meletus:[10] judging by what in the world does he say that I don't believe in the gods in whom the city believes—since both anyone else who happened to be present and Meletus himself, if he wished, used to see me sacri-

[8] Reading *tauta* ("these things") with R. B. Hirschig (*Miscellanea philologa et paedogogica* Fasc. 1:120, col. 14 [1850]) instead of *tautēn* ("this opinion") with the mss. Ollier prints the very difficult reading of the mss. but departs from it in his translation.

[9] The indictment appears to have been preserved in its original form in Diogenes Laertius (*Lives of the Famous Philosophers* 2.40). The charges as stated here seem to differ from those of the original indictment principally in two ways. First, where in the original Socrates is accused of having "introduced" (literally, "led in": *eisēgesthai*) strange *daimonia*, here the words "brought in" (literally, "carried in": *eispherein*) are substituted. Second, the corruption charge is here less clearly distinguished as a separate, second charge than it is in the original (as well as in the version of the indictment quoted in Xenophon's *Memorabilia* [1.1]).

[10] Meletus initiated the prosecution against Socrates, but he appears to have been in other respects the least important of Socrates' accusers. The Anytus who appears in Sections 29–31 below, on the other hand, seems to have been the most formidable of them. See Plato *Euthyphro* 2b; *Apology of Socrates* 19b1; and John Burnet on *Apology* 18b3 (*Plato's Euthyphro, Apology of Socrates, and Crito* [Oxford: Clarendon Press, 1979], 154).

ficing, at any rate, at the common festivals and on the public altars. (12) And how indeed would I be bringing in strange *daimonia* by saying that a sound from a god manifests itself to me, indicating what ought to be done? For doubtless others too make conjectures from sounds—some from cries of birds and others from sayings of human beings. And will anyone dispute with thunders either that they make sounds or that they are a very great omen?[11] And the priestess on the tripod at Delphi—doesn't she herself also announce the things from the god by means of a sound? (13) But doubtless both that the god foreknows what will be and that he forewarns whom he wishes—with respect to this too all say and believe just as I say. Yet, whereas others name what forewarns them "birds" and "sayings," and "signs" and "prophets," I call this a "*daimonion*" and I think that in naming it thus I speak both more truthfully and more piously than those who attribute to the birds the power of the gods. Indeed, that I do not speak falsely against the god I have this too as proof: though I reported the counsels of the god to many of my friends, never yet was I shown to have spoken falsely.' "[12]

(14) And [Hermogenes said that], when the jurors heard these things and raised a clamor—some disbelieving what was said, others being envious that he should receive from the gods too greater things than they themselves received—Socrates continued: " 'Come now, hear other things as well, so that those of you who wish may disbelieve still more that I have been honored by *daimones*: once, when Chaerephon asked in Delphi about me in the presence of many, Apollo responded that no human being was more free, more just, or more moderate than I.' "[13]

(15) And since the jurors clamored still more, as could be expected, when they heard these things in turn, [Hermogenes said that] Socrates continued: " 'But, men, the god said greater things in oracles

[11] The reading of the mss. Ollier reads *brontas* instead of *brontais:* "And will anyone dispute concerning thunders, either that they make sounds or that they are a very great omen?"

[12] The verb *pseudesthai* is translated throughout as "to speak falsely." It often means "to lie," but can also signify falsehood that is a result of error.

[13] Chaerephon appears in *Mem.* 2.3 and is mentioned as one of Socrates' associates at *Mem.* 2.2.48. The story of Chaerephon's consultation of the oracle is given somewhat differently in Plato *Apology of Socrates* 20e–21a.

about Lycurgus, who legislated[14] for the Lacedaemonians, than he said about me. For the god is said to have addressed him as he entered the inner temple, "I am pondering whether I ought to call you a god or a human being." He did not liken me to a god, but judged that I surpassed many human beings.[15] Nevertheless, do not rashly believe the god even in these things, but examine one by one the things the god said.'

(16) " 'Do you know anyone who is less enslaved to the desires of the body than I? And do you know any human being who is more free than I—I who accept from no one either gifts or wages? And whom would you be likely to believe more just than the one so well adapted to his present possessions as not to need in addition any of the possessions of others? And how could someone plausibly deny that I am a wise man—I, who from the very time that I began to understand what is said never yet ceased seeking and learning whatever good thing I could. (17) And don't the following things seem to you to be proofs that I was not toiling in vain? Many of the Athenian citizens who aim at virtue, and many foreigners, prefer to associate with me rather than with anyone else. And what shall we assert[16] is responsible for this: that although everyone knows that I least of all would be able to repay them, nevertheless many desire to give me some gift? And I am asked by no one to return benefits, but many admit to being in debt to me. (18) And during the siege,[17] while the others pitied themselves, I was in no way in greater straits than when the city was happiest. And while the others procure delights from the marketplace at great cost, I contrive, without expense, delights from the soul more pleasant than those. Yet, if in as many things as I have said about myself, no one would be able to convict me of speaking falsely, how then would I not justly be praised both by gods and by human beings?'

[14] Or, "had legislated." Cf. Herodotus 1.65.

[15] Reading *pollōn* with the mss. instead of *pollōi* with Johann Reuchlin (*Apologia, Agesilaus, Hieron* [Hagenau, 1520]), which would change the clause to: ". . . that I surpassed human beings by much [or by far]."

[16] Reading *ti phēsomen* ("what shall we assert"). Other mss. read *ti phēsomai* ("what shall I assert").

[17] See *Hellenica* 2.2 for Xenophon's account of this siege, which ended the Peloponnesian War.

(19) " 'But do you, Meletus, nevertheless assert that by engaging in these sorts of practices I corrupt the young? Doubtless we know what corruptions of the young are. Speak, if you know someone who, under my influence, has gone from piety to impiety, or from moderation to insolence, or from temperate living to extravagance, or from measured drinking to drunkenness, or from love of toil to softness, or who has yielded to another base pleasure.' "

(20) "But by Zeus," declared Meletus, "I know those whom you have persuaded to obey you rather than their parents!"

" 'As regards education at least,' " [Hermogenes said that] Socrates declared, " 'I admit it. For they know that this has been an object of care to me. But as regards health, human beings obey doctors rather than their parents. And doubtless in the assemblies, at least, all the Athenians obey[18] those who speak most sensibly rather than their relatives. In fact, don't you elect as generals whomever you believe to be most sensible in matters of war, in preference to both fathers and brothers—by Zeus, even in preference to yourselves?' "

" 'For this way, Socrates,' " [he said that] Meletus declared, " 'is both advantageous and customary.' "

(21) " 'Doesn't this seem to you to be amazing, then,' " [he said that] Socrates said, " 'that in the other actions the most excellent[19] do not receive merely equal treatment, but are preferred, yet I, since[20] I am judged by some to be best as regards the greatest good for human beings, namely education, for this I am being prosecuted by you on a capital charge?' "

(22) It is clear that more things than these were spoken both by him and by the friends who spoke out in his behalf. But I was not eager to say everything from the trial. For me it sufficed to make clear that, on the one hand, Socrates at that time[21] made it his goal above all else to appear neither impious as regards gods nor unjust as regards human beings; (23) and, on the other hand, that he did not think that he ought to hold out against dying[22] but believed that it

[18] The verb (*peithesthai*) translated here and throughout as "to obey," can also mean "to be persuaded (by)."

[19] Or, "the strongest" (*tous kratistous*).

[20] Reading *hoti* ("since") with Stephanus (*Xenophontis Opera* [Geneva, 1561]) instead of *ei* ("if") with one ms.

[21] Reading *tote* with the mss. instead of *to* with Reuchlin.

[22] Or, "to beg not to die."

was even an opportune moment for him to die then. And that this was his view became more manifest after he was convicted. For, to begin with, when he was bidden to propose a counterpenalty,[23] he neither proposed one himself nor permitted his friends to do so but said that to propose a counterpenalty belongs to one who admits to injustice. Then, when his companions wanted to steal him away from prison, he did not follow them but even seemed to make fun of them by asking whether they knew some spot outside of Attica to which death has no access.

(24) But when the trial was ending, [Hermogenes said that] Socrates said: " 'But, men, those who instructed the witnesses that they ought to break their oaths by giving false testimony against me, and[24] those who obeyed them—they must necessarily be aware of their own great impiety and injustice. But why should I be humbler than before I was condemned, since I was in no way proved to have done any of the things for which they indicted me? For I, at least, have been shown neither to sacrifice to strange *daimones* instead of Zeus and Hera and the gods associated with them, nor to swear by or name other gods. (25) And how could I corrupt the young by accustoming them to endurance and frugality? And as for the deeds for which the established penalty is death—temple-robbery, burglary, enslavement, and treason—not even the plaintiffs themselves said that I did any of these. So in my opinion, at least, it is something amazing how in the world it was shown to you that a deed deserving death had been done by me.'[25]

(26) " 'But that I die unjustly, not even on account of this should I feel humbled: this is shameful not to me but to those who condemned me. And Palamedes, who died in a similar way, also comforts me, for even now he still occasions much nobler songs than Odysseus, who unjustly killed him.[26] I know that, for me too, it will be borne out both

[23] In this case no penalty was prescribed by law. Instead, the jury had to choose between the alternative penalties proposed by the prosecution and the defense. Here, the prosecution proposed death as the fitting penalty.

[24] The omission in Ollier's text of the *kai* ("and") found in earlier editions is evidently a misprint, as his accompanying translation suggests.

[25] Following the quotation or periphrasis of Stobaeus (*Florilegium*). The difficult reading of the mss. would alter the translation given in the text as follows: ". . . my deed deserving death was shown to you."

[26] The traditional accounts of Palamedes' death vary considerably (cf. William Smith, *Dictionary of Greek and Roman Biography and Mythology* [London: John Murray,

by the time to come and by time past that I never did injustice to anyone or made anyone more base but benefited those who conversed with me by teaching without charge whatever good thing I could.' "

(27) Having said these things in a way that quite agreed with what had been said before, Socrates went away with beaming eyes and mien and gait. And [Hermogenes said that], when Socrates perceived those accompanying him crying, he said: " 'What's this? Are you really crying just now? Have you not long known that from the very time when I was born I have been condemned to death by nature? Now, indeed, if I perish prematurely while good things are flowing in, it is clear that I and my well-wishers must be pained; but if I end my life when difficult things are expected, I think that you all ought to be cheerful, on the assumption that I fare well.' "

(28) And a certain Apollodorus who was present—an ardent lover[27] of Socrates, but otherwise naive—then said: "But I, at least, Socrates, bear this with most difficulty, that I see you die unjustly."

And it is said that Socrates, after stroking Apollodorus' head, said: "Dearest Apollodorus, would you prefer to see me die justly or unjustly?" and that at the same time he laughed.

(29) It is said too that, when Socrates saw Anytus passing, he said: "This man is proud, on the grounds that he has accomplished something great and noble by killing me, because I, seeing that he was judged by the city to be worthy of the greatest offices,[28] said that he

1850], s.v., 3:92). According to another statement of Xenophon's Socrates, "everyone sings that Palamedes perished at the hands of Odysseus, who envied him on account of his wisdom" (*Mem.* 4. 2.23). See also the fragments of Gorgias' *Palamedes* (Hermann Diels and W. Kranz, *Die Fragmente der Vorsokratiker* [Hamburg: Rowohlt, 1957], 82 B 11A) and of Euripides' (August Nauck, *Tragicorum Graecorum Fragmenta* [Hildesheim: G. Olms, 1964], 578–590).

[27] Or, "follower." The noun is related to the verb "to desire" or "crave" (*epithumeō*), though not to the verb that means to love erotically (*eraō*).

[28] Anytus was chosen general in 409 B.C. He was in the same year unsuccessfully prosecuted for treason after the naval expedition under his command failed to relieve a besieged Athenian garrison. The failure was apparently due to bad weather, but Anytus had to win his acquittal by bribing the jury. He is said to have been the first of the Athenians to have done so (see Xenophon *Hellenica* 1.2.18; Aristotle *Constitution of the Athenians* 27.5; Diodorus Siculus 13.64; Plutarch *Coriolanus* 14.4). After the conclusion of the Peloponnesian War in 404 B.C., the victorious Spartans installed in Athens an oligarchic regime, later called the "Thirty Tyrants." Anytus was one of the most vigorous opponents of this oligarchy (Lysias 13.78; Xenophon *Hellenica* 2.3.42, 44) and hence became very important and powerful in Athens after its overthrow by the exiled democrats in 403 B.C.

ought not to educate his son to be a tanner.[29] How depraved this one is," he said, "since he appears not to know that whichever of us has accomplished more beneficial and nobler things for all time, that one is the victor. (30) But even Homer," [it is said that] he said, "ascribed to some of those at the end of life the power to discern what will be, and I too want to prophesy something. I was once briefly associated with the son of Anytus, and in my opinion he is not feeble in soul. So I assert that he will not persevere in the servile occupation that his father has prepared for him, but, on account of his lacking any serious supervisor, he will fall victim to some shameful desire and advance far in depravity."

(31) In saying these things he did not speak falsely: the youth, delighted by wine, did not cease drinking night or day, and finally became worthless to his city, to his friends, and to himself. In fact, Anytus, although he has died,[30] still has a bad reputation on account of the base education of his son and his own want of judgment.

(32) But as for Socrates, bringing envy upon himself by extolling himself in court, he made the jurors more willing to condemn him. Now in my opinion, he received a fate dear to the gods; for he left behind the most difficult part of life, and he obtained the easiest of deaths. (33) He also displayed his strength of soul, for when he recognized that to be dead was better for him than to live longer, he did not become soft in the face of death—just as he did not resist any other good thing—but accepted and completed it cheerfully.

(34) Indeed, I, when I consider the wisdom and the nobility of the man, cannot help but to make mention of him, and, in doing so, to praise him. And if one of those who aim at virtue came together with someone more helpful than Socrates, I believe that man worthy to be deemed most blessed.

[29] Anytus' family was said to have become wealthy through the manufacture of leather (Plato *Meno* 90a; scholium to *Apology of Socrates* 18b).

[30] According to one very late and doubtful story, Anytus was murdered in exile on account of his involvement in the death of Socrates (Themistius 20 [239c], but cf. Diogenes Laertius 2.43).

On the *Apology of Socrates to the Jury*

Thomas L. Pangle

That Xenophon's *Apology of Socrates to the Jury* deserves our attention, despite its now fashionable neglect, is easy to demonstrate. Together with Plato's *Apology of Socrates*, and to a lesser extent Xenophon's *Memorabilia*, it is the only substantial contemporary record we possess of the speech Socrates made in his own defense at his trial. Yet our interest in that speech is not merely or even primarily historical. The man generally credited (partly on the basis of Xenophon's testimony) with founding political philosophy[1] was sentenced to death, because of his philosophic activities, by a popular jury representing the city that was the home of perhaps the greatest democracy in history. What does this reveal about the essential and permanent character of the relationship between philosophy or political philosophy, as Socrates understood and practiced it, and civil society, especially democratic civil society? It is with this question in mind, and not in order to preserve an exact account of what occurred, that both Plato's and Xenophon's apologies seem to have been written. Certainly, neither work claims to be a verbatim report of what Socrates said, let

This is a revised version of an essay that first appeared as "The Political Defense of Socratic Philosophy: A Study of Xenophon's *Apology of Socrates to the Jury*," *Polity* 18 (1985): 98–114.

[1] Cicero *Academica* 1.4.15; *Tusculan Disputations* 5.4.10; *Brutus* 8.30–31; cf. Xenophon *Memorabilia* 1.1.12–15, 4.7.1–6 and Aristotle *On the Parts of the Animals* 642a28, *Metaphysics* 987b1ff., 1078b17ff. See also the discussion in W. K. C. Guthrie, *Socrates* (Cambridge: Cambridge University Press, 1971), 97–105.

alone what was said by his accusers and the friends who spoke on his behalf (§22).[2] In both cases the author is not a chronicler but a philosopher, whose dramatic reproduction of Socrates' defense forms a part of a corpus of Socratic dramas devoted not to a history of Socrates' actual words and deeds but to the poetic-philosophic presentation and justification of the Socratic way of life—as each student understood it—with a view to that life's lasting problems and achievements (see Plato *Second Letter* 314c). Through his highly selective and transformative re-creation of Socrates' defense speech, we may surmise that Xenophon means to guide our reflections on the permanent questions raised by his teacher's trial: What exactly are the sources of conflict between Socrates, or men of his type and way of life, and the rest of society? Can the conflict be muted or overcome? Can a "Socratic" speech be imagined which shows the way to a tenuous reconciliation, or a bridge, between the Socratic philosopher and society? If so, what sort of reconciliation or bridge?

From the very outset, Xenophon's *Apology* gives promise of helping to shed light on these questions. Its purpose, as stated in the opening sentence, is to recall the deliberation Xenophon's Socrates undertook, after he received his summons, concerning his defense and the termination of his life. Xenophon offers to take us behind the scenes, as it were, and give us access to the inner thoughts that dictated his Socrates' behavior in his last days. To be sure, Xenophon focuses on what he admits is only a part of Socrates' speech and deed, and hence intends to recall only a part of his deliberation—that which prompted his *megalēgoria* ("big talk," "boasting").[3] The "others" who have written about Socrates' defense and death have all "hit upon" or "touched on" this boastful speech; what others have only touched on Xenophon makes it his business to explain.

[2] Numbers in parentheses indicate section numbers of the *Apology of Socrates to the Jury*.

[3] Cf. John Burnet, *Plato's Euthyphro, Apology of Socrates, and Crito* (Oxford: Clarendon Press, 1963), 66 (= 146 of the 1979 paperback ed.): "It should be observed that *megalēgoria* is generally used in a bad sense, and that the Socrates of Hermogenes and Xenophon really is insufferably arrogant." The translation in the Loeb Library text is thus quite inaccurate as regards this crucial word. See also Guthrie, *Socrates*, 18–19.

The Puzzle: What Was Socrates' Purpose?

The most obvious reason why Socrates' boastful speech needs explanation is that it seems to have been rather imprudent—until one realizes that Socrates "already believed death to be preferable to life for himself" (§1). Xenophon speaks at the outset as if a chief factor in Socrates' deliberation was the latter's own self-interest. Certainly it is the likely imminence of his suffering the ills of old age that is Socrates' principal explicit reason for judging death to be now preferable; and Socrates welcomes the idea of the execution (i.e., being required to drink hemlock poison) because it affords "the death which has been judged by those in charge of this business to be the easiest" (§7). Yet Socrates goes on to add that such a death is also "least troublesome to friends, and productive in them of the most regret." In his understanding of his own welfare, then, Socrates includes his friends' attachment to him; moreover, in estimating what is best for himself, he takes into account not only his own welfare, narrowly defined, but also that of his friends. Shortly before, he had made it clear that in considering what is best he is concerned with whether or not he can continue to live "piously and justly," as he knows he has in his life heretofore (§5). But if Socrates' complex calculation of what was best for himself and others, given his advanced age, led him to welcome the prospect of the execution, and hence made his boastful speech not imprudent, what made such speech positively prudent? What was his purpose, such that "his boastful speech fitted his purpose" (§2)—such that his arrogant manner of speaking contributed to, and was not merely allowed by, that purpose?

Initially, the reader who is not careful may well sustain the impression that Xenophon is contending that the boastful talk is *fully* explained by Socrates' readiness, because of the imminent ills of old age, to undergo death by execution: that the simple, not to say simpleminded, thesis of Xenophon's *Apology* is that Socrates' reason for speaking in an arrogant manner was to incite the jury to impose on him the relatively painless death penalty, thus allowing him to escape the troubles of old age.[4] But a careful reading of the whole of the *Apology* dispels this impression.

[4] Thus Burnet, *Plato's Euthyphro,* 65–66 (=145–46 of the 1979 paperback ed.): Xenophon "excogitated the theory that Socrates deliberately provoked his condemna-

To begin with, Socrates is presented as concluding his account of the preferability of death for himself by denying that he intends directly to promote that death through his courtroom speech (§9). Socrates admits that what he intends to say may well "vex the jurors" and thereby heighten the likelihood of his conviction (see also §32); but he denies that *this* will be his purpose or intention in speaking as he plans.[5]

Besides, if Xenophon supposed that all that was required to explain fully the prudential reasons for the boastful speech was a proof that Socrates had previously decided that the trial offered a good opportunity to die, then it is hard to see why the work does not end in section 8 or 9. For by then he has presented the decisive evidence upon which the proof rests—namely, the testimony of Hermogenes about his conversation with Socrates. Why does Xenophon go on to devote most of the work to excerpts from Socrates' speech which illustrate the boastful speech, especially when "others" have already depicted it in their writing about the trial? And why, in doing so, does he continue to rely almost exclusively on the testimony of Hermogenes? We have, in fact, irrefutable evidence that Xenophon believed one could establish the proof in question without any quotations from the defense speech or any reference to subsequent comments and events: in the last chapter of the *Memorabilia,* Xenophon does just this. To prove that at the time Socrates himself preferred to die, he presents the same conversation with Hermogenes that is presented in sections 3–8 of the *Apology* (with minor alterations). Moreover, if we compare the two versions of the conversation with Hermogenes presented in the last chapter of the *Memorabilia* and in the *Apology,* we notice that the most remarkable difference between them is the utter absence in the former of any mention of Socrates' having talked in a boastful or arrogant manner at the trial. Xenophon can explain that Socrates had decided to accept the death penalty without making any reference to his decision to indulge in big talk. It would seem to follow, then, that in Xenophon's view the former decision does not necessarily imply, let alone explain, the latter.

---

tion in order to escape the troubles of old age . . . the *megalēgoria* of Socrates was something Xenophon felt bound to accept as a fact, though the justification of it was beyond the reach of his understanding."

[5] See Leo Strauss, *Xenophon's Socrates* (Ithaca: Cornell University Press, 1972), 138.

Finally, even if we were to discount as ironic or otherwise disingenuous Socrates' disclaimer of an intention, through his speech, to promote his conviction and execution, we would still find that Socrates' intention to bring on the death penalty fails to explain or justify the boastful speech. Doubtless the "big talk" did goad the jury, and thereby contributed substantially to Socrates' conviction and sentence. But was it the only, or even the most efficient, means to this end? If we attend to certain elements in the trial procedure that Xenophon highlights later on in the *Apology*, we see that such was not the case. In §23 Xenophon makes it clear that the procedure involved two separate stages: first, the jury decided the guilt or innocence of the accused; then, if it found him guilty, it determined his penalty. At the very beginning, in the indictment, the prosecution had to suggest a specific penalty (in Socrates' case, death by hemlock poison). The defendant, in the event of conviction, was offered the opportunity to make a counterproposal. The jury would then choose between the two suggestions. Thus, all Socrates had to do to receive the death penalty was to bring about a vote of conviction. This he could have done by offering a brief and palpably weak defense or by simply refusing to say anything, while letting the jury believe that he would do the normal thing, that is, propose a reasonably stiff counterpenalty. Even as it was, one must suppose that many members of the jury who voted to condemn never dreamed that Socrates would refuse to offer to go into temporary or permanent exile, or enter prison for a time, or propose some large fine to be paid by wealthier friends or relatives. Only after they had voted to condemn did it transpire, to their amazement, that Socrates offered no counterproposal (§23), and that hence their vote to convict was in fact a vote to execute. The boastful talk in the defense speech, not to mention the boastful talk Socrates allowed himself after the assessment of the penalty (§§24–26), was not necessary to achieve the death penalty. Arrogant speech was at most one of several possible courses of action that would have led or contributed to the death penalty.

What then *was* the deliberation that led to the strategy of boastful speech that Xenophon says it is his purpose to bring out in the *Apology*? Xenophon provides a crucial clue immediately after reproducing portions of Socrates' oration as it was remembered by Hermogenes. He begins by stressing that he has omitted a great deal of what was said in defense of Socrates, not only by Socrates' fellow pleaders but by Socrates himself. He then explains what intention guided his selection—and, by implication, what his intention is in the work as a whole: "For me it sufficed to make clear that, on the one hand, Socrates at that time [*tote*] made it his goal above all else [*peri pantos epoieito*] to appear neither impious as regards gods nor unjust as regards human beings; and, on the other hand, he did not think that he ought to hold out against dying but believed that it was even an opportune moment for him to die then" (§§22–23). The principal purpose which guided Socrates, *and which therefore explains his boastful talk*, was his intention to *appear* neither impious nor unjust. It follows that the truly arresting question Xenophon wants us to ponder is: what deliberation leads to the conclusion that arrogant boastfulness is the best means by which a philosopher like Socrates can appear neither impious nor unjust when accused by the city of impiety and corruption of the young? The suggestion is paradoxical, if only because the boasting obviously did not, and was not intended to, win the hearts of the jury. How can talk that infuriates the jury and seals Socrates' doom make him appear guiltless?

Hermogenes as the Key to the Work

I suggest that we seek our way to an answer by first raising a subordinate question: who was it above all others, and what sort of a person was he, before whom Socrates intended to appear in a favorable light by "talking big"? We need not look far; Xenophon has done everything in his power to spotlight one member of the audience at the trial, namely, Hermogenes, the son of Hipponicus. The *Apology* (in contrast to the *Memorabilia*) depicts Socrates not as he appeared to Xenophon but as he appeared to, and was remembered by, Hermogenes. Xenophon keeps this fact squarely before us, by couching most of the work in the awkward phraseology of "he said that Socrates said . . . and said that he said," and so forth. In the *Memorabilia* (4.8.11), Xenophon notes that he knows Socrates told "the others" the same "sort" of thing he told Hermogenes before the trial; but it is Hermogenes' account that he has singled out. In effect,

Xenophon tells us that if we wish to comprehend Socrates' purpose in "talking big," we need to know how that boastful talk, and its prelude and aftermath, struck Hermogenes: "Hermogenes, the son of Hipponicus, however, was a comrade of his and reported about him such things as make it clear that his boastful speech fitted his purpose" (§2). Socrates intended to make an impression primarily upon Hermogenes (and perhaps others akin to Hermogenes), and through him, upon others; Xenophon intends to foster that transmission.

Who, then, is Hermogenes and what does he represent? The other three Socratic writings of Xenophon show that he is a figure of some importance in the Socratic circle. In the *Symposium*, Hermogenes is one of the principal interlocutors. Near the beginning of Socrates' long speech on love in that work, when Socrates lightheartedly surveys some of the company, we find a vivid, if somewhat tongue-in-cheek, sketch of Hermogenes' personality:

> And as for Hermogenes, who among us doesn't know that he is melting away with love of gentlemanliness [*kalokagathia*], whatever in the world it may be? Don't you see how serious are his brows, how steady his eye, how measured his speeches, how gentle his voice, how cheerful his character? And although he associates with the most august gods as friends, do you see that he doesn't feel contempt for us human beings? (8.3)

Hermogenes comes to sight here as a man of considerable moral seriousness and pride, whose sense of dignity is enhanced by a belief in a very special, personal relationship with the gods—not necessarily all the gods, but surely "the most august." Yet, Hermogenes is evidently not quite a perfect gentleman. Socrates indicates this by characterizing him as one who is possessed by love for gentlemanliness, whatever it may be. As the immediate context shows, love as understood here is *eros*, the passionate longing for what one lacks. Hermogenes longs for the gentlemanliness he does not wholly possess. Indeed, Socrates' words suggest that Hermogenes, like Socrates himself, is not absolutely certain as to just "whatever gentlemanliness may be." In this respect Hermogenes is very different from Lycon, who is also a prominent figure at this drinking party and who later becomes one of Socrates' three accusers. Lycon has no love or erotic longing for gentlemanliness because he "knows" he is a gentleman. If he longs for anything, it is that his son, Autolycus, may grow up to become as perfect as his father (cf. 2.4–7; 3.12–13; 9.1) But in what respect is Hermogenes deficient as regards gentlemanliness? And how can his lack, or his sense of a lack, go together with his immense pride and his belief in his closeness to the most august gods?

Hermogenes is poverty-stricken. We learn from the *Memorabilia* (2.10) that when he was on the brink of financial ruin, Socrates saved him by discreetly bringing his plight, and his talents, to the attention of an acquaintance. Hermogenes thus lacks what Aristotle later called the "equipment" (*chorēgia*) necessary for the performance of many or most of the noble deeds of gentlemanly virtue. He has no estate to manage, he cannot afford a horse or even heavy armor, he cannot bestow entertainment or gifts, he cannot prove his taste by endowing magnificent temples or festivals or sacrifices, he cannot run for high political office. But if Hermogenes is so lacking in wherewithal, what led him to aspire to be a gentleman? What is more, how did he find the leisure, get the education, and form the tastes that allow him to associate with Socrates and his rather wealthy friends? In particular, what is he doing at a party at the house of Callias—in all likelihood the richest, and indubitably the most lavish, aristocrat in Athens?

The simple but paradoxical answer is that Hermogenes is the brother of Callias who, too, is the son, and also the sole heir, of Hipponicus. As such, Callias has not only untold riches but one of the most respectable lineages in Greece. His importance in civic affairs is attested by his family ties to both Pericles and Alcibiades, but most of all by his occupying, as a matter of family right, an unusually conspicuous sacerdotal office. As Socrates says near the end of his speech on love, addressing Callias: "For the greatest things belong to you: you are of a good family [*eupatridēs*], a priest of the gods of Erechtheus' descent, gods who led the army under Iacchus against the Barbarian. And now in the festival you make an appearance as priest that is more impressive than your ancestors" (8.40). Callias, as is abundantly clear from the *Symposium* (1.4; 4.62), made use of his position and wealth to become *the* patron of the Sophists, and to make his home into a kind of salon where the intellectually and politically most respected found entertainment (cf. Plato's *Protagoras; Cratylus*

391b–c; *Apology of Socrates* 20a). He was, in a word, the splendid pinnacle of Athenian upper-class society. It should perhaps come as no surprise that he also became a man of very dubious morals, around whom scandal swirled (see Andocides *On the Mysteries*).

It was into this prestigious world that Hermogenes was born, and from which—for reasons we do not quite know—he was disinherited (Plato *Cratylus* 391c). Hermogenes belongs, and yet does not belong, to the highest circles of conventional nobility. His extraordinary pride, we may surmise, is fueled by his understandable reaction against the rather low position in which civic and family convention places him. Similarly, his unique piety can be understood as a manifestation of his lofty refusal to accept the conventional estimation of his stature among gods and men, especially in contrast to that of his brother, the priest. The special character of Hermogenes' piety is brought into sharp relief by Xenophon earlier in the *Symposium*. At Socrates' urging, a playful contest is held in which a number of those present give speeches displaying that on which they most pride themselves. When it is Hermogenes' turn to state the subject of his speech, he gives the following response:

> "And you, Hermogenes," said Niceratus, "what do you exult in most of all?"—And he said, "The virtue and power of my friends and that, being of this sort, they are concerned with me." At this point everyone turned toward him, and many asked in unison whether he would make clear to them who these were. He said that he would not begrudge doing so. (3.14)

The friends turn out to be the gods—certain omniscient and omnipotent gods, common to Greeks and barbarians alike, whom Hermogenes refrains from mentioning (§13, and Plato's *Cratylus*, esp. 397c–d). After Hermogenes' brief speech on these unnamed gods and their care for him, which Xenophon says is the only wholly serious speech in the *Symposium*, Socrates initiates an exchange that Xenophon treats as part of this "seriously spoken *logos*."

> "Well there is nothing unbelievable in these things. Yet I for my part would gladly learn how it is that you tend to them and thus have them as friends."—"By Zeus," said Hermogenes, "very inex-

> pensively! For I praise them but spend no money; I always offer up something from what they give me; I speak as piously as I can; and I never wittingly lie when I have invoked them as witnesses."—"By Zeus," said Socrates, "if you, being of this sort, have them as friends, the gods too, it seems, are pleased by gentlemanliness!" (4.49)

Socrates, who lived in poverty, appears certain that poverty is no bar to gentlemanliness; and if Hermogenes is right about the gods, then the self-consciously incomplete or still "erotic" kind of gentlemanliness he and Hermogenes share may be perfectly pious. The impoverished Socrates and Hermogenes have in common an unconventional self-respect that is intimately linked with a claim to a special kind and degree of piety.

Xenophon's Teaching, I: The Political Lesson

We are now in a position to take our measure of Hermogenes. The picture emerging from Xenophon's varied presentation is that of an unphilosophic nobleman of the greatest high-mindedness, who has had many of the benefits of an aristocratic upbringing, but whose circumstances have induced him to take his proud distance from, and even to hold in some contempt, much of what is held to be conventionally respectable in terms of family, politics, and religion. This is not to say that he is a rebel against his city or his people; no one could possibly suspect him of indecency, sedition, or impiety. Yet, he stands at the margin, in a kind of noble aloofness. I suggest Xenophon wants to teach us that men of this kind, properly cultivated, can become reliable allies and important spokesmen for the Socratic philosopher—especially when "the chips are down." For to such men the philosopher, even or especially when he is in public disfavor, can appear as a kind of kindred spirit.

Socrates' independent and frugal or ascetic way of life, his propensity to question or voice wonderment at the customary notions of gentlemanliness and education for gentlemanliness, harmonize with Hermogenes' own reservations in these matters. Even more important, the unorthodox piety of a Socrates—his combination of avowed ignorance or cautious inquiry about the gods, together with the claim to possess a demonic voice by which he receives special guidance for himself and his friends—strikes a sympathetic chord. The fact that Socrates' heterodoxy, especially his demonic voice, eventually led him into conflict with the powers that be in society does not come as a great shock to Hermogenes. Moreover, Hermogenes is aware of the deficiencies of democratic legal procedure, and is therefore eager at first to prompt Socrates to devise a defense that will enable him to escape conviction "by any means necessary" (§§4, 8). He knows Socrates to be a great talker although he himself is capable neither of eloquence nor of quick-witted argument (cf. Plato *Cratylus* 408b). From his noteworthy elenchus of Socrates in the *Symposium* (6.3), it would appear that on occasion he could even be disapproving of Socratic loquaciousness. Yet, on the other hand, Hermogenes sees in Socrates a friend who can supply an awesomely articulate defense of their shared marginal but fiercely independent position in society. It seems altogether likely that he came to be delighted that circumstances at the time of the trial allowed Socrates finally to throw caution to the winds and speak his mind freely. On that great day, Socrates stood up and told off the entire city! At any rate, Xenophon gives the impression that Hermogenes retained a vivid memory of the trial and of what Socrates said prior to the trial, and did not hesitate to recall it for anyone who would listen. The vividness of the memory is not necessarily a sign of its accuracy. Apparently, what Hermogenes heard, or remembers having heard, was mainly the big talk—the proud and censorious words of his eloquent friend. Once we understand Hermogenes, we begin to realize that the account Xenophon provides by way of his memory is one that is almost bound to be distorted. What a man like Hermogenes remembers Socrates as saying—even what he actually heard and comprehended—is very different from what a Xenophon would have heard or what a Socrates would have said.

Yet Xenophon insists that we listen to hear how Socrates is remembered by a man like Hermogenes; he implies that Socrates wanted to be remembered, in part at least, as Hermogenes would remember him. Why? We have now seen why a man like Hermogenes would be attracted to a philosopher like Socrates; but why is Socrates drawn to Hermogenes? Why did Socrates, at the time of the trial and even in the years before, kindle and reciprocate the strong sympathy Hermogenes felt?

The first and most obvious (if the least important) reason is that a man like Hermogenes—with his education, energy, and loyalty—is of considerable practical usefulness. In the *Memorabilia,* Socrates speaks of him as follows:

> Now you know that Hermogenes is not wanting in judgment; and he would be ashamed if after being benefited by you he failed to benefit you in return. Indeed, one who serves voluntarily, whose mind is benevolently disposed, who is steadfast and capable of doing what he is bid, and who is not only capable of doing what he is bid but also has the power to be useful on his own initiative both in exercising foresight and in deliberating beforehand, is, I believe, equal in value to many servants. (2.10.3)

But of much more importance than the active assistance individuals like Hermogenes might render is the *reputation* that surrounds these men, a reputation with which the philosopher may prudently associate himself and his true friends. No one fears a Hermogenes; and if the belief in his harmlessness is tinged with a certain contempt, that contempt is no bar to the conviction that Hermogenes is a man of unquestionable probity, piety, and uprightness. Hermogenes is the perfect witness for Xenophon to appeal to when he rebuts those who accuse Socrates of lying about the existence of his demonic voice (*Memorabilia* 4.8). One may go further. To the public, a man like Hermogenes is almost the polar opposite of a man like Alcibiades. In the *Memorabilia* (1.2.48), when Xenophon seeks to refute those who adduce Critias and Alcibiades to show that Socrates corrupted young Athenian citizens, he offers a list of seven counterexamples of those who "consorted with him not in order to become popular public leaders or skillful in the courtroom, but in order to become gentlemen . . . not one of whom either in his youth or in his later years did anything wrong or incurred accusation": Hermogenes is at the center of the list.[6] After all, how could someone who is the close comrade of a man like Hermogenes ever be justly suspected of impiety? Hermogenes and men like him are living proof that proud, even assertive, unorthodoxy as regards the divinities, and as regards education in gentlemanliness, is by no means a necessary sign of corruption. By associating with such men, the philosopher secures some protection for himself and his students. And by leaving behind such men as his outspoken defenders even after his legal execution, the philosopher continues to gain some important protection for his enterprise and his surviving students (like Xenophon). Thus, in the long run, Socrates' big talk is directed, by way of Hermogenes, to the city as a whole.

Moreover, the image Xenophon's Socrates leaves is not merely that of a strange comrade of, or kindred spirit to, the pious and moral Hermogenes. It is also, much more dramatically, the image of a man admired, even worshipped, by Hermogenes because of his godlike self-sufficiency and Olympian pride. Now there are many in the city who share a portion, at least, of Hermogenes' spirit or taste, and admire—if only grudgingly—this kind of spiritual autonomy. For these, the image Xenophon's Hermogenes presents may well provoke, eventually, a sense of remorse. In other words, precisely the image of pride, verging on arrogance, which initially goads the city to kill Socrates may in years to come redouble the regret of some—and compel them to think twice before they vent their anger on other proud, unorthodox philosophers. In addition, there may always be a few truly "proud men"—in Aristotle's sense of "the perfect gentlemen"—who, because of their own stature and reserve, would never become followers of Socrates, but who might well come to see something admirable in him by way of the depiction presented by Hermogenes. Last but not least, this particular depiction of the philosopher as a man of almost divine inner independence is one that may awaken the longing or *eros* of young people with genuine

[6] Without Hermogenes, the list is rather thin: of the other six, three are foreigners (Simmias, Cebes, Phaedondas—cf. Plato *Phaedo* 59c), two are the brothers Chaerecrates and Chaerophon, the latter of whom was publicly accused of atheism along with Socrates in Aristophanes' *Clouds*, and one is Socrates' neighbor and old family friend Crito, whose n'er-do-well son Critoboulus Socrates sought to educate without great success (cf. *Symposium* 4.23–28; *Memorabilia* 1.3.8–13; 2.6; *Oeconomicus*; Plato *Euthydemus* 306d).

philosophic potential. Hermogenes, this would mean to say, is also the unwitting carrier of a message of seduction to souls considerably superior to his own.

We must not overlook, however, the peculiar difficulties or dangers a man like Hermogenes presents, and which Xenophon shows Socrates trying gently to alleviate. However sound the judgment of such a man may be in general, he is constitutionally liable to an assertion of his dignity and independence which may verge on imprudent insolence. In the particular case of Hermogenes, the political risk is lessened by his limited abilities as a speaker. Nevertheless, the example of public arrogance with which Socrates closed his life might prove a dangerous precedent for Hermogenes and his type—were it not for the fact that Socrates went to great lengths to stress to Hermogenes the essential precondition for his unrestrained speech, namely, his own certainty, corroborated by the divine sign, that for his own good, and at that time, death had become preferable to continued life. We can now appreciate the perfect appropriateness—with a view to the effect on Hermogenes and others like him—of the peculiar mixture of arrogant disdain and hardheaded calculation which Socrates evinces in the *Apology*. The continual need for the careful calculation of one's own interest was doubtless one of the major lessons Socrates strove always to inculcate in Hermogenes as well as in other noble men whose tendency to headstrong or thoughtless pride needed restraint (consider book 2 of the *Memorabilia*, chaps. 7–end). Certainly Socrates' demonic voice and, therefore, his piety represent a kind of divine inspiration that was *never* at odds with his personal well-being (see §§5, 8, 33). As for Hermogenes' other, less dangerous proclivities—his heavy moralism, his tendency to withdraw into an unphilanthropic isolation—the *Symposium* reveals, with Xenophon's characteristic deftness, the manner in which Socrates sought to correct these vices and make of someone like Hermogenes a more convivial and useful member of society.[7]

[7] In Plato's Socratic writings, Hermogenes makes an appearance twice: once as a member of the group that was present at Socrates' death (*Phaedo*) and, more important, as the chief interlocutor of one of the longer dialogues, the *Cratylus*. The vivid portrait of Hermogenes in the *Cratylus* confirms and complements Xenophon's depiction. The *Cratylus* is the dialogue devoted to the theme of language, especially names and nouns, and more precisely Greek names and nouns. In it Socrates leads Hermogenes back from an overly enthusiastic attachment to nature and overly scornful atti-

We must finally observe that the usefulness and importance of Hermogenes as a spokesman for Socrates is fully actualized, not through any efforts of Socrates himself, but through the rhetorical genius of Xenophon. For taken by himself, Hermogenes is too much a figure of contempt to attract great respect or repute for Socrates. Hermogenes' report of Socrates is immortalized not because it is by Hermogenes, but because it is by Xenophon—a man whose noble exploits in war, and whose educative writings in peace, established him as a figure bound to attract the respect and even the awe of future generations of proud gentlemen. The Hermogenean portrait of Socrates is delivered to us, or to the world in general, as a portrait that is primarily Xenophontic—that is, advertised, presented, and vouched for by the famous leader of men and noble teacher of gentlemanly souls. Whether and to what extent this observation indicates a decisive incompleteness in Socrates' own strategy in defense of his circle must here remain an open question.

Xenophon's Teaching, II: The Justice or Virtue of the Socratic Philosopher

Thus far, I have described the lesson Xenophon conveys as regards a key aspect of the Socratic philosopher's political prudence. But this lesson points, beyond itself, to another and ultimately more significant dimension of the work. Xenophon's Hermogenes provides us with more than the lively image of one of Socrates' more important bridges to, and defenses against, the fervent beliefs of the political community. A man like Hermogenes focuses on, and through his report highlights for us, crucial truths about Socrates' extraordinarily proud or independent posture toward political society at large: truths that in any other context would be imprudent for Xenophon to

---

tude toward convention (derived, perhaps, in part from a study of Anaxagoras) to a new respect for Greek tradition, especially the names of the Greek gods and heroes. Socrates accomplishes this partly by appealing to the teachings of Euthyphro (cf. the *Euthyphro*). The opinions of a Euthyphro are the antidote to the bent of a Hermogenes: Hermogenes is the extreme opposite, in one sense, of a fanatic traditionalist or "bible-belt preacher" like Euthyphro.

present so plainly. It is chiefly this deeper level of Xenophon's teaching in the *Apology* that Leo Strauss[8] has addressed with his characteristic penetration—and also with his characteristic "avoidance of prolixity." Given the extraordinary difficulty and compactness of Strauss's discussion, it would not be redundant to explain and enlarge somewhat the points he has made.

In order to reach the truth of what Socrates says about himself in the *Apology*, we must bear in mind that he is here presented as indulging in a kind of boastfulness or *alazoneia* calculated, in the short run, to enrage most of his immediate audience, but to gratify men like Hermogenes. That is, Socrates is shown as exaggerating his independence from, and his disdain for, civil society. Now it is fair to say that in his other three writings Xenophon mostly avoids such boastfulness or exaggeration, both in what he says in his own name and in what he puts in the mouth of Socrates. On its face, this might seem to imply that the *Apology* is by far the least reliable of what Shaftesbury[9] has called the "system" of Xenophon's Socratic writings. But that this conclusion is too hasty becomes apparent as soon as we recollect that Socrates was famous for speaking of himself in an ironic manner. That is, Socrates usually exaggerated in the opposite sense from the way he is shown exaggerating in Xenophon's *Apology*: he generally indulged in the graceful vice of untrue self-deprecation, by which he partially masked his own sense of superiority to his fellowmen (*eirōneia*: see Aristotle *Nicomachean Ethics* 1127a12–b33). He did this because he "spent his life" paying heed to how he might defend himself (*Memorabilia* 4.8.4; *Apology* §3), or because he was, like Odysseus, a "safe speaker" or "safe orator"—that is, one who spoke with a view to inducing in most of his listeners the maximum of agreement with his statements (*Memorabilia* 4.6.15). It is almost certain that the "orator" Xenophon, in his writings in his own name—and especially in the *Memorabilia*, whose explicit purpose is the defense of Socrates against any and all suspicions of illegality or injustice—followed this example. On the basis of these observations I pose the following heuristic question: may not the truth about the

[8] Strauss, *Xenophon's Socrates*, 129–140.

[9] Anthony Ashley Cooper, Third Earl of Shaftesbury, *Characteristics of Men, Manners, Opinions, and Times* (Indianapolis: Bobbs-Merrill, 1964), 2:309.

Xenophontic Socrates' understanding of his relation to civil society lie somewhere between the impression given by the *Apology* and the impression given by Xenophon's other three Socratic writings? Or, put another way, must we now allow the *Apology* weight out of all proportion to its brevity and lack of certain superficial charms, when we balance it against the other Xenophontic reports of Socrates?

Let me illustrate the thrust of this question by concentrating on a few of Socrates' most thought-provoking statements in the *Apology*. In the course of explaining to Hermogenes prior to the trial that the time was right for his life to end, Socrates is reported to have said that up to that time he would acknowledge no human being to have lived a better life than he. The reason he gives is that his life has contained what is most pleasant (§5). This leads us to wonder how Socrates conceives the relation between the good and the pleasant. For he seems here to measure the good by the pleasant. In Xenophon's rendering of the same remark in the *Memorabilia* (4.8.6), he has Socrates formulate it so as to make clear the qualitative distinction between the good and the pleasant. But perhaps that distinction begins to blur a bit under careful scrutiny.

The greatest pleasure, whose possession seems to insure the good life for a human being, is a kind of knowledge, namely, the knowledge Socrates has had that his *entire* life has been lived piously and justly. In the *Memorabilia,* where no big talk is allowed, Xenophon reformulates this remark so as to have Socrates say more humbly that the greatest pleasure is a kind of perception, namely, the keen perception Socrates has that he is steadily improving. It is possible to perceive one's steady improvement while still not knowing whether one is pious and just, and it is surely possible, or even probable, that one's sense of improvement includes the awareness that at a younger age one was in some way deficient in piety or justice. Is it conceivable, as the *Apology* implies, that Socrates never felt such a deficiency (see below, n. 10)? This much is clear: in the *Apology* Socrates speaks as if there were no period in his life which he would find morally regrettable or even questionable. The young Socrates was no less pious and just than the old. He offers no apology whatsoever for the investigations in which he was once engaged, and which prompted Aristophanes' satire. This despite the fact, as he admits elsewhere, that in that period of his life he had no idea what a gentleman's way of life was and, what is more, had no wish to inquire (*Oeconomicus* 6.13–17; 11.1–6). Indeed, in the *Apology* as a whole, Socrates would seem to minimize or omit as insignificant those changes in his life which one might otherwise suppose to betoken what is usually called the "Socratic revolution," or the metamorphosis from the "pre-Socratic" Socrates to the one who founded political philosophy. He makes no reference to his being married or having children; he does not say a word to refute the rumored charges that he is a "thinker of the things in the heavens," of the "most useless things," such as "the distance between fleas' feet" (*Symposium* 6.6–8; *Memorabilia* 1.1.11–16; *Oeconomicus* 11.3); he confirms, rather than denies, the charge that he is a teacher who displaces the authority of the parents as regards education. Is he then, even at the time of his death, perhaps not so different from the man Aristophanes blew up into comic proportions? Recall that the Clouds, like Hermogenes, loved Socrates not for his wisdom—in that respect they favored Prodicus—but for his swagger and his self-esteem (Aristophanes *Clouds* 360–65).

But if Socrates can affirm that he was pious and just his whole life, what does he understand his piety and his justice to have consisted in? I will limit myself to considering some of the *Apology*'s most striking comments about the philosopher's *justice*. Socrates speaks first of his justice when he explains what he meant when he said he had spent his life preparing to defend himself: that preparation consisted of "going through life never doing anything unjust" (§3). Could it be that Socrates understands his, or the philosopher's, justice to be simply refraining from wrongdoing? Does he not believe the philosopher is under an obligation to take a positive role in the city—if not as a ruler, then at least as a citizen and parent, and if not even that, then at least as a benevolent doer of good deeds? In the *Memorabilia,* Xenophon reports the same remark differently. There Socrates is reported to have said that his lifelong preparation to defend himself consisted in "going through life doing nothing else except investigating the just things and the unjust things, doing the just things and refraining from doing the unjust" (4.8.4). This is more or less in accord with the tone of the *Memorabilia* as a whole, the bulk of which (that is, 1.3–end) is devoted to showing that Socrates benefited those who associated with him (including his immediate family), and that he was therefore just, not merely in the negative sense of avoiding wrongdoing, but in the much fuller sense of being a benefactor of society (see the concluding summation: 4.8.11). But perhaps the enormous help Socrates gave to those friends who "made use of" him in their quest for virtue did not benefit, quite as much, his family or society in general as the *Memorabilia,* taken by itself, would have us believe. Perhaps the "justice" of Socrates to those who used him is somewhat further removed from what is ordinarily called justice—that is, concern for the common good of society—than it initially appears. In the *Oeconomicus,* Xenophon presents a conversation between the philosopher Socrates and a "perfect gentleman," in the course of which Socrates asks the gentleman whether he ever feels the need to make any preparations for defending himself. The relatively narrow scope of Socrates' activities on behalf of society becomes more visible when we contrast what we have heard him say, either in the *Memorabilia* or in the *Apology,* with the reply the perfect gentleman gives:

> Well, don't I seem to you, Socrates, to be continually practicing my defense, inasmuch as I do injustice to no one, but rather benefit as many people as I can? And don't I seem to you to practice myself in lodging accusations against people, by keeping a watchful eye out for certain persons who commit injustice against many, in private dealings, and also against the city, while they do no good to anyone? (11.22)

Socrates speaks next of his justice when, in the course of refuting the impiety charge, he claims that the Delphic Oracle once announced that no human being was more liberal, more just, or more moderate than he (§14). Socrates explains and justifies the oracle's praise of his justice with the following argument: "whom could you reasonably hold to be more just than he who is so satisfied with what he has that he needs in addition nothing that belongs to anyone else?" A few sentences later Socrates gives an almost shocking illustration of what this "satisfaction" means. Near the end of the Peloponnesian War, during the siege whose sufferings prefigured the tragic defeat of Athens by Sparta, "the others were grief-stricken for themselves, while my life went on without any greater concern than when the city enjoyed its greatest happiness" (§18). What underlies Socrates' "justice" is his nigh-Olympian independence from the needs and fears which prompt men to compete with, but also to help, one another in the city. As a matter of fact, a close consideration of what Socrates says here about each of his moral virtues, other than wisdom, shows that the heart of these virtues is "liberality" (*eleutheria*: §9)—understood not as generosity, or the disposition to give appropriate gifts to appropriate persons, but rather as freedom, or noble independence from the ordinary desires for security, pleasure, prosperity, and political success. A man like Hermogenes can conceive of such liberality as the heart of almost all moral virtues, and in particular justice.

It is true, of course, that immediately after this exposition of his wisdom and moral virtues Socrates turns to a refutation of the charge that he was a corrupter of the youth and asserts that, far from corrupting them, he served them as an expert in education, which is "the greatest good for human beings" (§§19–21). Without a doubt, Socrates believed he had done great benefit to some of the young (§26). But in doing them that good did he make them more loyal and effective rulers or citizens or family members? And therefore, did he benefit them in the eyes of the city or with a view to the common good? He admits that he made the young obey him rather than their own parents when it came to education, the "greatest good." Moreover, he speaks in the *Apology* as if what *he* means by "education" is distinct not only from medicine but also from the practical judgment (*phronesis*) that qualifies one to take the lead in the political assembly or in military affairs. Once again, this noteworthy admission or exaggeration must be placed in the balance against the rather different impression we receive from passages in the *Memorabilia* (like 4.8.4). No wonder the god at Delphi, as Socrates in the *Apology* readily concedes, preferred Lycurgus, the lawgiver or founder, to Socrates the philosopher.

From the *Apology* we learn little about the core of what Socrates meant by "education," or his "wisdom" (§16). We discern with lucidity only certain important externals, such as the fact that Socrates himself possessed, and had the power to induce in some of his students, a remarkable "endurance and frugality" (§25), or that he had the capacity to accept without tears "the death sentence nature imposed on me at the time I came into being" (§27). We do not penetrate to the heart of Socratic wisdom because we see Socrates in the light cast by the mind of Hermogenes, a man who has practically no insight into Socrates' deepest needs and joys: unlike Charmides, Hermogenes never caught a glimpse of Socrates dancing alone (*Symposium* 2.15–19).[10] What Hermogenes does perceive, and hold in awe—what he mistakes for the peak of the philosophic existence—is the philosopher's magnificent and divinely inspired transcendence of political life. The picture Xenophon chose to present in the *Apology* may exaggerate not least in that it has Socrates talk and act as if he felt a pride or reverence for his own soul like that a Hermogenes aspires to feel. Socrates plays in this work the role of what Aristotle later called the "man of greatness of soul." But this aspect of the *Apology* must also be balanced against what we learn from the other Socratic writings. In the *Oeconomicus* and *Memorabilia*, Xenophon allows the reader to discern Socrates' lack of manliness or of pride, but he compensates by stressing the philosopher's justice—understood as his concern to aid his fellowman. In the *Apology*, on the other hand, we get a deeper insight into the character of the philosopher's justice; this disclosure is compensated for by the stress laid on Socrates' manliness and pride.

[10] This observation, the observation that Socrates' boasting in the *Apology* downplays the virtue that is by far the most estimable to him personally, points the way to a resolution of the apparent contradiction between the *Apology* and the *Memorabilia* with regard to the question of whether or not Socrates progressed in virtue: Socrates made enormous progress in the most important respect, in wisdom—as the implicit equation of education and his wisdom signals; but he did not progress to an appreciable extent in piety and justice, because his own life as a citizen underwent no change that was fundamental, or more than tactical. This presupposes, of course, that knowledge of piety and justice—of the nature of piety and justice—is not the same thing as being pious and just, or that the virtue of piety and the virtue of justice as here understood are not simply knowledge.

TWO

Oeconomicus

Translated by Carnes Lord

CHAPTER 1

(1) I once heard him discourse on the management of the household as well, in about these words.

"Tell me, Critoboulus," he said, "is management of the household the name of a certain kind of knowledge, as medicine, smithing, and carpentry are?"

"It seems so to me, at least," said Critoboulus.

(2) "Then just as we are at no loss to say what the work of each of these arts is, can we say also what the work of household management is?"

"It seems, at any rate," said Critoboulus, "that it is the part of a good household manager to manage his own household well."

(3) "But if someone were to entrust another's household to him," said Socrates, "could he not manage that, if he wanted to, as well as he does his own? For the one who knows carpentry can do equally for another what he does for himself; and so too, presumably, can the skilled household manager."

This translation is reprinted, in slightly revised form, from Leo Strauss: *Xenophon's Socratic Discourse: An Intrepretation of the* Oeconomicus. The original translation was made, by permission of the Clarendon Press, Oxford, from the Oxford Classical text, *Xenophontis Opera Omnia,* vol. 2 (2d ed., Oxford: Clarendon Press, 1921), edited by E. C. Marchant. All deviations from the readings of that text are specifically noted. The *oikonomikos* is the "skilled household manager," not merely the "household manager" (*oikonomos*) mentioned in 1.2 and 1.15.

"It seems so to me, at least, Socrates."

(4) "Is it possible, then," said Socrates, "for one who knows this art, even though he happens to have no wealth himself, to manage another's household, just as a builder can build another's house, and earn pay for it?"

"Yes, by Zeus, and he would earn a lot of pay," said Critoboulus, "if on taking over, he were able to do what's necessary and, in producing a surplus, increase the household."

(5) "But what in our opinion is a household? Is it just the house, or is whatever one possesses outside the house also part of the household?"

"To me, at any rate," said Critoboulus, "it seems that whatever someone possesses is part of his household, even if it isn't in the same city as the possessor."

(6) "Don't some men possess enemies?"

"Yes, by Zeus; and some, at least, have a great many."

"Shall we say the enemies are also their possessions?"

"But it would be ridiculous," said Critoboulus, "if the one who increases enemies should in addition earn pay for it."

(7) "Because, of course, it was our opinion that a man's household is whatever he possesses."

"Yes, by Zeus," said Critoboulus, "at least if what he possesses is good; for whatever is bad, by Zeus, I do not call a possession."

"You, then, appear to call possessions whatever is beneficial to each."

"Very much so," he said, "and whatever is harmful I hold to be loss rather than wealth."

(8) "If, therefore, someone buys a horse he doesn't know how to use and hurts himself in a fall, the horse isn't wealth for him?"[1]

"No, at least if wealth is a good."

"Then not even the earth is wealth for the human being who works it in such a way as to suffer loss in working it."

"No, the earth isn't wealth either, if it brings hardship instead of nourishment."

(9) "And isn't it the same with sheep: if someone suffers loss through not knowing how to use them, the sheep aren't wealth for him?"

[1] Etymologically, *chrēsthai* ("to use") is related to *chrēma* ("wealth") as *ktasthai* ("to possess") is related to *ktēma* ("possession").

"It seems so to me, at least."

"You, then, as it appears, believe that whatever benefits is wealth, while whatever harms is not."

"Just so."

(10) "Then the same things are wealth for the one knowing how to use each of them and not wealth for the one not knowing how; just as flutes are wealth for the one knowing how to play the flute in a manner worth mentioning, while for the one not knowing how they are nothing more than useless stones, as long as he doesn't sell them. (11) And thus it looks to us as though the flutes are wealth for those not knowing how to use them only when they sell them, and not when they don't sell them but keep them in their possession."

"Neither of us can disagree with this argument, Socrates, since it was said that whatever is beneficial is wealth. So unsold flutes are not wealth, for they aren't useful, but sold ones are wealth."

(12) To this Socrates said: "At least, if he knows how to sell. For should he sell them and in turn receive something he didn't know how to use, they wouldn't be wealth even when sold, at least according to your argument."

"You appear to be saying, Socrates, that not even money is wealth if one doesn't know how to use it."

(13) "And you seem to me to agree that whatever can benefit someone is wealth. Well, what if someone were to use his money to buy a prostitute, and through her he became worse in body, worse in soul, and worse in regard to his household—in what way would the money still be beneficial to him?"

"In no way, unless, of course, we are going to say that the so-called pig bean,[2] which brings madness to all who eat of it, is wealth."

(14) "Then unless one knows how to use money, let him thrust it so far away, Critoboulus, that it isn't even wealth. As for friends, if one knows how to use them so as to be benefited by them, what shall we assert they are?"

"Wealth, by Zeus," said Critoboulus, "and worth much more than oxen, if indeed they are more beneficial than oxen."

(15) "Then enemies too are wealth, at least according to your argument, for whoever is able to benefit from them."

[2] "Pig bean" is a literal translation of *hyoskyamos* ("henbane").

"It seems so to me, at any rate."

"It is the part of the good household manager, therefore, to know how to use enemies so as to benefit from enemies."

"Most emphatically."

"And of course you see, Critoboulus," he said, "how many households of private men have been increased through war, and how many through tyrannies."[3]

(16) "These things seem to me, at least, nobly[4] spoken, Socrates," said Critoboulus; "but what does it look like to us when we see some who have both the kinds of knowledge and the resources which they might put to work to increase their households, and we perceive that they're unwilling to do it, and see that as a result their knowledge is of no benefit to them? What else than that for them the kinds of knowledge are not wealth, and neither are the possessions?"

(17) "Is it slaves, Critoboulus," said Socrates, "you are attempting to discuss with me?"

"No, by Zeus," he said, "not I, but rather men of whom some at least are reputed to be very wellborn; some of these I see have the kinds of knowledge that belong to war, others those that belong to peace, yet they are unwilling to put them to work—I suppose for this reason, that they do not have masters."

(18) "And how is it they have no masters," said Socrates, "if in spite of the fact that they pray for happiness and want to do the things from which good will result for them, they are nevertheless prevented from doing so by the rulers?"

"And just who are these invisible rulers of theirs?" said Critoboulus.

(19) "But by Zeus," said Socrates, "they are not invisible at all, but rather quite manifest. And surely it doesn't escape your notice that

[3] A translation of the Oxford text of this sentence reads: "how many households of private men have been increased through war, and how many of tyrants." This alteration seems warranted neither by the evidence of the manuscripts nor by the sense of the passage. At most, one might change *tyranniōn* ("tyrannies") to *tyrannōn* ("tyrants"). In any case, the contrast is not between tyrants and private men, which would not be in point here, but between two situations in which private men "benefit from enemies."

[4] *Kalōs*, the first appearance in the *Oeconomicus* of this important term. It refers either to external beauty or beauty of character and will be consistently rendered as "beautiful" ("beautifully," etc.) or "noble" ("nobly," etc.); in a few instances, the translation "fine" ("finely," etc.) has seemed more appropriate (7.36, 17.4, 19.16, and 20.20).

they are most wicked, that is, if you hold that laziness and softness of soul and neglect are wicked. (20) And there are other deceiving mistresses, pretending to be pleasures—dice-playing and human associations without benefit—which in time become obvious even to the deceived as pains with a mere gloss of pleasure, and which, when they are in control, keep men from beneficial works."

(21) "But others, Socrates," he said, "are not prevented from working by these things; on the contrary, they apply themselves quite vigorously to their work and to devising means of income, and yet at the same time they deplete the households and are continually without means."

(22) "These too are slaves," said Socrates, "and slaves indeed to harsh masters, some to gluttony, some to lust, some to drunkenness, some to foolish and expensive ambitions—all of which rule the human beings they control so harshly as to compel them, while they see them in their prime and capable of working, to spend on their desires whatever they may gain from work; and when their masters perceive that they are no longer capable of working due to age, they abandon them to grow old miserably and attempt to use others in turn as slaves. (23) It is no less necessary, Critoboulus, to fight for freedom against them than against those who attempt to enslave by arms. Enemies, when they are gentlemen and have enslaved others, have in fact compelled many to become better by moderating them and have made them live in greater ease in the time remaining to them; but these mistresses never cease to plague the bodies, the souls, and the households of human beings as long as they rule over them."

CHAPTER 2

(1) Thereupon Critoboulus spoke somewhat as follows. "As regards such things, it seems to me I've heard enough of what you have to say. On examining myself I seem to find I am fairly continent in such matters, so that if you advise me about what I might do to increase my household, it seems to me I wouldn't be prevented from doing it, at least by those things you call mistresses. Be confident,

then, and give me your good advice; or do you charge us, Socrates, with being sufficiently rich already, and do we seem to you to need no additional wealth?"

(2) "Not I," said Socrates. "But if you're speaking of me as well, I seem to need no additional wealth and indeed to be sufficiently rich; but you, Critoboulus, you seem to me to be very poor, and, yes, by Zeus, there are times when I greatly pity you."

(3) And Critoboulus spoke, laughing. "And how much—by the gods—do you, Socrates," he said, "suppose your possessions would bring if they were sold, and how much mine?"

"I suppose," said Socrates, "that my house and all my property[5] would bring quite easily five minas, if I chanced on a good buyer; but I know with some accuracy that your things would bring more than a hundred times that."

(4) "And though you understand this, you still believe you need no additional wealth, while you pity me for my poverty?"

"My things are sufficient to provide enough for me," he said, "but with the pomp you have assumed and your reputation, even if you had an addition of three times what you possess now, it seems to me it wouldn't be sufficient for you."

(5) "How so?" said Critoboulus.

Socrates declared: "First, because I see you are compelled to make frequent and great sacrifices, as otherwise, I suppose, neither gods nor human beings could put up with you; then, because it's appropriate for you to receive many foreigners, and to do so with magnificence; and then, because you must feast the citizens and treat them well, or be bereft of allies. (6) And again I perceive that the city orders you to accomplish great things—breeding of horses and training of choruses, support of the gymnasia, public commands; and if war should come, I know they will order you to support a trireme and to contribute so much that you will be hard put to sustain it. And should you seem to have performed some one of these things inadequately, I know the Athenians will punish you no less than they would if they caught you stealing something of theirs. (7) In addition I see that you, supposing yourself to be rich and therefore neglecting

[5] *Ta onta,* literally, "the beings" or "the things that are." Every instance of "property" in the text is *ta onta.*

to devise means to wealth, apply your thought to the affairs of a boyfriend, as though that were possible for you. For these reasons I pity you, lest you suffer some irreparable evil and end up in the worst poverty. (8) As for me, if I need anything more for myself, I know you too understand that there are some who would help me and who could, by supplying a very little, overwhelm my way of life with a deluge of abundance; but your friends, though what they have is more sufficient for their condition than what you have is for yours, nevertheless look to you as a source of benefits."

(9) And Critoboulus spoke. "To these things, Socrates, I have no response; rather it's time for you to take command of me, before I become really pitiable."

After having heard this, Socrates spoke. "And doesn't it seem a wonderful thing you are doing, Critoboulus—that you should have laughed at me a little while ago when I asserted I was rich, as though I didn't know what a rich man was, and then not given up until you had refuted me and made me admit to possessing not the hundredth part of your things, while now you bid me take command of you and make it my concern[6] that you don't become altogether and in truth a poor man?"

(10) "It's because I see, Socrates," he said, "that you know one enriching work: how to produce a surplus. I expect that one who saves something from a little could very easily produce a large surplus from much."

(11) "Don't you remember, then, what you were saying a moment ago in the argument—when you wouldn't permit me to utter a sound—that horses wouldn't be wealth for the one not knowing how to use them, and neither would the earth nor sheep nor money nor any single thing that one didn't know how to use? It's from such things that income derives; yet how do you suppose I will know how to use any one of them when, to begin with, I've never possessed any of them?"

[6] This is the first occurrence in the dialogue of the verb *epimeleisthai*, meaning, roughly, "to be concerned with," "to take care that," "to be careful," "to be diligent." The verb as well as the noun derived from it, *epimeleia*, are of central importance in Ischomachus' education of his wife and stewards. Wherever possible these terms are translated, respectively, "to be diligent," and "diligence"; otherwise, "to be concerned" or "to concern oneself," and "concern." The related terms *amelein* and *ameleia* are rendered, respectively, "to neglect" or "to be negligent," and "neglect."

(12) "But it seemed to us that, even if someone happened to have no wealth of his own, there could still be a knowledge of household management. What then prevents you from knowing as well?"

"The very thing, by Zeus, that would prevent a human being from knowing how to play the flute, that is, if he had never possessed flutes himself and another had never made provision for him to learn on his. This is just my situation in regard to household management. (13) For I myself have never possessed the instrument—wealth—with which to learn, nor has another ever provided me with his own to manage, except for you who are now willing to provide yours. But, surely, those who are just learning to play the lyre usually ruin the lyres; if I were to undertake to learn household management in your household, I would perhaps utterly ruin it for you."

(14) To this Critoboulus said: "At any rate you're trying eagerly, Socrates, to avoid being of any benefit to me in carrying on more easily my necessary affairs."

"No, by Zeus," said Socrates, "not at all; on the contrary, I shall very eagerly explain to you whatever I know. (15) But I suppose if you had come for fire and I had none, you wouldn't blame me if I led you to some other place where you could get it; and if you asked me for water and I, having none myself, took you to some other place and took you to it, I know you wouldn't blame me for that either; and if you wished to learn music from me, and I pointed out to you some who were much cleverer in music than I and would be grateful if you were willing to learn from them, how, again, could you blame me for doing this?"

(16) "I couldn't justly blame you, Socrates."

"Then I'll point out to you, Critoboulus, certain others who are much cleverer than I in those things you persist in wanting to learn from me. I admit I have been diligent in finding those in the city who are the most knowledgeable in each kind of thing. (17) For on learning that among those who are in the same line of work some were very poor and others very rich, I wondered greatly, and it seemed worthwhile to me to investigate why this should be. On investigating it, I found that these things happen quite properly. (18) I saw those who act at random suffering loss, and I noticed that those who are diligent and apply their minds do things more quickly, more easily, and more profitably. From these, I suppose, you too could learn, if you wanted to and the god did not oppose you, how to become an extremely clever money-maker."

CHAPTER 3

(1) After having heard this, Critoboulus spoke. "Now then," he said, "I won't let you go, Socrates, until you have shown what you promised in the presence of these friends here."

"What, then, Critoboulus," said Socrates, "if I first show you, with respect to houses, some who build useless ones for a great deal of money, and others who for much less build ones that have everything that's necessary—will I seem to display[7] to you one of the works of household management[8]?"

"Very much so," said Critoboulus.

(2) "And what if after this, and following on this, I display to you some who possess very many belongings of every sort and yet don't have them for use when they need them and don't even know when they're secure, and who as a result are themselves greatly harassed and harass the servants in turn, and others who possess no more, but even less, yet have them always ready for use when they need them?"

(3) "Is anything else the cause of this, Socrates, than that by the first everything is thrown down by chance, while by the others each kind of thing is kept in order in a place?"

"Yes, by Zeus," said Socrates, "and not in just any chance place; rather, wherever it's appropriate, there each kind of thing is ordered separately."

"In speaking of this, also," said Critoboulus, "you seem to me to be talking about a part of household management."

(4) "What, then," he said, "if I display to you, in respect to servants, certain places where all of them are tied down, so to speak,

[7] "Display" translates *epideiknunai;* "show," *apodeiknunai.* The latter term conveys a suggestion of demonstrative proof; the former, of rhetorical virtuosity. Both are compounds of *deiknunai,* "point out," which first occurs in 2.15–16.

[8] The expression *tōn oikonomikōn* here and in 3.3 could also mean "of those skilled in household management."

and yet frequently run away, and others where they are released and yet are willing to work and to remain—won't I seem to display to you a work of household management that is worth looking at?"

"Yes, by Zeus," said Critoboulus, "certainly."

(5) "And also, in respect to those who farm very similar farms, some claiming they have been destroyed by farming who in fact are very poor, and others having abundantly and nobly all they need from farming?"

"Yes, by Zeus," said Critoboulus. "For perhaps they squander, spending not only on what's necessary but also on what brings harm to themselves and the household."

(6) "Perhaps there are some like this too," said Socrates. "But I'm speaking not of them but rather of those who have nothing even for the necessary expenses, though they claim to be farmers."

"And what would be the cause of this, Socrates?"

"I'll take you to them as well," said Socrates; "by looking you'll doubtless learn it."

"By Zeus," he said, "at least if I'm able."

(7) "In looking you must test yourself, to see whether you understand. Now I've known you to get up very early in the morning and go a very long way on foot to look at comedies and eagerly persuade me to join in the looking; but not once did you ever invite me to this other kind of work."

"I must look ridiculous to you, Socrates."

(8) "But far more ridiculous to yourself, by Zeus," he said. "And what if I display to you some who, through horsemanship, have been brought to poverty as regards even the necessary things, and others who are very well off through horsemanship and take pride in the profit?"

"I too see such people and I know both sorts, yet I do not any more on that account become one of those who profit."

(9) "That's because you look at them as you look at tragedies and comedies—not, I suppose, in order to become a poet but rather that you may take pleasure in seeing or hearing something. And perhaps it's right this way, as you don't want to become a poet; but since you are compelled to make use of horsemanship, don't you suppose you would be a fool not to consider how you might avoid being merely

a layman[9] in this work, especially as the same horses are both good for using and profitable for selling?"

(10) "Is it colt-breaking[10] you suggest I do, Socrates?"

"No, by Zeus, no more than I suggest you buy children and equip them to be farmers; but it seems to me there are certain ages at which both horses and human beings are immediately useful as well as susceptible to improvement. I can also display some who use the women they marry in such a way as to have them as coworkers in increasing the households, and others in a way that for the most part ruins them."

(11) "Must one fault the man or the woman[11] for this, Socrates?"

"When sheep fare badly," said Socrates, "we usually fault the shepherd, and when a horse behaves badly, we usually speak badly of the horseman; as for the woman, if she has been taught the good things by the man and still acts badly, the woman could perhaps justly be held at fault; on the other hand, if he doesn't teach the noble and good things but makes use of her though she is quite ignorant of them, wouldn't the man justly be held at fault? (12) In any event, speak the whole truth to us, Critoboulus," he said, "for you are in the presence of friends. Is there anyone to whom you entrust more serious matters than to your wife?"

"No one," he said.

"And is there anyone with whom you discuss fewer things than your wife?"

"There aren't many, in any case," he said.

(13) "Did you marry her when she was a very young girl and had seen and heard as little as possible?"

"Yes, indeed."

"Then it's even more wonderful if she knows anything of what she ought to say or do than if she goes wrong."

(14) "Those who you say have good wives, Socrates—did they themselves educate them?"

[9] *Idiōtēs*, a private individual as opposed to a public figure (cf. 1.15); hence, an unskilled person as opposed to an expert.

[10] There is a play in Greek on the words for "colt-breaking" (*pōlodamnein*) and "selling" (*pōlēsis*).

[11] *Anēr* and *gynē*, in this as in other contexts, mean also or primarily "husband" and "wife." Wherever possible *anēr* is translated "man"; it signifies the male in the emphatic sense, the "real man" as opposed to the ordinary "human being" (*anthrōpos*).

"There's nothing like investigating the matter. I'll introduce you to Aspasia,[12] who will display all these things to you more knowledgeably than I. (15) But I hold that a woman who is a good partner in the household is a proper counterweight to the man in attaining the good. For while the possessions usually come into the house through the man's actions, they are expended for the most part in the course of the woman's housekeeping; and when these things turn out well, the households increase, but when done badly, the households diminish. (16) And I suppose I could also display to you those who put to work, in a manner worth mentioning, each of the other kinds of knowledge, if you hold that something further is needed."

Chapter 4

(1) "But why must you display all of them, Socrates?" said Critoboulus. "It's not easy to get possession of the kinds of workers that are necessary in all the arts; nor is it possible to become experienced in them; but the kinds of knowledge that are reputed to be the noblest and would be especially suitable for my concern—these you must display for me, as well as those who practice them, and you yourself must do what you can to benefit me in these matters by teaching me."

(2) "You speak nobly, Critoboulus," he said. "For indeed those that are called mechanical are spoken against everywhere and have quite plausibly come by a very bad reputation in the cities. For they utterly ruin the bodies of those who work at them and those who are concerned with them,[13] compelling them to sit still and remain indoors,[14] or in some cases even to spend the whole day by a fire. And when the bodies are made effeminate, the souls too become much more diseased. (3) Lack of leisure to join in the concerns of friends and of the city is another condition of those that are called mechanical;

[12] The most famous courtesan and mistress of Pericles, noted for her intellectual attainments.

[13] A distinction seems intended here between the workers and those who are merely "concerned" with the work, i.e., overseers of some kind. Cf. 4.10 and 5.4.

[14] Literally, "to sit and nourish themselves with shadows."

those who practice them are reputed to be bad friends as well as bad defenders of their fatherlands. Indeed in some of the cities, especially those reputed to be good at war, no citizen is allowed to work at the mechanical arts."

(4) "Then as for us, Socrates, which do you advise we make use of?"

"Should we be ashamed," said Socrates, "to imitate the king of Persia? For they say he believes farming and the art of war are among the noblest and most necessary concerns, and concerns himself emphatically with both of them."

After having heard this, Critoboulus spoke. (5) "Do you take this too on trust, Socrates," he said, "that the king of Persia concerns himself in some way with farming?"

"If we investigate the matter as follows, Critoboulus," said Socrates, "perhaps we may learn whether in some way he does concern himself with it. We agree he is emphatically concerned with the works of war, since it is he who gives orders to the rulers of however many nations send him tribute, regarding just how many horsemen and archers and slingers and targeteers each must maintain, that they may be sufficient both to control the ruled and to defend the country should enemies invade it. (6) Apart from these he maintains guards in the citadels, and the rulers are ordered in addition to provide maintenance for these garrisons. Every year the king holds an inspection of the mercenaries and the others he has ordered to be in arms, bringing together at various points of assembly all except those in the citadels. Those near his own residence he surveys himself; those further away he sends trusted officers to examine; (7) and whichever rulers of garrison and field troops[15] and the satraps look to have the full number as ordered and provide them equipped with splendid horses and arms, these rulers he increases with honors and enriches with great presents; but whichever rulers he finds have neglected the garrisons or looked to their own profit, these he punishes harshly and, removing them from rule, appoints others more diligent. In doing these things, then, it seems to us he is indisputably concerned with the works of war. (8) Again, whatever part of the

[15] "Garrison commanders" (*phrourarchoi*) and "commanders of a thousand" (*chiliarchoi*); the latter term may also designate the rule of a (Persian) military district. Xenophon goes on to suggest that these are "rulers" (*archontes*) not only in name.

country he rides through he surveys himself, and scrutinizes, and what he doesn't survey himself he examines by sending out trusted officers. And whichever rulers he perceives have provided that the country is well inhabited and that the earth is productive and replete with crops and with every kind of tree that it bears, these he enlarges with new territory, adorns with presents, and rewards with seats of honor; but whichever he sees have an inactive[16] country and few human beings, whether through harshness or arrogance or neglect, these he punishes and, removing them from rule, appoints other rulers. (9) In doing these things, then, does he seem any less concerned that the earth be made productive by its inhabitants than that it be well guarded by the garrisons? The rulers he has ordered to each thing are, furthermore, not the same, but certain ones rule the inhabitants and the workers and collect taxes from them, and certain others rule the armed garrisons.[17] (10) And if the ruler of the garrison doesn't sufficiently defend the country, the one who rules the inhabitants and is concerned with the works brings an accusation against him on the ground that the people cannot work because of the lack of a guard; but if the ruler of the garrison provides peace for the works, while the ruler provides but few human beings and an inactive country, then the ruler of the garrison brings an accusation against him. (11) For those who work the land badly will hardly be able either to maintain the garrisons or to pay taxes. But wherever a satrap is appointed, he concerns himself with both these things."

(12) Thereupon Critoboulus spoke. "If the king indeed acts in this way, Socrates, it seems to me at least that he concerns himself no less with the works of farming than with those of war."

(13) "But again, in addition to this," said Socrates, "in whatever countries the king resides, or wherever he travels, he is concerned that there be gardens, the so-called pleasure gardens,[18] filled with all the noble and good things that the earth wishes to bring forth, and in these he himself spends most of his time, when the season of the year doesn't preclude it."

[16] *Argos*, "inactive" or "lazy" (as in 1.19, 16.4), is the opposite of *energos*, "productive"; both are related to the word for "work," *ergon*.

[17] In the Oxford text this phrase is emended to read, in translation: "both the armed [troops] and the garrisons."

[18] Xenophon uses the Persian word *paradeisoi*.

(14) "By Zeus, Socrates," said Critoboulus, "but the king necessarily concerns himself that the pleasure-gardens, where he spends time, be as beautifully equipped as possible with trees and all the other beautiful things that the earth brings forth."

(15) "And some assert, Critoboulus," said Socrates, "that when the king gives presents, he first sends for those who have proved themselves good in war, on the ground that there would be no benefit in plowing very much if there were no defenders; and that secondly he sends for those who cultivate their lands in the best manner and make them productive, saying that not even the brave could live if there were no workers. (16) It is also said that Cyrus, a king of the highest reputation, once told those who were called to receive presents that he himself should justly take the presents for both these things; for he was best, he said, both in cultivating the land and in protecting what was cultivated."

(17) "Cyrus, at any rate," said Critoboulus, "took no less pride, Socrates, if he said these things, in making his lands productive and cultivating them than he did in being a skilled warrior."

(18) "Yes, by Zeus," said Socrates, "and Cyrus, it seems, had he lived, would have become an excellent ruler; of this there were many proofs provided, but particularly the fact that during the march against his brother, in the fight for the kingdom, it is said that no one deserted Cyrus for the king, while tens of thousands came from the king to Cyrus.[19] (19) I regard it also as a great proof of virtue in a ruler when others willingly obey him[20] and are willing to remain with him even in terrible dangers. Cyrus' friends fought with him while he lived, and when he was dead they all died fighting near his corpse, except Ariaios; for Ariaios happened to have been ordered to the left wing.[21] (20) It was this Cyrus who is said to have received Lysander[22] with many marks of friendship when he came bringing presents from

[19] This seems to refer to the younger Cyrus, Xenophon's contemporary and friend and leader of the revolt against his brother, the Persian king Artaxerxes.

[20] Or, "when others are readily persuaded [*peithōntai*] by him."

[21] Compare *Anabasis* 1.8.5 and 1.9.31. The commander of all Cyrus' non-Greek troops and his chief lieutenant, Ariaios fled the battle as soon as he learned of Cyrus' death. Later he exchanged oaths of fidelity with the Greeks who had fought under Cyrus, but soon afterward deserted them altogether.

[22] Lysander was a Spartan and commander of the Peloponnesian fleet during the last years of the Peloponnesian War. The occasion and circumstances of his meeting with Cyrus, which took place in 407, are described by Xenophon in the *Hellenica*

the allies—as Lysander himself once said in relating the story to a certain host in Megara—and in particular, he said, he displayed to him the pleasure garden in Sardis. (21) After Lysander had wondered at it—that the trees should be so beautiful, the plantings so regular, the rows of trees so straight, the angles so beautifully laid, and that so many pleasant scents should accompany them as they walked—wondering at these things, he spoke. 'I, Cyrus, am full of wonder at the beauty of everything,[23] but much more do I admire the one who has measured out and ordered each kind of thing for you.' (22) On hearing this, Cyrus was pleased and spoke. 'All these things, Lysander, I measured out and ordered myself, and there are some of them,' he said that he said, 'that I even planted myself.' (23) And Lysander said that, looking at him and seeing the beauty of the clothes he wore, perceiving their scent and also the beauty of the necklaces and bracelets and the other ornaments he was wearing, he had spoken and said: 'What do you mean, Cyrus? You planted some of these with your own hands?' (24) And Cyrus had replied, 'Do you wonder at this, Lysander? I swear to you by Mithras: as long as I'm healthy, I never go to dinner until I have worked up a sweat either by practicing some work of war or farming, or at any rate by always devoting my ambition[24] to some one thing.' (25) And Lysander himself said that on hearing this he took Cyrus' right hand and spoke: 'You, Cyrus, seem to me to be justly happy, for you are happy while being a good man.' "

Chapter 5

(1) "This, Critoboulus, I relate," said Socrates, "because not even the altogether blessed can abstain from farming. For the pursuit of farming seems to be at the same time some soft pleasure, an increase

---

(1.5.1ff.); its main object was to secure Persian assistance in the prosecution of the war against Athens. Xenophon does not, however, make mention in the *Hellenica* of the incident related here.

[23] In the Oxford text this phrase is emended to read, in translation: "the beauty of everything here" or "of all these things" (*panta tauta*). The insertion of *tauta* is without manuscript authority.

[24] Here and throughout, "ambition" could be translated as, "love of honor."

of the household, and a training of the bodies so that they can do whatever befits a free man. (2) First, the earth bears, to those who work it, what human beings live on, and it bears in addition what they take pleasure in experiencing; (3) then, it provides that with which they adorn altars and statues and are adorned themselves, together with the most pleasant scents and sights; then, it either brings forth or nourishes all manner of sauces[25]—for the art of sheep breeding is linked to farming—that they may have something with which, by sacrificing, to win over the gods, as well as something to use themselves. (4) But though providing the good things most abundantly, it doesn't yield them up to softness but accustoms all to bear the cold of winter and the heat of summer. It exercises those who work with their own hands and adds to their strength, and it produces a kind of manliness even in those who are merely concerned with farming, causing them to rise early in the morning and compelling them to move about vigorously. For in the country as in town, the most important actions have always their proper season. (5) Then, if someone wants to defend the city as a horseman, farming is most sufficient for helping to maintain a horse, or if one is a foot soldier, it provides a vigorous body. The earth also in some degree helps encourage a love of the toil in the hunt, since it provides the dogs with an easy source of nourishment and at the same time supports wild animals. (6) And not only are the horses and dogs benefited by farming, but they benefit the country in turn, the horse by carrying the caretaker[26] to his concerns early in the morning and allowing him to return late, and the dogs by keeping wild animals from damaging the crops or the sheep and by helping to give safety to solitude. (7) Further, the earth stimulates in some degree the farmers to armed protection of the country by nourishing her crops in the open for the strongest to take. (8) What art makes men more fit for running, throwing, and jumping than does farming? What art brings more gratification to those who work at it? What affords a more pleasant welcome to the one concerned with it—inviting whoever comes along to take whatever he requires? What welcomes foreigners with more abundance? (9) Where

[25] The Greek word (*opson*) signifies whatever is eaten with bread, i.e., both meat and vegetables.

[26] Evidently, the master. Xenophon uses a poetic and somewhat strange expression (*ho kēdomenos*), literally, "the one who is troubled," "the one who is concerned [for]."

are there more facilities than in the country for passing the winter with an abundance of fire and warm baths? And where can one spend a summer more pleasantly than in the country, amid waters and breezes and shade? (10) What else provides more suitable first offerings for the gods or shows ampler feasts? What is more beloved by servants, more pleasant for the wife, more sharply missed by children, or more gratifying to friends? (11) It would seem wonderful to me if any free human being possessed anything more pleasant than this or found a concern at once more pleasant and of greater benefit in life. (12) Furthermore, the earth, being a goddess, teaches justice to those who are able to learn, for she gives the most goods in return to those who attend to her best. (13) Then if those engaged in farming and educated to vigor and manliness should at some time be deprived of their works by a multitude of invaders, they would be able—if a god didn't prevent them—being well prepared both in soul and in body, to go into the country of the preventers and take what they needed to maintain themselves. For in war it is often safer to seek to maintain oneself with arms rather than with the instruments of farming. (14) At the same time farming educates in helping others. For in fighting one's enemies, as well as in working the earth, it is necessary to have the assistance of other human beings. (15) The one who is going to farm well, then, must provide himself with eager workers who are willing to obey him; and the one who leads against enemies must devise means to accomplish the same things, by giving presents to those who act as the good ought to act and by punishing those who are disorderly. (16) The farmer must often exhort his workers no less than the general his soldiers; and slaves require good hopes no less than the free, but rather more so, that they may be willing to remain. (17) Whoever said that farming is the mother and nurse of all the other arts spoke nobly indeed. For when farming goes well, all the other arts also flourish, but wherever the earth is compelled to lie barren, the other arts almost cease to exist, at sea as well as on the earth."

(18) After having heard this, Critoboulus said: "In regard to these things, Socrates, you seem to me, at least, to speak nobly; but in regard to most of the things of farming,[27] it's impossible for a human

[27] Literally, "the things of the farming [art]." The adjective is used, as is common in Greek, with a substantive absent but understood: probably either "knowledge" or "art" is intended.

being to exercise forethought: sometimes hail, frost, drought, violent rains, blights, and often indeed other things wreck what has been nobly conceived and done; sometimes a herd of sheep raised in the noblest manner is most miserably destroyed by disease."

(19) After having heard this, Socrates said: "But I for my part supposed you knew, Critoboulus, that the gods are lords of the works of farming no less than of those of war. Those who are at war you see, I suppose, trying to win over the gods before undertaking warlike actions, and consulting them by means of sacrifices and auguries as to what must or must not be done; (20) but in regard to the actions of farming, do you suppose it any less necessary to propitiate the gods? Know well," he said, "that moderate men attend to the gods out of regard for their crops—the wet and the dry alike—and their oxen and horses and sheep and indeed all their possessions."

CHAPTER 6

(1) "In regard to these things, Socrates," he said, "you seem to me to speak nobly, in suggesting that one attempt to begin every work with the gods' help, since the gods are lords of the works of peace no less than those of war. We shall attempt to do it. But speaking from where you left off in your account of household management, attempt to go through what remains of it for us; for having heard what you've said, I now seem to see rather better than before what I must do in order to make a living."

(2) "What then," said Socrates, "if we first recapitulate what we have gone through and agreed upon, that we may attempt in the same way, if we are at all able, to go through the rest so as to agree upon it?"

(3) "It's a pleasant thing, at any rate," said Critoboulus, "for partners in speeches to go through what they have discussed and agree, as it is for partners in wealth to go over the accounts without dispute."

(4) "Then," said Socrates, "it seemed to us that household management is the name of some kind of knowledge, and the knowledge itself looked to be that by which human beings are enabled to increase households; a household then looked to us to be the totality of

possessions, a possession we asserted to be whatever would be beneficial for the life of each, and beneficial things were found to be all things that one knows how to use. (5) Then as it seemed impossible for us to learn all the kinds of knowledge, we joined the cities in repudiating the so-called mechanical arts, because they seem to ruin the bodies utterly and because they enervate the souls. (6) One would have the clearest proof of this, we asserted, if, as enemies were invading the country, one were to seat the farmers and the artisans apart from one another and question each as to whether it seemed better to defend the country or, giving up the earth altogether, to guard the walls. (7) Those who are bound to the earth we supposed would vote to defend it, while the artisans would vote not to fight at all but rather to sit still as they had been educated to do, neither toiling nor risking danger. (8) We came to the conclusion that for the gentleman the most excellent[28] kind of work and the best kind of knowledge is farming, by which human beings supply themselves with the necessary things. (9) For that kind of work seemed to be at once the easiest to learn and the most pleasant to work at; it seemed to produce at once the most beautiful and most robust bodies, and as for the souls, it seemed least of all to cause any lack of leisure for joining in the concerns of friends and cities. (10) It seemed to us further that farming incites to bravery those who work at it, by bringing forth and nourishing the necessary things outside the fortifications. This manner of living is, as a result, held in highest repute by the cities, for it seems to provide the best and best-willed citizens to the community."

(11) And Critoboulus: "I seem to be quite sufficiently persuaded, Socrates, that farming is indeed the noblest and best and most pleasant way to make a living; but as to what you asserted earlier—that you had learned the causes of some people's farming in such a way as to have everything they need from farming, and in abundance, and of others' working in such a way that farming is not at all lucrative for them—of both these things, it seems to me, I would be pleased to hear you speak, so that we may do what is good and avoid what is harmful."

[28] The Greek word (*kratistos*) can mean "best" in the sense of having the upper hand or of being strongest; "most excellent" will always translate the word in the superlative degree, "superior" the comparative (*kreittōn*).

(12) "What then, Critoboulus," said Socrates, "if I relate to you from the beginning how I once came together with a man who seemed to me really to be one of those men to whom the name of gentleman is justly applied?"

"I would like very much to hear it," said Critoboulus, "as I too desire to become worthy of that name."

(13) "I'll tell you, too," said Socrates, "how I came to the consideration of it. A very short time was sufficient for me to go around to the good carpenters, the good smiths, the good painters, the sculptors, and all the others like them, to see the works of theirs that were reputed to be beautiful.[29] (14) But as regards those who have the solemn name of gentleman, that I might investigate whatever sort of work they do to be worthy of being called by it, my soul very much desired to come together with one of them. (15) And first, because the 'noble' is added to the 'good,'[30] whenever I saw a noble-looking man, I would go up to him and try to learn whether I could see the 'good' connected to the 'noble.' (16) But this was not the case, for I seemed to learn that some of those who were noble in outward form were quite depraved in their souls. It seemed best, then, to disregard the noble looks and to go instead to one of those called gentlemen. (17) Since I had heard Ischomachus named a gentleman by everyone—by men and women, foreigners and townsmen alike—it seemed best to try to come together with him."

CHAPTER 7

(1) "Seeing him then one day sitting in the colonnade of Zeus the Deliverer, I went over to him, and as he seemed to me to be at leisure, I sat down with him and spoke. 'Why are you sitting like this, Ischomachus, you who are so unaccustomed to leisure? For I mostly see you either doing something or at least hardly at leisure in the market place.'

[29] Or, "noble"; see n. 4 above.

[30] The phrase *kalos kagathos [anēr]*, "gentleman," means literally "noble and good [man]." Throughout this passage Socrates plays on the ambiguity of *kalos*, which may mean "external beauty" as well as "nobility" (see n. 4 above).

(2) " 'Nor would you see me now, Socrates,' said Ischomachus, 'if I hadn't made an appointment to meet some foreigners here.'

" 'When you aren't doing this sort of thing,' I said, 'by the gods, how do you spend your time and what do you do? For I would like very much to inquire whatever it is you do in order to be called a gentleman, since you don't spend your time indoors, and the condition of your body hardly looks like that of one who does.'

(3) "And Ischomachus, laughing at my asking what he did to be called a gentleman and rather pleased, or so it seemed to me, spoke. 'I don't know whether some call me by that name when discussing me with you, but surely when they call me to an exchange[31] for the support of a trireme or the training of a chorus, no one,' he said, 'goes looking for "the gentleman," but they summon me clearly,' he said, 'by the name Ischomachus and by my father's name.[32] As to what you asked me, Socrates,' he said, 'I never spend time indoors. Indeed,' he said, 'my wife is quite able by herself to manage the things within the house.'

(4) " 'It would please me very much, Ischomachus,' I said, 'if I might also inquire about this—whether you yourself educated your wife to be the way she ought to be, or whether, when you took her from her mother and father, she already knew how to manage the things that are appropriate to her.'[33]

(5) " 'How, Socrates,' he said, 'could she have known anything when I took her, since she came to me when she was not yet fifteen, and had lived previously under diligent supervision in order that she might see and hear as little as possible and ask the fewest possible questions? (6) Doesn't it seem to you that one should be content if she came knowing only how to take the wool and make clothes, and had seen how the spinning work is distributed among the female attendants? For as to matters of the stomach, Socrates,' he said, 'she came to me very nobly educated; and to me, at any rate, that seems to be an education of the greatest importance both for a man and a woman.'

[31] *Antidosis.* There was an Athenian law according to which a man charged with a public duty could challenge someone he believed richer than himself either to take on the duty or to exchange his property for that of the challenger.

[32] I.e., by his patronymic: "Ischomachus, the son of . . ."

[33] The expression can also mean "the things that belong to her."

(7) " 'And in other respects, Ischomachus,' I said, 'did you yourself educate your wife to be capable of being diligent about what's appropriate to her?'

" 'By Zeus,' said Ischomachus, 'not until I had sacrificed and prayed that I might succeed in teaching, and she in learning, what is best for both of us.'

(8) " 'Didn't your wife sacrifice with you and pray for these same things?' I said.

" 'Certainly,' said Ischomachus; 'she promised before the gods that she would become what she ought to be, and made it evident that she would not neglect the things she was being taught.'

(9) " 'By the gods, Ischomachus,' I said, 'relate to me what you first began teaching her. I'd listen to you relating these things with more pleasure than if you were telling me about the noblest contest in wrestling or horsemanship.'

(10) "And Ischomachus replied: 'Well, Socrates,' he said, 'when she had gotten accustomed to me and had been domesticated to the extent that we could have discussions, I questioned her somewhat as follows. "Tell me, wife, have you thought yet why ever it was that I took you and your parents gave you to me? (11) That it was not for want of someone else for us to sleep with—this is obvious, I know, to you too. Rather, when I considered for myself, and your parents for you, whom we might take as the best partner for the household and children, I chose you, and your parents, as it appears, from among the possibilities[34] chose me. (12) Should a god grant us children at some point, we will then consider, with respect to them, how we may educate them in the best possible manner; for this too is a good common to us—to obtain the best possible allies and supporters in old age; (13) but for the present this household is what is common to us. As to myself, everything of mine I declare to be in common, and as for you, everything you've brought you have deposited in common. It's not necessary to calculate which of us has contributed the greater number of things, but it is necessary to know this well, that whichever of us is the better partner will be the one to contribute the things of greater worth." (14) To this, Socrates, my wife replied:

[34] The expression could also mean either "from among capable men," i.e., men of some wealth and position (cf. 11.10), or "according to their [i.e., the parents'] capabilities."

"What can I do to help you?" she said. "What is my capacity? But everything depends on you: my work, my mother told me, is to be moderate." (15) "By Zeus, wife," I said, "my father told me the same thing. But it's for moderate people—for man and woman alike—not only to keep their property in the best condition but also to add as much as possible to it by noble and just means." (16) "Then what do you see," said my wife, "that I might do to help in increasing the household?" "By Zeus," I said, "just try to do in the best manner possible what the gods have made you naturally capable of and what the law praises." (17) "And what are these things?" she said. "I for my part suppose they are things of no little worth," I said, "unless, of course, the leading bee in the hive also has charge of works of little worth. (18) For it seems to me, wife," ' he said that he had said, ' "that the gods have used great consideration in joining together the pair called male and female so that it may be of the greatest benefit to itself in its community. (19) First, that the races of living things may not be extinguished, the pair is brought together for the production of children; then, from this pairing it is given to human beings at least to possess supporters in old age; and further, the way of life of human beings is not, as is that of herds, in the open air, but evidently needs shelter. (20) Still, if human beings are going to have something to bring into the dwellings, someone is needed to work in the open air. For plowing the fallow, sowing, planting, and herding are all works of the open air, and from them the necessary things are gotten. (21) But when these things have been brought into the dwelling, someone is needed to keep them secure and to do the works that need shelter. The rearing of newborn children also needs shelter; shelter is needed for the making of bread from the crop, and similarly for the working of clothes from wool. (22) Since, then, work and diligence are needed both for the indoor and for the outdoor things, it seems to me," ' he had said, ' "that the god directly prepared the woman's nature for indoor works and indoor concerns.[35] (23) For he equipped the man, in body and soul, with a greater capacity to endure cold and heat, journeys and expeditions, and so has ordered

[35] The construction of this sentence in Greek could lead one to believe that something has dropped out of the text at this point. The Oxford editor makes the following conjecture, which, however, lacks manuscript authority: "and that of the man for outdoor ones."

him to the outdoor works; but in bringing forth, for the woman, a body that is less capable in these respects," ' he said that he had said, ' "the god has, it seems to me, ordered her to the indoor works. (24) But knowing that he had implanted[36] in the woman, and ordered her to, the nourishment of newborn children, he also allotted to her a greater affection for the newborn infants than he gave to the man. (25) Since he had also ordered the woman to the guarding of the things brought in, the god, understanding that a fearful soul is not worse at guarding, also gave the woman a greater share of fear than the man. And knowing too that the one who had the outdoor works would need to defend himself should someone act unjustly, to him he gave a greater share of boldness. (26) But because it's necessary for both to give and to take, he endowed both with memory and diligence in like degree, so that you can't distinguish whether the male or the female kind has the greater share of these things. (27) As for continence in the necessary things, he endowed both with this too in like degree; and the god allowed the one who proved the better, whether the man or the woman, to derive more from this good. (28) Since, then, the nature of each has not been brought forth to be naturally apt for all of the same things, each has need of the other, and their pairing is more beneficial to each, for where one falls short the other is capable. (29) Now," I said, "wife, as we know what has been ordered to each of us by the god, we must, separately, do what's appropriate to each in the best manner possible. (30) The law too praises these things," ' he said that he had said, ' "in pairing man and woman; and as the god made them partners in children, so too does the law appoint them partners.[37] And what the god made each to be more capable of by nature, the law shows to be noble as well. It is a nobler thing for the woman to stay indoors than to spend time in the open, while it is more disgraceful for the man to stay indoors than to concern himself with outdoor things. (31) But when someone acts in a way contrary to what the god has brought forth, perhaps in causing some disorder he is noticed by the gods and pays the penalty for

[36] The words for "implant" and "bring forth" have the same root, being related to the word for "nature" (*physis*).

[37] In the Oxford text this phrase is emended to read, in translation: "so too does the law appoint them partners in the household." The insertion of the words for "in the household" is without manuscript authority.

neglecting his own works or for doing the woman's works. (32) And it seems to me," I said, "that the leader of the bees also toils in this way to accomplish the works that the god has ordered her to do." "In what way," she said, "are the works of the leader of the bees similar to the works I must do?" (33) "In that she remains in the hive," I said, "and doesn't let the bees be inactive but sends them to the work whenever some are needed to work outside; she knows what each of them brings in, receives it, and keeps it secure until it is needed for use. When the season for using it comes around, she distributes to each what is just. (34) She also has charge of the weaving of the cells inside, to see that they are beautifully and quickly woven, and when the offspring are born, she is concerned with their nourishment; and once the young are fully grown and able to work, she sends them out as a colony, with one of them as leader." (35) "Will it be necessary, then," said my wife, "for me to do these things as well?" "It will be necessary," I said, "for you to remain indoors and to send out those of the servants whose work is outside; as for those whose work is to be done inside, these are to be in your charge; (36) you must receive what is brought in and distribute what needs to be expended, and as for what needs to be set aside, you must use forethought and guard against expending in a month what was intended to last a year. When wool is brought to you, it must be your concern that clothes be made for whoever needs them. And it must be your concern that the dry grain be fine and fit for eating. (37) There is one thing, however," I said, "among the concerns appropriate to you, that will perhaps seem less agreeable: whenever any of the servants become ill, it must be your concern that all be attended." "By Zeus," said my wife, "that will be most agreeable, at least if those who have been well tended are going to be grateful and feel more good will than before." (38) I admired her reply,' said Ischomachus, 'and spoke: "Isn't it through this kind of forethought that the leader of the hive so disposes the other bees to her that when she leaves the hive, not one of the bees supposes they must let her go, but rather they all follow?" (39) My wife replied: "I wonder whether the works of the leader[38] are not rather yours than mine. For my guarding and distribution of the in-

[38] Ischomachus' wife uses the masculine article (*ho*) with *hēgemōn* ("leader") where previously Ischomachus had used only the feminine (*hē*), in the sense "queen bee."

door things would look somewhat ridiculous, I suppose, if it weren't your concern to bring in something from outside." (40) "On the other hand," I said, "it would look ridiculous for me to bring anything in if there weren't someone to keep secure what had been brought in. Don't you see," I said, "how those who are said to draw water with a leaking jar are to be pitied, since they seem to toil in vain?" "By Zeus," said my wife, "they are miserable indeed, if this is what they do." (41) "Other private concerns will prove pleasant for you, wife," I said, "as when you take someone who knows nothing of spinning and make her knowledgeable, so that she is worth twice as much to you; or when you take someone who knows nothing of housekeeping or waiting and make her a knowledgeable, trusted, and skilled waiting maid, worth any sum; or when you're allowed to treat well those who are both moderate and beneficial to your household, and to punish anyone who looks to be wicked. (42) But the most pleasant thing of all: if you look to be better than I and make me your servant, you will have no need to fear that with advancing age you will be honored any less in the household, and you may trust that as you grow older, the better a partner you prove to be for me, and for the children the better a guardian of the household, by so much more will you be honored in the household. (43) For the noble and good things," I said, "increase for human beings, not ripening like the beauties of youth,[39] but through the exercise of the virtues in life." I seem to remember that the first things I discussed with her were of this sort.' "

CHAPTER 8

(1) " 'Did you notice, Ischomachus,' I said, 'that she was stirred to greater diligence by these things?'

" 'Yes, by Zeus,' said Ischomachus. 'I know she once became very upset, and blushed deeply, when she was unable to give me one of the things I had brought in when I asked for it. (2) Seeing she was ir-

[39] "Ripening like the beauties of youth" translates *ōraiotēs*, a word of rare occurrence and uncertain meaning. It suggests seasonableness, ripeness, and beauty.

ritated, I spoke. "Don't be discouraged, wife," I said, "because you can't give me what I happen to ask for. It is indeed clear poverty not to have a thing to use when it's needed; at the same time our present want—to look for something and be unable to find it—is certainly a less painful thing than not to look for it at all, knowing it's not there. But you aren't at fault in this," I said; "rather I am, since I handed over these things to you without having determined an order where each kind of thing should be put, so that you would know where to put them and where to find them again. (3) There is nothing, wife, so useful or noble for human beings as order. A chorus consists of human beings; when each acts in a chance way, a confusion appears that is unlovely even to look at, but when they act and speak in an ordered manner, the same ones seem worth looking at and worth hearing as well. (4) And, wife," I said, "a disordered army is a thing of the greatest confusion, the easiest prey for its enemies, and for its friends a most inglorious and useless sight—mules, heavy-armed soldiers, baggage carriers, light-armed soldiers, horsemen, and wagons, all together; for how could they march if they were constantly getting in one another's way, the slow marcher obstructing the fast marcher, the fast marcher colliding with someone who is standing still, the wagon blocking the horseman, the mule blocking the wagon, the baggage carrier blocking the heavy-armed soldier? (5) And if they had to fight, how could they ever do it in this condition? The ones who were compelled to flee before their attackers would be apt to trample the ones actually under arms. (6) An ordered army, on the other hand, is the noblest sight for friends and the most appalling for enemies. What friend wouldn't look with pleasure on a large number of heavy-armed soldiers marching in order, or wonder at the horsemen riding in ordered groups? What enemy wouldn't be terrified by the sight of heavy-armed soldiers, horsemen, targeteers, archers, and slingers, all distinctly arranged and following their rulers in an orderly way? (7) For when they march in order, though there be tens of thousands of them, all march calmly, as one man; the empty spaces are always filled by those coming up from behind. (8) And why else is a trireme laden with human beings a fearful thing for enemies and for friends a thing worth looking at, unless it is because it sails quickly? And how else do those who sail in it keep out of one another's way unless it's by sitting in order, bending forward in order, drawing back in order, and embarking and disembarking in order? (9) Disorder is the sort of thing, it seems to me, that would result if a farmer threw together in one place his barley and wheat and peas, and then, when he needed barley cakes or bread or sauce, had to separate them grain by grain instead of having them already distinctly arranged for use. (10) If you would rather avoid this confusion, wife, and want to know how to manage our property accurately, how to find easily whatever is needed for use, and how to oblige me by giving me whatever I ask for, then let us choose a place that is appropriate for each kind of thing and, after putting it there, let us teach the waiting maid to take the thing from there and to put it back again. In that way we shall know what's secure and what isn't; for the place itself will miss the thing that isn't there, a glance will indicate what needs attention, and the knowledge of where each thing is will put it quickly into our hands, so that we'll be at no loss when it comes to using it." (11) And I saw what seemed to be the noblest and most accurate ordering of implements, Socrates, when I went to look over that large Phoenician ship; I saw there a very great number of implements divided within a very small space. (12) For doubtless,' he said, 'it takes a great many implements—wooden things and ropes—to launch and land the ship, and it sails with much so-called suspended rigging; it is armed with many devices for use against enemy ships, carries arms for the men, and brings for each common mess all the implements that human beings use in the house. Besides all this, it is loaded with the cargo that the owner transports for profit. (13) And everything I have mentioned,' he said, 'is kept in a place not much larger than a room proportioned for ten couches. I noticed that everything is kept in such a way that nothing obstructs anything else or requires anyone to search for it, or is inaccessible or so difficult to remove as to cause a delay when needed for some sudden use. (14) I found that the boatswain, the so-called man of the prow, knew so well the place of each kind of thing that he could say, without being there, just where everything was kept and how many there were of each kind, and no less exactly than the knower of letters could say how many letters are in "Socrates" and what their order is. (15) I saw this same one,' said Ischomachus, 'inspecting at his leisure all the things that would have to be used on the ship. And wondering at this examination,' he said, 'I asked him what he was doing. He spoke: "Stranger," he said, "I'm examining how the things in the ship are kept, in case anything should happen," he said, "or in case anything is missing or is awkwardly placed. (16) For when the god raises a storm at sea," he said, "there's no time to search for whatever may be needed or to get out something from an awkward place. The god threatens and punishes the slack. If only he doesn't destroy those who have not gone wrong, one should be very content; and if he preserves those who serve very nobly, one should know much gratitude," he said, "to the gods." (17) Having observed, then, the accuracy in this arrangement, I said to my wife that we would be very slack indeed if those in ships—which, after all, are small—find places for their things and preserve the order among them, even when they are roughly tossed about, and are able even in moments of panic to find what is needed, whereas we, who have large and distinct storerooms in our house for each kind of thing and indeed have a house on solid ground, cannot find a noble place for each of our things where they may readily be found—how could this be anything but great unintelligence on our parts? (18) That an ordered arrangement of implements is a good, then, and that it is easy to find in the house an advantageous place for each kind of thing, has been established. (19) But how noble it looks, too, when shoes of any kind are set out in a regular manner; it is noble to see clothes of any kind when they are sorted, as also bedcovers, bronze kettles, the things pertaining to the table, and—what of all things would be most ridiculed, not indeed by the solemn man but by the wit—even pots have a graceful look when distinctly arranged. (20) Indeed, all other things look somehow nobler when they are kept in order.[40] Each kind of thing looks like a chorus of implements, and even the space between them looks noble, as everything has been kept out of it—just as a circular chorus is not only itself a noble sight, but even the space within it looks pure and noble. (21) If I am speaking the truth, wife," I said, "it will be possible for us to try these things without suffering much loss or going to much trouble. Nor should we be discouraged, wife," I said, "by the difficulty of finding someone who can learn the places and remember to

[40] "Order" here translates the Greek *kosmos,* which often means simply "ornament" (as in 4.23 and 9.6). The usual word for "order," *taxis,* and its derivatives (as in 8.18 and 8.22–23), connote by contrast primarily military order.

replace each kind of thing. (22) For doubtless we know that the whole city has ten thousand times what we have, yet when you tell any one of the servants to buy something for you in the marketplace, he is never at a loss—every one of them evidently knows where he has to go for each kind of thing. The cause of this," I said, "is nothing other than that everything is kept ordered in its place. (23) But if someone goes looking for another human being—who may at the same time be looking for him—he frequently gives up before finding him. And the cause of this is nothing other than that there is no ordered place where each is to meet." As regards the order of the implements and their use, I seem to remember discussing with her things of this sort.' "

CHAPTER 9

(1) " 'What then, Ischomachus?' I said. 'Did your wife seem to heed to what you were so seriously teaching her?'

" 'What else did she do if not promise, at any rate, to be diligent, manifest her very great pleasure, as though she had found some easy means out of a difficulty, and ask me to order things separately as quickly as possible in the way I had stated?'

(2) " 'How, then, Ischomachus,' I said, 'did you separately order them for her?'

" 'What else seemed best to me if not to show her first the capacity of the house? For it is not adorned with decorations, Socrates; the rooms were planned and built simply with a view to their being the most advantageous receptacles possible for the things that would be in them, so that each called for what is suitable to it. (3) The bedroom, being in an interior part of the house, invited the most valuable bedcovers and implements; the dry parts of the dwelling, the grain; the cool places, the wine; and the well-lighted places, the works and implements that need light. (4) And I displayed to her the areas for the daily use of human beings, furnished so as to be cool in summer and warm in winter. And I displayed to her the house as a whole, and how it lies open to the south—obviously, so as to be well exposed to the sun in winter and well shaded in summer. (5) Then I pointed out to her the women's apartments, separated from the men's by a bolted door, so that nothing may be taken out that shouldn't be and so that the servants may not produce offspring without our knowledge. For the useful ones, for the most part, feel even more good will once they have had children, but when wicked ones are paired together, they become only more resourceful in their bad behavior. (6) When we had gone through these things,' he said, 'we then proceeded to separate our belongings according to tribes.[41] We began first,' he said, 'by collecting whatever we use for sacrifices. After this we distinguished the woman's ornaments for festivals, the man's dress for festivals and war, bedcovers for the women's apartments, bedcovers for the men's apartments, shoes for women, shoes for men. (7) Another tribe consisted of arms, another of instruments for spinning, another of instruments for breadmaking, another of instruments for cooking, another of the things for bathing, another of the things for kneading bread, another of the things for the table; and all these things were further divided according to whether they were used every day or only for festivals. (8) We also set apart the monthly expenses from those calculated on a yearly basis; for in this way we could better see how things would come out at the end. And when we had sorted our belongings according to tribes, we took each kind of thing to its appropriate place. (9) After this, as to the implements the servants use from day to day—those for making bread, for cooking, for spinning, and others of this sort—we pointed out to those who would be using them where each must go, handed them over, and gave orders that they be kept secure. (10) Those we use for festivals, for entertaining foreigners, or only from time to time we handed over to the housekeeper, and after pointing out to her their places and counting and making lists of the various kinds of things, we told her to give each what he needed of them, to remember what she had given someone, and when she had got it back, to return it to the place she had taken it from. (11) We chose as housekeeper the one who upon examination seemed to us most continent as regards food, wine, sleep, and associating with[42] men, and who, in addition, seemed to have a good memory and the forethought to avoid being

[41] In this context the sense seems to be classes or kinds of things (*phulē*). See also 9.7–8.

[42] Or, "intercourse."

punished by us for negligence and to consider how, by gratifying us in some way, she might be honored by us in return. (12) We taught her also to feel good will toward us, sharing our delights when we were delighted in some way, and when there was something painful, inviting her aid. We further educated her to be eager to increase the household, making her thoroughly acquainted with it and giving her a share in its prosperity. (13) And we inspired justice in her, honoring the just more than the unjust and displaying to her that they live richer and freer lives than the unjust. We then installed her in the place. (14) But in addition to all these things, Socrates,' he said, 'I told my wife that there would be no benefit in any of this unless she herself was diligent in seeing that the order belonging to each thing remains. I taught her that in the cities subject to good laws the citizens do not think it enough merely to have noble laws, but in addition choose guardians of the laws to examine them, to praise the one who acts lawfully, and to punish the one who acts contrary to the laws. (15) Then,' he said, 'I suggested that my wife consider herself a guardian of the laws regarding the things in the house; that she inspect the implements whenever it seems best to her, just as a garrison commander inspects his guards; that she test whether each thing is in a noble condition, just as the council tests horses and horsemen; and that, like a queen, she praise and honor the deserving, to the limit of her capacity, and rebuke and punish the one who needs such things. (16) In addition,' he said, 'I taught her that she could not be justly annoyed if I gave her many more orders in regard to our possessions than I gave to the servants, displaying to her that the servants share in their master's wealth only to the extent that they carry it, attend to it, or guard it, and that no one of them is allowed to use it unless the lord gives it to him, whereas everything is the master's to use as he wishes. (17) To the one deriving the greatest benefit from its preservation and the greatest harm from its destruction belongs the greatest concern for a thing—this I declared to her.'

(18) " 'What then?' I said. 'After your wife had heard these things, Ischomachus, did she at all heed you?'

" 'What else did she do,' he said, 'if not tell me I didn't understand her correctly if I supposed that in teaching her to be concerned with our property I had ordered her to do something hard. For as she told me,' he said, 'it would have been much harder if I had ordered her to neglect her own things than if she were required to concern herself with the goods of the household. (19) For just as it seems natural,' he said, 'for a sensible[43] woman to be concerned for her offspring rather than to neglect them, so she said she believes that it's more pleasant for a sensible woman to be concerned for those of the possessions that delight her because they are her own than to neglect them.' "

Chapter 10

(1) "On hearing that his wife had replied to him in this way," said Socrates, "I spoke. 'By Hera, Ischomachus,' I said, 'you display your wife's manly understanding.'

" 'There are other instances of her high-mindedness that I am willing to relate to you,' said Ischomachus, 'instances of her obeying me quickly in some matter after hearing it only once.'

" 'In what sort of thing?' I said. 'Speak; for to me it is much more pleasant to learn of the virtue of a living woman than to have had Zeuxis display for me the noble likeness of a woman he had painted.'

(2) "Ischomachus then says: 'Well once, Socrates,' he said, 'I saw she had applied a good deal of white lead to her face, that she might seem still fairer than she was, and some dye, so that she would look more flushed than was the truth, and she also wore high shoes, that she might seem taller than she naturally was. (3) "Tell me, wife," I said, "would you judge me more worthy to be loved as a partner in wealth if I showed you our property itself, didn't boast of having more property than is really mine, and didn't hide any part of our property, or if instead I tried to deceive you by saying I have more property than is really mine and by displaying to you counterfeit money, necklaces of gilt wood, and purple robes that lose their color, and asserting they are genuine?" (4) She broke in straightway. "Hush," she said; "don't you become like that; if you did, I for my part could never love you from my soul." "Haven't we also come together, wife," I said, "as partners in one another's bodies?" "Human

[43] Or, "sensible," "sober."

beings say so, at least," she said. (5) "Would I then seem more worthy to be loved," I said, "as a partner in the body, if I tried to offer you my body after concerning myself that it be healthy and strong, so that I would really be well complexioned, or if instead I smeared myself with vermilion, applied flesh color beneath my eyes, and then displayed myself to you and embraced you, all the while deceiving you and offering you vermilion to see and touch instead of my own skin?" (6) "I wouldn't touch vermilion with as much pleasure as I would you," she said, "or see flesh color with as much pleasure as your own, or see painted eyes with as much pleasure as your healthy ones." (7) "You must believe, wife," 'Ischomachus said that he had said,' "that I too am not more pleased by the color of white lead or dye than by your color, but just as the gods have made horses most pleasant to horses, oxen to oxen, and sheep to sheep, so human beings suppose the pure body of a human being is most pleasant. (8) Such deceits may in some way deceive outsiders and go undetected, but when those who are always together try to deceive one another they are necessarily found out. For either they are found out when they rise from their beds and before they have prepared themselves, or they are detected by their sweat or exposed by tears, or they are genuinely revealed in bathing." '

(9) " 'By the gods,' I said, 'what did she reply to this?'

" 'What else,' he said, 'was her reply, if not that she never did anything of the sort again and tried always to display herself suitably and in a pure state. At the same time she asked me if I could not advise her how she might really come to sight as beautiful and not merely seem to be. (10) I advised her, Socrates,' he said, 'not always to sit about like a slave but to try, with the gods' help, to stand at the loom like a mistress, to teach others what she knew better than they, and to learn what she did not know as well; and also to examine the breadmaker, to watch over the housekeeper in her distribution of things, and to go about and investigate whether each kind of thing is in the place it should be. In this way, it seemed to me, she could both attend to her concerns and have the opportunity to walk about. (11) And I said it would be good exercise to moisten and knead the bread and to shake out and fold the clothes and bedcovers. I said that if she exercised in this way, she would take more pleasure in eating, would become healthier, and so would come to sight as better complexioned in truth. (12) And a wife's looks, when in contrast to a waiting maid she is purer and more suitably dressed, become attractive, especially when she gratifies her husband willingly instead of serving him under compulsion. (13) On the other hand, women who always sit about in pretentious solemnity lend themselves to comparison with those who use adornments and deceit. And now, Socrates,' he said, 'know well, my wife still arranges her life as I taught her then and as I tell you now.' "

Chapter 11

(1) "Then I spoke. 'Ischomachus, I seem to have heard enough for the present concerning the works of your wife, for which indeed you both deserve much praise. But as to your own works,' I said, 'tell me now of them, in order that you may take pleasure in relating the things for which you are highly reputed and that I may be very grateful to you after hearing fully about the works of the gentleman and after understanding them, if I can do so.'

(2) " 'But by Zeus, Socrates,' said Ischomachus, 'it will be a very great pleasure for me to tell you about my constant doings, so that you may also correct me if in anything I do not seem to you to act nobly.'

(3) " 'But how could I justly correct an accomplished gentleman,' I said, 'especially as I am a man who is reputed to be an idle talker and to measure the air and who is reproached for being poor—which seems to be the most foolish accusation of all? (4) And I would have been greatly discouraged by this charge, Ischomachus, if I had not recently encountered the horse of Nicias, the newcomer, and seen the numerous onlookers who were following it and heard some of them speaking about it; whereupon I approached the groom and asked him if the horse had much wealth. (5) He looked at me as though I had not asked a sane question, and spoke: "How could a horse have wealth?" I was relieved then on hearing that it is lawfully permissible for a poor horse to become good if it has a soul by nature good. (6) Therefore, as it is permitted me to become a good man, you must fully relate your works so as to enable me, insofar as I can learn by

listening, to imitate you, beginning tomorrow. That is a good day,' I said, 'to begin in virtue.'

(7) " 'You're joking, Socrates,' said Ischomachus, 'but I'll relate to you anyway the practices with which, as far as I can, I try to occupy my life. (8) Since I seem to have learned that the gods do not by law permit human beings to prosper unless they understand what they ought to do and are diligent in accomplishing it, and that nevertheless they grant only to some of the prudent and diligent to be happy, and not to others, I therefore begin by attending to the gods, and I try to pray to them and act in such a manner that it may be by law permitted me to acquire health, strength of body, honor in the city, good will among my friends, noble safety in war, and noble increase of riches.'

(9) "And I, having heard this: 'Is it then a matter of concern with you to be rich, Ischomachus, and having much wealth, to have also the troubles that come from concerning yourself with it?'

" 'What you ask of is certainly a matter of concern with me,' said Ischomachus, 'for it seems to me a pleasant thing, Socrates, to honor the gods magnificently, to aid friends when they need something, and to see that the city is never unadorned through lack of wealth on my account.'

(10) " 'These are noble things you speak of, Ischomachus,' I said, 'and particularly suited to a capable man. Indeed how could it be otherwise? For there are many human beings who cannot live without being in need of others, and many are content if they can provide only what is enough for themselves. But as to those who not only can manage their own households but even produce a surplus that enables them to adorn the city and relieve their friends, how could one hold that they are not men of weight and strength? (11) There are indeed many of us who can praise this sort,' I said, 'but you, Ischomachus, tell me what you began with—how you concern yourself with health and the strength of the body, and how it is permitted you to save yourself nobly in war. As for your money-making,' I said, 'it will be sufficient if we hear of that later.'

(12) " 'But as it seems to me, Socrates,' said Ischomachus, 'these things all follow on one another. For when someone has enough to eat, he stays healthier, it seems to me, if he works it off in the right manner, and in working it off, he also becomes stronger. If he trains

in military matters, he can save himself more nobly, and if he is diligent in the right manner and doesn't grow soft, it is likely he will increase his household.'

(13) " 'I follow you this far, Ischomachus,' I said, 'when you assert that the human being who works off a meal and is diligent and trains himself is more apt to acquire the good things, but as to the kind of toil that is necessary for keeping up one's condition and strength, and as to how one ought to train in military matters, or how one must be diligent in producing a surplus so as to aid friends and strengthen the city—it is with pleasure,' I said, 'that I would learn these things.'

(14) " 'I have accustomed myself, Socrates,' said Ischomachus, 'to rising from my bed at an hour when I can expect to find indoors anyone it happens I need to see. And if there is something I need to do in the city, I use the opportunity to walk there; (15) but if there's no necessity for being in the city, the boy takes my horse into the fields, and I use the occasion for a walk along the road to the fields—which is perhaps a better thing, Socrates, than a walk under a colonnade. (16) When I come to the fields, I examine the work in hand and correct it, if I have something better to suggest, whether it is planting they happen to be doing or plowing the fallow or sowing or gathering in the crops. (17) After this I usually mount my horse and practice a kind of horsemanship as similar as possible to the horsemanship necessary in war, avoiding neither traverses, slopes, ditches, nor streams, though concerned not to lame my horse in the process. (18) When this is done, the boy gives the horse a roll and leads it home, at the same time taking with him into town whatever we need from the country; and I return home, sometimes walking, sometimes at a run, and clean myself up. I then take my morning meal, Socrates, eating just enough to pass the day without being either empty or overfull.'

(19) " 'By Hera, Ischomachus,' I said, 'to me, at any rate, these things are very agreeable. For to make use at the same time of your arrangements regarding health and strength, your training for war, and your concern for riches—all this seems to me quite admirable. (20) And you have given sufficient proofs that you concern yourself with each of these things in the right manner; for we see you generally healthy and strong, with the gods' help, and we know you are

spoken of as one of the most skilled in horsemanship and one of the very rich.'

(21) " 'All the same, Socrates,' he said, 'in doing these things I am greatly slandered[44] by many—perhaps you supposed I was about to say I am called a gentleman by many.'

(22) " 'But I was going to ask you about this too, Ischomachus,' I said: 'whether you make it a concern of yours to be able to give an account of yourself or to receive one from another if you should ever need it.'

" 'Do I not seem to you, Socrates,' he said, 'to practice constantly these very things—to say in my defense that I do not act unjustly toward anyone and treat many well as far as I am able, and to practice accusing human beings by learning that some act unjustly both toward many in private and toward the city and treat no one well?'

(23) " 'But if you are also practiced in interpretation, Ischomachus,' I said, 'clarify this further for me.'

" 'I never cease to practice speaking, Socrates,' he said. 'For either I listen to one of the servants accusing someone or defending himself and I try to cross-examine him, or I blame someone before my friends or praise someone, or I reconcile certain of my intimates by teaching them it is more advantageous to be friends than enemies; (24) or else when we are in the presence of a general, we censure someone, or defend someone who had been unjustly faulted for something, or accuse one another if someone has been unjustly honored. And frequently we deliberate as to what we desire to do, and praise these things, and as to the things we don't want to do, we blame them. (25) Up to now, Socrates,' he said, 'I have many times submitted to a judgment as to what I must suffer or pay.'

" 'Whose judgment, Ischomachus?' I said. 'For this had escaped my notice.'

" 'My wife's,' he said.

" 'And how do you plead your case?' I said.

" 'Very decently, when it's advantageous to tell the truth; but when untruth would be handier, Socrates, by Zeus I am not able to make the worse argument the stronger.'

[44] I.e., the victim of extortion (*sychophantesthai*). Strictly speaking, "sycophants" were those who threatened to bring formal judicial actions against wealthy citizens unless they received a payoff (see *Mem*. 2.9 and *Symp*. 4.30).

"And I spoke: 'Perhaps, Ischomachus, you cannot make the untruth true.' "

Chapter 12

(1) " 'But don't let me detain you, Ischomachus,' I said, 'if you want to go away.'

" 'By Zeus, Socrates,' he said, 'you're not detaining me. I wouldn't go away in any case until the market was over.'

(2) " 'By Zeus,' I said, 'you're certainly apprehensive about losing your name for being called a gentleman. For now there are perhaps many matters that require your concern, and yet because you made a promise to some foreigners, you are waiting for them, in order not to prove untruthful.'

" 'But those things you speak of, Socrates,' said Ischomachus, 'aren't neglected by me, for I have stewards in the fields.'

(3) " 'When you need a steward, Ischomachus,' I said, 'do you try to learn where there's a man who is a skilled steward and attempt to buy him, just as when you need a carpenter you learn—I well know—where to look for a skilled carpenter and attempt to get him into your possession, or do you educate the stewards yourself?'

(4) " 'By Zeus, Socrates,' he said, 'I try to educate them myself. For if someone is to be sufficiently diligent when I am away, what must he know other than what I know myself? If I myself am fit to command the works, doubtless I may teach another what I know.'

(5) " 'Then mustn't he first feel good will toward you and yours,' I said, 'if he is going to be sufficient in your place? For without good will what benefit is there in a steward's having any kind of knowledge?'

" 'None, by Zeus,' said Ischomachus, 'but good will toward me and mine is the first thing I try to teach.'

(6) " 'By the gods,' I said, 'how can you teach just anyone you want to feel good will toward you and yours?'

" 'Generosity, by Zeus,' said Ischomachus, 'whenever the gods give us an abundance of some good.'

(7) " 'Are you saying, then,' I said, 'that those who enjoy your goods come to feel good will and want to do something good for you in return?'

" 'I see this as the best instrument, Socrates, for securing good will.'

(8) " 'And if he comes to feel good will toward you, Ischomachus,' I said, 'will he then be a fit steward? Don't you see that while so to speak all human beings feel good will toward themselves, many of them aren't willing to be very diligent in acquiring the good things that they want?'

(9) " 'But by Zeus,' said Ischomachus, 'when it's stewards of this sort I want to appoint, I teach them to be diligent.'

(10) " 'By the gods,' I said, 'how? For I supposed diligence was something that could in no way be taught.'

" 'Nor is it possible, Socrates,' he said, 'to teach diligence to all without exception.'

(11) " 'For whom, then,' I said, 'is it possible? Try in every way to indicate to me clearly who they are.'

" 'First, Socrates,' he said, 'you couldn't make anyone diligent who is incontinent in regard to wine; for intoxication inspires forgetfulness of everything that needs to be done.'

(12) " 'Is it only those who lack continence in this, then,' I said, 'who are incapable of diligence, or others as well?'

" 'No, by Zeus,' said Ischomachus, 'but also those who lack continence in regard to sleep; for no one could do in his sleep what needs to be done or make others do it.'

(13) " 'What then?' I said. 'Will these be the only ones incapable of being taught this diligence by us, or are there others in addition?'

" 'It seems to me, at least,' said Ischomachus, 'that those who are mad lovers of the sexual[45] cannot be taught to be more diligent about any other thing than they are about this; (14) for it is not easy to find a hope or a concern more pleasant than the concern for one's favorite, nor is there any punishment so harsh as being kept from one's beloved when there is something to be done. So I give up on those I understand to be of this sort and don't even try to make them diligent.'

[45] Literally, "Aphrodite."

(15) " 'What then?' I said. 'Are those who are in love with profit also incapable of being educated to diligence in the works of the field?'

" 'No, by Zeus,' said Ischomachus, 'not at all, but they are very well disposed to such diligence; for nothing else is needed than to point out to them that diligence is profitable.'

(16) " 'And as for others,' I said, 'who are continent in the things you suggest and who are temperate lovers of profit,[46] how do you teach them to be diligent in the way you want them to be?'

" 'It's very simple, Socrates,' he said. 'When I see they are diligent, I praise them and try to honor them, and when I see they are negligent, I try to do and say things that will sting them.'

(17) " 'Come, Ischomachus,' I said, 'turn the argument from the diligence of the educated and clarify something about education—whether it's possible for one who is himself negligent to make others diligent.'

(18) " 'No, by Zeus,' said Ischomachus, 'no more than it's possible for someone who is himself unmusical to make others musical. For when the teacher himself sets a bad example in something, it is hard to learn from him to do it in a noble way, and if the master sets an example of negligence, it is hard for the attendant to become diligent. (19) To speak concisely: I seem to have learned that the servants of a bad master are always useless; on the other hand, I have seen the servants of a good master act badly, though not without being punished. But whoever wants to make them diligent must be skilled in surveying and inspecting, be willing to show gratitude to the one who is the cause of things nobly done, and not shrink from imposing a proper penalty on the one who is negligent. (20) It seems to me that the barbarian's reply was a noble one,' said Ischomachus, 'when the king of Persia, having chanced upon a good horse and wanting to fatten it as quickly as possible, asked one of those who seemed to be clever in regard to horses what most quickly fattens a horse, and he is said to have answered, "the master's eye." And so in other things, Socrates,' he said, 'it is under the master's eye that noble and good works are done.'"

[46] In 12.15, Socrates, following Ischomachus, speaks of "erotic love" (*erōs*); in 12.16 he replaces the erotic lovers of profit by temperate, "friendly lovers" of profit—not *erōs* but *philia*, the term ordinarily translated "love" in the dialogue. Words related to *erōs* occur elsewhere only in 6.12, where the verb *eran* is translated "desire."

CHAPTER 13

(1) " 'When you have impressed upon someone, and with particular firmness, that he must be diligent in the way you want,' I said, 'is he then fit to become a steward, or will there be some other thing to be learned in addition if he is to be a fit steward?'

(2) " 'Yes, by Zeus,' said Ischomachus, 'it still remains for him to understand what is to be done and when it is to be done and how; for if he does not, how is a steward any more beneficial than a doctor who is diligent in visiting his patient day and night and yet doesn't know what would be advantageous for him?'

(3) " 'And if he learns the work that is to be done,' I said, 'will he need anything in addition, or will this be your perfect steward?'

" 'I suppose he must learn at least to rule the workers,' he said.

(4) " 'Then do you,' I said, 'educate the stewards to be fit to rule?'

" 'I try, at least,' said Ischomachus.

" 'But how, by the gods,' I said, 'do you educate them in this matter of ruling human beings?'

" 'In a very ordinary way, Socrates,' he said, 'so that you will perhaps laugh on hearing it.'

(5) " 'This is not a laughing matter, Ischomachus,' I said. 'For whoever is able to make rulers of human beings can evidently teach them also to be masters of human beings, and whoever can make them masters can make them also kings. And so the one who can do this seems to me to be worthy of great praise rather than laughter.'

(6) " 'Other living things, Socrates,' he said, 'learn to obey in these two ways: by being punished when they try to disobey, and by being well treated when they serve eagerly. (7) Colts, at any rate, learn to obey the colt breakers by getting something that's pleasant to them when they obey and getting into trouble when they disobey, until they become subservient to the mind of the colt breaker; (8) and puppies, though they are far inferior to human beings both in mind and tongue, nevertheless learn in some way to run in a circle and do somersaults and many other things. For when they obey, they get something they need, and when they are negligent, they are punished. (9) As for human beings, it's possible to make them more obedient by speech as well, by displaying to them how advantageous it is for them to obey; and yet for slaves the education that seems fit only for

beasts is effective also in teaching them to obey, for in gratifying their bellies to the extent they desire, you can accomplish much with them. But the ambitious natures among them are spurred by praise as well. For some natures are as hungry for praise as others are for food and drink. (10) These things, then, which I myself do in the expectation of having more obedient human beings for my use, I teach to those I want to appoint as stewards, and I second them also in the following ways: I make sure that the clothing and the shoes I must supply to the workers are not all alike, but rather some are worse and some better, so that I may be able to honor the superior one with the better things and give the worse things to the worse. (11) For it seems to me, Socrates,' he said, 'that it is a great discouragement to the good when they see that the work is done by themselves and yet that they receive the same as those who aren't willing to toil or risk danger when there is need of it. (12) I myself, therefore, in no way consider that the better and the worse deserve to receive equal things, and when I see that the stewards have given the most excellent things to those who are worth the most, I praise them, but if I see someone being honored before others through flattery or some other favor that benefits no one, I do not neglect the matter, Socrates; rather I reprimand the steward and try to teach him that what he is doing is not to his own advantage.' "

Chapter 14

(1) " 'But when he has become fit to rule for you, Ischomachus,' I said, 'so as to make the others obedient, do you then consider him the perfect steward, or does the one who has everything you've spoken of still need something in addition?'

(2) " 'Yes, by Zeus,' said Ischomachus, 'he must abstain from the master's things and not steal anything. For if the one who manages the crops should dare to make off with them, and the works ceased to be lucrative, what benefit would there be in entrusting him with the farming concerns?'

(3) " 'Do you then undertake to teach this justice as well?' I said.

" 'Certainly,' said Ischomachus, 'but I find it's a teaching not all readily obey. (4) Nevertheless, taking some things from the laws of

Dracon and some from those of Solon, I try,' he said, 'to lead the servants to justice. For it seems to me,' he said, 'that those men laid down many of their laws with a view to the teaching of this sort of justice. (5) For it is written there that, if someone is caught in the act, he is to be punished for the theft and imprisoned, and those who resist may be put to death. It's evident,' he said, 'that in writing these things, they wanted to make sure that base profit would not be lucrative for the unjust. (6) Adopting some things, then, from these laws,' he said, 'and using others from the laws of the king of Persia as models, I try to make the servants just in regard to what they have under their management. (7) For the first kind of law only punishes those who go wrong, but the laws of the king not only punish those who act unjustly, but they also benefit the just; so that when they see the just becoming rich, many of those who are unjust and lovers of profit are very careful to refrain from acting unjustly. (8) But if I perceive some,' he said, 'who try to act unjustly though they have been well treated, I make it clear that I have no use for anyone so incorrigibly greedy. (9) On the other hand, if I learn of some who are induced to be just, not only through having more than others as a result of their justice, but also through desiring my praise, I treat them as free men, not only enriching them but honoring them as gentlemen. (10) For it seems to me it is in this, Socrates,' he said, 'that the ambitious man[47] differs from the man who loves profit—in his willingness to toil when there is need of it, to risk danger, and to abstain from base profits, for the sake of praise and honor.' "

CHAPTER 15

(1) " 'But when you have inspired in someone a desire that the good things be yours, and you have inspired in the same one a diligence in securing them for you, when in addition you have seen to it that he possesses knowledge as to how each kind of work is to be done so as to provide greater benefits, when in addition you have made him fit to rule, and when finally he is as pleased for you as you

[47] Literally, "the man who loves honor."

would be for yourself at exhibiting the most bountiful harvest possible, I will no longer ask whether someone of this sort still needs something in addition; for it seems to me a steward of this sort would already be worth very much. But Ischomachus,' I said, 'don't omit this one thing, which we passed over very lazily in the argument.'

(2) " 'What?' said Ischomachus.

" 'Doubtless you were saying,' I said, 'that it is most important to learn how each kind of work must be performed; there would be no benefit in diligence, you asserted, if one didn't know what must be done and how it must be done.'

(3) "Then Ischomachus spoke. 'Are you suggesting I teach you the art of farming itself, Socrates?'

" 'It is perhaps this art that makes those rich who know it,' I said, 'while those who don't know it live a poor life no matter how much they toil.'

(4) " 'Now, Socrates,' he said, 'hear of the philanthropy of this art. For as it is most beneficial and pleasant to work at, the noblest and most beloved of gods and human beings, and in addition the easiest to learn, how can it be anything but well-bred? For doubtless we call those living things well-bred that are noble, great, beneficial, and at the same time gentle toward human beings.'

(5) " 'I seem to have learned sufficiently what you were saying, Ischomachus,' I said, 'as regards what the steward must be taught; I seem to have learned in what way you asserted you made him feel good will toward you, and in what way diligent, a fit ruler, and just. (6) But when you said that the one who is going to concern himself with farming in the right manner must learn what is to be done and how and when, for each kind of thing—these things, it seems to me,' I said, 'we have passed over somewhat lazily in the argument. (7) It is as if you should say that the one who is going to be able to write down what is dictated to him and read what is written must know letters. Had I heard this, I would have heard indeed that one must know letters, but I suppose I wouldn't know letters any better for knowing this. (8) In the same way, I am by now readily persuaded that the one who is going to concern himself with farming must know it, but I don't know how to farm any better for knowing this. (9) But if it should seem best to me right now to take up farming, I

would seem to be like the doctor who visits his patients and examines them and yet doesn't know what would be advantageous for them. So that I may not be of this sort, then,' I said, 'teach me the works of farming themselves.'

(10) " 'But really, Socrates,' he said, 'farming is not as difficult to learn as the other arts, where the one who is being taught must wear himself out in the learning before the work he does is worth what it takes to feed him; but partly by seeing others at work and partly by listening, you would know straightway, and well enough to teach someone else, if you wanted to. And I think you yourself know very much about it,' he said, 'without being aware of it. (11) For the other artisans in some way conceal the most important features of their arts; among farmers, on the other hand, the one who plants in the noblest manner would be very pleased if someone watched him do it, and similarly with the one who sows in the noblest manner; and if you asked him about something that was nobly done, he would not conceal from you how he did it. (12) And so it appears, Socrates,' he said, 'that farming also renders those who are engaged in it extremely well-bred in their characters.'

(13) " 'That's a noble preface,' I said, 'and not such as to turn your listener from questioning. As it is easy to learn, then, you must on that account describe it to me much more fully. It is not a disgrace for you to teach something that is easy, and rather more disgraceful by far for me not to know it, especially if it happens to be useful.' "

CHAPTER 16

(1) " 'First of all, Socrates,' he said, 'I want to display this to you: that part of farming is not at all hard which is called most complicated by those who describe farming most accurately in speech and who do the least work themselves. (2) For they assert that one who is going to farm in the right manner must know the nature of the earth.'

" 'And they are right to say it,' I said. 'For the one not knowing what the earth has the power to bear would not, I suppose, know what he ought to sow or plant.'

(3) " 'It's possible to understand what it can and cannot bear,' said Ischomachus, 'simply by looking at the crops and trees on another's land. And once someone understands this, there is no advantage in fighting against the god. For he wouldn't obtain more of the necessary things by sowing and planting what he himself needs rather than what the earth is pleased to bring forth and nourish. (4) But if the earth cannot display its capacity on account of the laziness of the owners, it is often possible to understand more of the truth about it from a neighboring place than from inquiring of a neighboring human being. (5) And even lying waste it displays its nature, for if it brings forth beautiful wild products, it can, if tended, bear beautiful domesticated ones. Thus even those who are not very experienced in farming can understand the nature of the earth.'

(6) " 'Well it seems to me, Ischomachus,' I said, 'that I am sufficiently reassured as to this: that I mustn't abstain from farming out of fear that I don't understand the nature of the earth. (7) Indeed, I remember the practice of fishermen,' I said, 'whose work is at sea, who don't stop to look and don't even slacken their course as they sail by the fields, and yet who, when they see the crops in the earth, do not hesitate to declare which kind of earth is good and which bad, and to criticize the one and praise the other. And, in fact, for the most part I see them declaring the same kind of earth to be good as do those who are very experienced in farming.'

(8) " 'At what point, then, Socrates,' he said, 'do you want me to begin reminding you of farming? For I know I'll tell you many things concerning how to farm that you already know.'

(9) " 'It seems to me, Ischomachus,' I said, 'that I would be pleased to learn first—what particularly becomes a man who is a philosopher—how I might work the land, if I wanted to, so as to get the greatest amount of barley and wheat.'

(10) " 'Do you know, then, that it's necessary to prepare the fallow[48] for sowing?'

" 'I do know it,' I said.

(11) " 'What if we began to plough the earth in winter?' he said.

" 'It would be mud,' I said.

" 'Does the summer seem better to you?'

[48] The word here translated "fallow" (*neos*) can also mean "youth."

" 'The earth will be too hard for the team,' I said.

(12) " 'Probably the work ought to be begun in the spring,' he said.

" 'It's likely,' I said, 'that the earth will be easier to spread if it is plowed at that time.'

" 'And it is then, Socrates,' he said, 'that the undergrowth, being turned up, provides manure for the earth, while it has not yet shed its seeds so as to bring forth more. (13) For I suppose you understand this too, that if the fallow is going to be good, it must be purified of weeds and baked as much as possible by the sun.'

" 'Certainly,' I said, 'and I believe it must necessarily be this way.'

(14) " 'Do you hold, then,' he said, 'that these things can come about in any other way than by turning over the earth as often as possible during the summer?'

" 'I know with some accuracy,' I said, 'that there is no other way to keep the weeds from taking root or to dry them out with the heat, or to have the earth baked by the sun, than to work it with the team in the middle of the summer and in the middle of the day.'

(15) " 'And if human beings should make the fallow by digging up the ground,' he said, 'isn't it quite evident that they also must separate the earth and the weeds?'

" 'And scatter the weeds over the surface,' I said, 'that they may dry out, and turn the earth, that the raw part of it may be baked.' "

CHAPTER 17

(1) " 'As regards the fallow, Socrates,' he said, 'you see how the same things seem best to both of us.'

" 'They seem best indeed,' I said.

" 'But as regards the season for sowing, Socrates,' he said, 'do you know any other way than to sow in that season that all the human beings before us who have tried it, and all those who try it now, understand to be the most excellent? (2) For when the autumnal times comes, all human beings, I suppose, look to the god to find out when he will send rain to the earth and allow them to sow.'

" 'Indeed, Ischomachus,' I said, 'all human beings understand this, and they don't willingly sow in dry ground—because, evidently, those who sow before the god bids them to have to wrestle with many punishments.'

(3) " 'Then all human beings,' said Ischomachus, 'are of like mind in these matters.'

" 'As regards what the god teaches,' I said, 'it happens that all think alike, as for example in winter it seems better to all to wear heavy clothing, if they are able, and it seems better to all to light a fire, if they have wood.'

(4) " 'But in this matter of sowing,' said Ischomachus, 'many differ, Socrates, as to whether the early sowing is the most excellent or the middle, or the latest.'

" 'And the god,' I said, 'does not manage the year in an orderly way; rather one year is finest for the early sowing, another for the middle, another for the latest.'

(5) " 'Do you believe it's superior, then, Socrates,' he said, 'for someone to choose one of these sowings, whether he has much or little seed to sow, or rather to begin with the earliest sowing and continue right through the latest?'

"And I spoke. (6) 'To me, Ischomachus, it seems most excellent to share it among all the sowings. For I believe it is much superior always to have enough grain rather than to have very much at one time and not enough at another.'

" 'In this at any rate, Socrates,' he said, 'you, the student, are of like mind with me, the teacher, even when you are the first to declare your mind.'

(7) " 'What of this?' I said. 'Is there a complicated art to casting the seed?'

" 'By all means, Socrates,' he said, 'let's examine this too. That the seed must be cast from the hand you know, I take it,' he said.

" 'I have seen it,' I said.

" 'But there are some who can cast it evenly,' he said, 'and others who cannot.'

" 'In this, then,' I said, 'the hand needs practice, like the hand of a lyre player, so that it will be able to serve the mind.'

(8) " 'Certainly,' he said. 'But what if the earth is in some places lighter and in others heavier?'

" 'What do you mean?' I said. 'That the lighter is the weaker, and the heavier the stronger?'

" 'I mean that,' he said, 'and I ask you this question: would you give equal seed to each kind of earth, or to which kind would you give more?'

(9) " 'I for my part hold to adding more water to the stronger wine,' I said, 'and to imposing greater burden on the stronger human being if something needs to be carried; and if certain persons needed maintenance, I would order the more capable to maintain more of them. But as to whether weak earth becomes stronger,' I said, 'when someone puts a greater crop in it—as would be the case with oxen—this you must teach me.'

(10) "Ischomachus spoke, laughing. 'But you're joking, Socrates,' he said. 'Know well, however,' he said, 'after you've put the seed in the earth, and after the first shoots appear from the seed during that time when the earth takes much nourishment from heaven, if you plow them in again, they become food for the earth, which then has strength instilled in it, as if from manure; but if you allow the earth to go on nourishing the seed until you have the crop, it is hard for the weak earth to bring much of a crop to maturity. It is hard also for a weak sow to nourish many stout pigs.'

(11) " 'Do you mean, Ischomachus,' I said, 'that less seed must be put into the weaker earth?'

" 'Yes, by Zeus,' he said, 'and you agree, Socrates, when you say you hold that all weaker things should be ordered to do less.'

(12) " 'For what purpose, Ischomachus,' I said, 'do you send out hoers to work on the grain?'

" 'Doubtless you know,' he said, 'that there is much rain in winter.'

" 'How could I not know it?'

" 'Let us suppose, then, that some of the grain is covered with mud as a result of the rain, and that some of it is exposed at its roots by the flow of water. And often weeds spring up with the grain as a result of the rain and choke it.'

" 'It's likely,' I said, 'that all these things happen.'

(13) " 'Does it seem to you, then,' he said, 'that the grain needs some assistance under these circumstances?'

" 'Very much so,' I said.

" 'What does it seem to you they could do to assist the muddied grain?'

" 'They could remove the earth,' I said.

" 'And what of the grain that has been exposed at its roots?' he said.

" 'They could replace the earth around it,' I said.

(14) " 'What if the weeds springing up with the grain should choke it,' he said, 'and rob it of its nourishment, just as useless drones rob the bees of the nourishment they have worked to get and to store up?'

" 'One should cut out the weeds, by Zeus,' I said, 'just as one should expel the drones from the hive.'

(15) " 'Does it seem plausible to you, then,' he said, 'that we should send out hoers?'

" 'Certainly. But I am reflecting, Ischomachus,' I said, 'on the effect of introducing good likenesses. For you aroused me much more against the weeds by speaking of drones than you did by speaking of the weeds themselves.' "

Chapter 18

(1) " 'But after this,' I said, 'the likely thing is reaping. Teach me what you know about this too.'

" 'Unless, that is,' he said, 'you manifestly know the same things about it as I do. You know that the grain must be cut.'

" 'How could I not know it?' I said.

" 'When you cut it, then,' he said, 'do you stand with your back to the wind or facing it?'

" 'Not facing it,' I said; 'for I suppose it is hard on the eyes and the hands to reap with the husk and the sharp ears blowing in one's face.'

(2) " 'And would you cut the ears at the top,' he said, 'or close to the earth?'

" 'If the stalk of grain was short, I, at least,' I said, 'would cut lower down, that the chaff might be more fit for use; if it was tall, I hold I would do right to cut it in the middle, that the threshers might not be troubled with added toil or the winnowers with something they do not need. As for what is left in the earth, I believe it would benefit the earth if it were burned, or if thrown in with the manure, would swell the manure supply.'

(3) " 'You see, Socrates,' he said, 'you are caught in the act: you know the same things about reaping that I do.'

" 'Probably I do,' I said, 'and I want to consider whether I know also about threshing.'

" 'Certainly you know,' he said, 'that they thresh the grain with beasts of burden.'

(4) " 'How could I not know?' I said. 'And I know that oxen, mules, and horses are alike called beasts of burden.'

" 'And you believe they know only how to tread the grain when they are driven?' he said.

" 'What else would beasts of burden know?' I said.

(5) " 'But that they will cut just what is required, and that the threshing will be even—to whom does this belong, Socrates?'

" 'Evidently,' I said, 'to the threshers. For by turning over what is untrodden and throwing it under their feet, it is evident they would keep the threshing floor even and quickly finish the work.'

" 'You are not at all behind me,' he said, 'in understanding these things.'

(6) " 'And after this, Ischomachus,' I said, 'we will purify the grain by winnowing it.'

" 'Tell me, Socrates,' said Ischomachus, 'do you know that if you begin to the windward side of the threshing floor, your chaff will be carried over the whole floor?'

" 'That is a necessity,' I said.

(7) " 'It's likely, then,' he said, 'that it will fall on the grain.'

" 'It would be quite something,' I said, 'if the chaff were carried across the grain to the empty part of the threshing floor.'

" 'But what if one begins winnowing,' he said, 'from the lee side?'

" 'It is evident,' I said, 'that the chaff would end at once in the chaff receiver.'

(8) " 'But when you have purified the grain,' he said, 'as far as the middle of the floor, will you winnow the remaining chaff while the grain is still spread out, or after you have heaped the purified portion in a narrow space in the center?'

" 'After I have heaped up the purified grain, by Zeus,' I said, 'so that my chaff may be carried to the empty part of the threshing floor and I may not have to winnow the same chaff twice.'

(9) " 'You, Socrates,' he said, 'might even be able to teach another how the grain may be most quickly purified.'

" 'I know these things,' I said, 'without being aware of it. And for some time I have been thinking whether I might know how to pour gold, play the flute, and paint, without being aware of it. For no one taught me these things any more than farming; but I see human beings practicing the other arts, just as I have seen them farming.'

(10) " 'Haven't I been telling you for some time,' said Ischomachus, 'that farming is the most well-bred art, because it's the easiest to learn?'

" 'Come, Ischomachus,' I said, 'I know that; for I know the things pertaining to sowing, though without having been aware that I knew them.' "

Chapter 19

(1) " 'Is the planting of trees,' I said, 'part of the art of farming?'

" 'It is,' said Ischomachus.

" 'How is it, then,' I said, 'that I knew the things pertaining to sowing but don't know the things pertaining to planting?'

(2) " 'Don't you know them?' said Ischomachus.

" 'How could I?' I said. 'I know neither in what kind of earth one should plant nor to what depth one should dig for the plant nor how wide or tall the plant should be when put in nor how the plant should be placed in the earth in order to grow best.'

(3) " 'Come, then,' said Ischomachus, 'learn what you don't know. I know you've seen the kinds of trenches they dig for plants,' he said.

" 'Many times,' I said.

" 'Have you ever seen one of them deeper than three feet?'

" 'Never, by Zeus,' I said, 'deeper than two and a half.'

" 'What of this: have you ever seen one more than three feet in width?'

" 'Never, by Zeus,' I said, 'more than two.'

(4) " 'Come, then,' he said, 'answer me this: have you ever seen one less than a foot in depth?'

" 'Never, by Zeus,' I said, 'less than one and a half. For the plants would be uprooted in digging about them,' I said, 'if they were planted too near the surface.'

(5) " 'You know this sufficiently, then, Socrates,' he said, 'that they do not dig deeper than two and a half feet or less than one and a half.'

" 'I must necessarily have seen this,' I said, 'since it's so obvious.'

(6) " 'What of this?' he said. 'Do you recognize drier and wetter earth when you see it?'

" 'The earth around Lycabettus and that similar to it,' I said, 'seems to me to be dry, and the earth in the Phalerian marsh and that similar to it, to be wet.'

(7) " 'Would you then dig a deep pit for the tree in the dry earth,' he said, 'or in the wet?'

" 'In the dry earth, by Zeus,' I said; 'for if you dug a deep one in the wet earth, you would find water, and you wouldn't be able to plant in water.'

" 'You seem to me to speak nobly,' he said. 'But once the pits are dug—have you ever seen when each kind of plant ought to be put in them?'

(8) " 'Certainly,' I said.

" 'Then as you want them to grow as quickly as possible, do you suppose that if you put prepared earth under it, the vine cutting would take root faster through this soft earth than through unworked earth in hard ground?'

" 'It's evident,' I said, 'that it would sprout more quickly through prepared than through unworked earth.'

(9) " 'Earth would then have to be put under the plant.'

" 'How could it not be?' I said.

" 'But do you believe that the cutting would rather take root if you placed it upright, looking toward heaven, or if you placed it on its side in the prepared earth, like an overturned gamma?'

(10) " 'That way, by Zeus,' I said, 'for there would be more eyes beneath the earth; it is from the eyes that I see the plants sprouting up above. And I believe the eyes beneath the earth do the same thing. With many shoots growing in the earth, the plant would, I believe, sprout quickly and vigorously.'

(11) " 'As regards these matters,' he said, 'you happen to understand the same things I do. But would you just scrape together the

earth around the plant,' he said, 'or would you pack it down firmly?'

" 'I would pack it down, by Zeus,' I said, 'for if it weren't packed down, I know well that the rain would turn the unpacked earth to mud, and the sun would dry it up completely; so there would be a danger that during the rains the plants would rot from dampness, or that there would be too much heat at the roots and they would wither from dryness or from the porousness of the earth.'[49]

(12) " 'As regards the planting of vines also, Socrates,' he said, 'you happen to understand all the same things I do.'

" 'Should one plant the fig in the same way?' I said.

" 'I suppose so,' said Ischomachus, 'and all the other fruit trees. For why would you reject the noble procedures in the planting of the vine that pertain to the other plantings?'

(13) " 'How shall we plant the olive, Ischomachus?' I said.

" 'You are testing me in this too,' he said, 'which you know best of all. For you surely see that a deeper pit is dug for the olive, as it is dug mostly along the roadsides; you see that stems belong to all the young plants; you see,' he said, 'that mud covers the heads of all the roots, and that the upper part of every plant is protected.'

(14) " 'I see all these things,' I said.

" 'Since you see them, then,' he said, 'what is it you don't understand? Are you ignorant, Socrates,' he said, 'of how to place shells over the mud?'

" 'By Zeus,' I said, 'there is nothing you say that I am ignorant of, Ischomachus, but I am thinking again why ever it was, when you asked me some time ago whether in general I knew how to plant, that I denied it. For I seemed to have nothing to say regarding how one should plant; but since you have undertaken to question me on each thing by itself, I answer the very things that you—who are said to be a clever farmer—assert you understand yourself. (15) Is it the case, then, Ischomachus,' I said, 'that questioning is teaching? For I just now understand how you questioned me: by leading me through what I know, you display to me that what I didn't know is similar to it and persuade me, I suppose, that I know that too.'

[49] The Greek phrases for "during the rains" and "or from the porousness of the earth" are bracketed in the Oxford text, though apparently with no manuscript authority.

(16) " 'If, then, in regard to a piece of money,' said Ischomachus, 'I questioned you as to whether it was fine or not, would I be able to persuade you that you knew how to distinguish the fine from the counterfeit piece? Or if I questioned you about flute players, would I be able to persuade you that you knew how to play the flute—or about painters, or about others of this sort?'

" 'Perhaps,' I said, 'for you persuaded me that I am a knower of farming, though I know no one ever taught me this art.'

(17) " 'It isn't so, Socrates,' he said; 'but some time ago I told you that farming is such a philanthropic and gentle art that it makes those who see and hear of it at once knowers of it. (18) For it teaches many things itself,' he said, 'about how one may use it in the noblest manner. The vine running up trees, whenever it has a tree nearby, straightway teaches that it must be supported; by spreading its leaves while its bunches are still tender, it teaches that shade must be provided for whatever is at that season exposed to the sun; (19) by shedding the leaves when it's time for the grapes to be sweetened by the sun, it teaches that it must be stripped and the fruit brought to ripeness; and through its productivity, by showing forth some mature bunches while bearing others that are still unripe, it teaches that each must be gathered as it swells to maturity, in the same way that figs are gathered.' "

CHAPTER 20

(1) "Then I spoke. 'If the things pertaining to farming are so easy to learn, Ischomachus, and all know equally well what ought to be done, how is it that all do not do equally well, but rather some live in abundance and have a surplus, while others cannot provide even the necessary things but run into debt besides?'

(2) " 'I'll tell you, Socrates,' said Ischomachus. 'It isn't the knowledge or the ignorance of the farmers that causes some to be well off and others to be poor; (3) you wouldn't hear any argument,' he said, 'to the effect that the household is ruined because the sower didn't sow evenly, or because he didn't plant in straight rows, or because being ignorant of what kind of earth bears vines, someone planted

them in infertile soil, or because someone was ignorant of the good that comes from preparing the fallow for sowing, or because someone was ignorant of how good it is to mix manure with earth; (4) but it is more usual to hear this: "The man doesn't get any grain from his fields because he isn't diligent in sowing them or in providing manure"; or "The man has no wine because he isn't diligent in planting the vines or in getting the ones he has to bear fruit"; or "The man has neither olives nor figs because he isn't diligent and does nothing to get them." (5) Such things, Socrates, are the cause of the differences between farmers and their faring so differently, rather than the fact that some seem to have invented something wise for use in the work. (6) So it happens that some generals are better and others worse in certain works of strategy, though they don't differ from one another in mind but rather clearly in diligence. For what all the generals understand—and most private men—only some of the rulers act on, while some do not. (7) For example, all understand that in war it's better for the marchers to march in an orderly manner if they are to fight well when there is need of it. But though they understand this, some act on it, and some don't. (8) All know it's better to post guards day and night before the camp. But some are diligent in doing this, and some are not diligent. (9) And when they pass through narrow places, isn't it very difficult to find someone who does not understand that it's superior to occupy commanding positions beforehand than not to? But here again some are diligent in doing it, and some are not. (10) And all say that manure is best in farming, and they see that it's readily available; yet though they know with accuracy how it becomes available and how easily a lot can be gotten, some are diligent in seeing that it is collected, and some neglect it entirely. (11) Again, the god above provides rain, all the hollow places are filled with water, and the earth provides weeds of every kind, of which the earth must be purified by the one who is going to sow; but if someone should throw the weeds he has removed into the water, time itself would produce those things in which the earth takes pleasure. For what kind of weed, what kind of earth, does not become manure in stagnant water? (12) And what sort of attention the earth needs—whether it is too damp for sowing or too salty for planting—everyone understands, as well as how water may be drained by ditches and how a salty soil may be corrected by mixing with it any number of unsalty materials whether moist or dry; but as regards these things, some are diligent, and some are not. (13) Even if someone were in every way ignorant of what the earth can bear, and had never had an opportunity to see its crops and plants or to hear the truth about it from anyone, isn't it still much easier for every human being to test the earth than to test a horse, and much easier indeed than to test another human being? For it doesn't show itself deceptively, but reveals simply and truthfully what it can do and what it cannot. (14) It seems to me that the earth excellently scrutinizes those who are bad and lazy by providing what is easily learned and understood. For it's not possible with farming, as it is with the other arts, for the ones who don't work at it to make the excuse that they don't know it, since all know that the earth does well when it is well treated; (15) but laziness as regards the earth is a clear accusation of a bad soul. For no one persuades himself that a human being would be able to live without the necessary things; but he who neither knows no other money-making art nor is willing to farm obviously intends to live from stealing or robbing or begging, or is altogether irrational.' (16) He said that it makes a great difference as to whether farming is lucrative or not when someone with a number of workmen is diligent in seeing to it that his workers remain at work the entire time, and another isn't diligent in this respect. 'For it easily makes a difference when one man of ten works the entire time, as it makes a difference when another man leaves before the time is up. (17) Indeed, to let human beings take it easy in their work during a whole day easily makes a difference of half the whole amount of work. (18) Just as in traveling it sometimes happens that two human beings, though both are young and healthy, differ from each other in speed by as much as a hundred stadia in two hundred when one does what he set out to do and keeps walking, while the other, idle and easy in his soul, lingers at fountains and shady places, looks at the sights, and hunts soft breezes. (19) In the same way, as regards work, there is a great difference in what is accomplished by those who do what they have been ordered to do, and those who don't do it but find excuses for not working and are allowed to take it easy. (20) To perform one's work in a noble way, or to be diligent in a bad way, makes as much difference as to be wholly at work or wholly inactive. When those who are digging to purify the vines of weeds dig in such a manner that the weeds come up in greater numbers and finer than before, how could you deny that this is laziness? (21) These, then, are the things that wreck households, much more than any great deficiencies in knowledge. For, when constant expenditures flow from the households while the work isn't lucrative with respect to the expenditures, one ought not to wonder if there is want instead of a surplus. (22) For those who are capable of diligence, however, and who farm with utmost vigor, my father taught me, and himself practiced, a most effective way of making money from farming. He never allowed me to buy land that had been worked previously, but whatever through neglect or the incapacity of its possessors lay inactive and unplanted—this he encouraged me to buy. (23) For he used to say that cultivated land costs a great deal of money and permits of no improvement; he held that what permits of no improvement does not provide the pleasures of that which does, and supposed that every possession or creature on its way to becoming better affords a greater delight. But nothing shows greater improvement than inactive land when it becomes fertile. (24) Know well, Socrates,' he said, 'we have by now made many pieces of land worth many times their old value.[50] And this invention, Socrates,' he said, 'is worth so very much and is so very easy to learn that now that you have heard of it, you know it as well as I do, and you may go away and teach it to another, if you want to. (25) Indeed, my father neither learned it from anyone nor meditated very deeply to find it out; he used to say that he desired land of that sort because of his love of farming and his love of toil, in order to have something to do and at the same time to feel pleasure while being benefited. (26) For you see, Socrates,' he said, 'it seems to me that my father was by nature the Athenian most in love with farming.'

"And I, on hearing this, asked him: 'Did your father then keep in his possession the land he had worked, Ischomachus, or did he sell it if he could get a lot of money for it?'

" 'He sold it, by Zeus,' said Ischomachus; 'but he bought other land at once, inactive land, because of his love of work.'

(27) " 'You are saying, Ischomachus,' I said, 'that by nature your father was really no less a lover of farming than the merchants are

[50] The word for "value" (*timē*), here as in 20.28, means literally "honor."

lovers of grain. For the merchants, from an excessive love of grain, sail the Aegean, the Euxine, and the seas of Sicily in search of the place they hear has the greatest quantity of it; (28) and when they have gotten as much as they can, they bring it across the sea, stowing it in the ship they sail in themselves. And when they need money, they don't dispose of it at random wherever they happen to be, but rather wherever they hear that grain is particularly valued and highly regarded by human beings, there they take it and to them they offer it. In a similar way, somehow, your father appears to have been a lover of farming.'

(29) "Ischomachus spoke in response to this. 'You're joking, Socrates,' he said; 'but I hold that those who sell the houses they have built and then build others are no less lovers of housebuilding.'

" 'By Zeus, Ischomachus,' I said, 'I swear to you, I trust what you say: all believe by nature that they love those things by which they believe they are benefited.' "[51]

CHAPTER 21

(1) " 'But I am thinking, Ischomachus,' I said, 'how well you have shaped your whole argument to aid your contention; for you contended that the art of farming is the easiest of all to learn, and I am now in every way persuaded, by all you've said, that this is indeed the case.'

(2) " 'By Zeus,' said Ischomachus, 'but, Socrates, as regards what is common to all actions—to farming, politics, household management, and war—I mean ruling, I agree with you that some men differ very much from others in mind; (3) in a trireme, for example,' he said, 'which needs a full day's rowing to cross the open sea, some of the boatswains are able to say and do such things as whet the souls of human beings and cause them to toil willingly, while others are so lacking in mind that they accomplish the voyage in more than twice the time. In the one case the boatswain and those who obey him

[51] In the Oxford text the first *nomizein* ("believe") is bracketed, with some slight manuscript authority. Its deletion would make the translation of the whole sentence read: "by nature they love those things by which they believe they are benefited."

leave the ship dripping sweat and full of praise for one another, while the others arrive without having worked up a sweat, hating their supervisor and being hated by him. (4) And generals differ from one another in the same way,' he said, 'for some provide soldiers who aren't willing to toil or risk danger, who don't consider it worth their while to obey and don't do so except by necessity, but rather take pride in opposing the ruler; these same generals provide soldiers who don't know enough to be ashamed if some disgraceful thing happens to them. (5) But the divine, good, and knowing rulers, when they take over these same soldiers, and often others as well, make of them soldiers who are ashamed to do anything disgraceful, who suppose it is better to obey, who are indeed, one and all, proud to obey, and who toil undiscouraged when toil is needed. (6) Just as a love of toil may arise in private men, so in a whole army under good rulers there may arise both a love of toil and an ambition to be seen doing some noble act by the ruler himself. (7) Rulers toward whom their followers are disposed in this way are the ones who become the strongest rulers, not, by Zeus, those who excel the soldiers in bodily condition, who excel in javelin-throwing or archery, who have the best horses, and who risk danger in the forefront of the cavalry or of the targeteers, but rather those who are capable of inspiring the soldiers to follow them through fire and through every danger. (8) One might justly call these great-minded, and many who follow them understand it; indeed, he may plausibly be said to march with a strong arm whose mind so many arms are willing to serve, and he really is a great man who can do great things by means of the mind rather than by means of strength. (9) In the same way in private work, whether the one in charge is a steward or a supervisor, those who can make the workers eager, energetic, and persevering in the work are the ones who accomplish the most good and produce a large surplus. (10) But, Socrates,' he said, 'if the master—who can harm the bad workers and honor the eager ones to the greatest degree—himself appeared at the work and the workers did nothing remarkable, I would not admire him, but if on seeing him they were stirred, and he filled each of the workers with spirit, a love of victory vis-à-vis one another, and each with the ambition[52] to be the most ex-

[52] Or, "love of honor" (see n. 24 above).

cellent, then I would assert he had something of a kingly character. (11) And this is the greatest thing, it seems to me, in any work where something is achieved by human beings, in farming as in any other. Yet I do not say, by Zeus, that it's possible to learn by seeing it or hearing of it once, but I assert that the one who is going to be capable of it needs education, a good nature, and most of all, to become divine. (12) For it seems to me that this good—to rule over willing subjects—is not altogether a human thing, but, rather, divine; it is clearly given only to those who have been genuinely initiated into the mysteries of moderation; but tyrannical rule over unwilling subjects, it seems to me, they give to those whom they believe worthy of living like Tantalus in Hades, who is said to spend unending time in fear of a second death.' "

On the *Oeconomicus*

Wayne H. Ambler

The *Oeconomicus* does not immediately appear to have been designed to be revealing of Socrates' deepest secrets, but it does show how he helped his friends and how devoted he was to gentlemanliness ("nobility together with goodness"). The ostensible purpose of the dialogue is to help his young but irresponsible friend Critoboulus to change his ways and more effectively manage his household (and the considerable property it includes). Toward this end, Socrates must first persuade Critoboulus that he is on the brink of economic ruin and that Socrates can help him avert it. Socrates' inimitable elenchus allows him to succeed quickly in this effort, as Critoboulus signals by saying, "it's time for you to take command of me, before I become really pitiable" (2.9). Nor does Socrates rest content with this; he compels Critoboulus to see and admit his difficulties also on two subsequent occasions (3.7, 11–13).

Once he has impressed upon Critoboulus the urgency of his problem and hence prepared him to face it, Socrates outlines a curriculum consisting of six main subjects (chapter 3), defends farming in such a way as to lead Critoboulus to conclude that "farming is indeed the noblest and best and most pleasant way to make a living," and interests him in hearing Socrates describe his encounter with "one of

This essay has been improved by attention to *Xenophon's Socratic Discourse: An Intrepretation of the Oeconomicus* by Leo Strauss (Ithaca: Cornell University Press, 1970) and Christopher Bruell's "Strauss on Xenophon's Socrates," *Political Science Reviewer* 14 (1984): 263–318. These challenging works discuss issues that this introductory essay has not even raised.

those men to whom the name gentleman is justly applied" (6.11–12). Approximately two-thirds of the *Oeconomicus* is devoted to Socrates' description of his encounter with Ischomachus, who has "the solemn name of gentleman" (6.13). Socrates clearly intends Critoboulus, who professes an erotic longing to be worthy of the name "gentleman" (6.12), to be encouraged and guided by the inspiring example of Ischomachus. Thus Xenophon, in the longest Socratic conversation recorded in his works, shows Socrates to be helpful to his friends and to be an admiring student of the perfect gentleman. In marked contrast to the Socrates of Aristophanes' *Clouds*, to which play the *Oeconomicus* alludes more than once, Socrates here is scarcely discernible as a philosopher; is openly respectful of the gentleman, the model of moral, religious, and free political life; and certainly does not try to recruit the Athenian youth for a way of life that is not suitable to them and is harmful to their families and neighbors. Socrates lacked the wherewithal to be a gentleman himself, but this did not stop him from praising the gentleman and what he represents (11.11).

In showing how Socrates was beneficial to his friends and that he was very much concerned with gentlemanliness, the *Oeconomicus* advances the work of the *Memorabilia*, whose defense of Socrates prominently features these two themes. Indeed, the opening words of the *Oeconomicus* are the same as those that begin the discussion of friendship in the *Memorabilia*, and it would appear to be possible to place the *Oeconomicus* in this larger work (*Mem.* 2.4.1). Inasmuch as the *Memorabilia* shows Socrates appealing to the ideals of gentlemanliness but does not show him in a direct encounter with the gentleman, however, the *Oeconomicus* can help us understand better just how Socrates assesses and promotes these ideals and the longings that accompany them (*Mem.* 1.2. 2–3; 1.6.14).

But Socrates was notorious for his irony, and it would be too much to expect that he announce his every employment of it. There are, however, several instances of open playfulness in the *Oeconomicus*, and they are one of the ways by which Xenophon compels us to examine more carefully the thesis that Socrates was entirely in earnest in his endeavor to help Critoboulus and in his deference to the perfect gentleman. Even some of the main features of the dialogue point us in this direction.

Although Critoboulus' very real economic difficulties are the occasion for the introduction of Socrates' narration of his encounter with Ischomachus, it really cannot have been the case that they were Socrates' guiding concern throughout the dialogue. Socrates stresses that he originally sought out Ischomachus as part of his own investigations into the relationship between the noble and the good (6.13–17), not as a model for imitation or even out of pure admiration. As Socrates understood it, at least, an encounter with the gentleman was required by his philosophical quest. It is true that Socrates does say he might try to imitate Ischomachus, but even the serious Ischomachus sees this as a joke (11.6–7). Ischomachus is similarly aware that there is something fishy about Socrates' professed interest in learning how to farm (although he does persuade himself that Socrates might like to become a teacher of farming!). Even though Socrates narrates his conversation with Ischomachus, he never interrupts his narration to offer special instruction to Critoboulus.[1] Nor do we ever hear that Socrates' narration of his encounter with Ischomachus had any effect on its nominal addressee. Indeed, once Ischomachus' name is mentioned, there is never again a reference to Critoboulus. Everything but some aspects of the occasion for the narration suggests that Socrates was retelling his conversation to convey his *understanding* of the gentleman, an understanding whose importance may eclipse even that of the playful Critoboulus' financial difficulties. None of this is to deny that Socrates is concerned with Critoboulus' moral and economic improvement, but the character of the *Oeconomicus* as a whole suggests the priority of other issues.[2]

It may be unlikely that Socrates would bother to recount his investigation of the gentleman to poor Critoboulus, but Xenophon lets us know that he himself and other friends were listening carefully to Socrates' remarks (1.1; 3.12, 1). They may well have been moved by other than financial needs, and even by longings like Socrates' own desire to understand the combination of nobility and goodness rep-

[1] He does, however, offer such comments on Ischomachus' character as that he was "rather pleased" to hear himself praised (7.3; cf. 11.1). Socrates' editorial comments point out what kind of man Ischomachus was rather than enforce the importance of imitating him.

[2] The extent of Socrates' interest in Critoboulus' moral reformation is indicated also at *Symposium* 4.23–24.

resented by the gentleman. As the very first sentence of the *Oeconomicus* implies, it is Socrates and his discourse that is the abiding subject of the author's interest, not household management per se. Should it turn out that Socrates fails to reform Critoboulus, it is possible that he made progress on another front, in the education of his silent friends. Surely the *Memorabilia* is correct to insist that Socrates was beneficial to his friends, but which friends he benefits and how he benefits them is not always obvious.

Nor, even prior to the point at which Ischomachus takes center stage, is it quite so clear that Socrates is guided primarily by the goal of helping Critoboulus. Certainly it is striking that as soon as Critoboulus calls for Socrates to take command over him, Socrates begins to deny that he is able to give him the assistance whose need he has just demonstrated (2.9–14). Quite properly accused by Critoboulus of trying to weasel out of helping him, Socrates agrees at least to show to Critoboulus others who are allegedly more clever than he is in the matters Critoboulus wants to learn (2.16). This promise is then made more specific in chapter 3, when Socrates' promised curriculum is to include field trips to see the successes and failures in six different areas of household management. We never read that these promises are kept, and the full burden of Critoboulus' education seems to fall on Socrates' narration of his conversation with Ischomachus. Perhaps the importance of such promises is overshadowed by other considerations in the economy of Socrates' life.

Socratic Economics

Once open to the possibility that Socrates' remarks are intended not only for Critoboulus, one may see more clearly that the first chapter would be a curious start for a work whose purpose is to admire and foster the gentlemanly citizen of a republican regime. Socrates here transforms Critoboulus' view of property and wealth with a swiftness and sureness that is reminiscent of his treatment of Polemarchus' view of justice in Book 1 of the *Republic*.[3] In both cases,

[3] Plato *Republic* 331e–332a. See also *Mem*. 4.2.12–18.

notions that are shaped by law or convention are quickly transformed under the power of the premise that one should do what is beneficial or good above all. Strict repayment of debts may entail actions that are positively harmful, so justice cannot demand them; we might spend our money in ways that only harm us, so this cannot be true property (1.13–14). Like justice in the *Republic,* property must be good in order to be property. Hence Socrates can conclude, "Then unless one knows how to use money, let him thrust it so far away, Critoboulus, that it isn't even wealth" (1.14).

This clear and important point is accompanied by the implication that knowing what is best is not easy. The difficulty of gaining money is overshadowed by the difficulty of knowing how to use it. This first principle of Socratic economics, that property is not really property unless it is beneficial to us—a principle with the potential to reveal the poverty of usual notions of wealth and the folly of ordinary economic activity, which are largely indifferent to what benefits us in our souls[4]—establishes the context within which the gentleman's economic activity will be considered. By these exacting standards, Critoboulus will find it difficult to be rich, no matter how much money he may acquire.

A comparison with the Polemarchus section of the *Republic* also helps to highlight what might be called the economic character of the text before us. Whereas Polemarchus is quickly led to the view that justice is benefiting friends and harming enemies (and, later, to the view that the just man harms no one at all, 335d), Critoboulus is led to the view that household management is the art of being benefited by both friends and enemies. Neither the unselfish nor the punitive aspects of Polemarchus' remarks are represented here; one's own benefit—in soul, body, and household—is the operative principle, and the good household manager will be able to profit from friends and enemies alike. If it appeared at first as though household management was a topic unworthy of serious interest, this was because our notion of household management was much narrower than that of Socrates. Socratic household management has emerged as the all-embracing art of securing gain or benefits wherever they may be found.

[4] Socrates' concern for what is beneficial to our souls is indicated in 1.13 and 23.

Socrates also advances a view of slavery and freedom which is independent of legal categories, for it is based rather on the liberty of the individual from such masters and mistresses as laziness, softness of soul, neglect, and dice-playing (1.19–23). Citizens whom the law regards as free may in fact be wretched slaves in their souls, and such slaves should rejoice in the event they come to be enslaved by worthy human rulers. Of course Socrates does not deny the desirability of legal or political freedom, but he does imply that it is not beneficial for those who do not first enjoy what we might call moral or psychological liberty. Neither, of course, is Socratic economics, whose practice requires these various kinds of continence. Notwithstanding Critoboulus' amusing proclamation that he is already continent, or at least fairly continent, it is unlikely that he can become a practitioner of Socratic economics.[5] This sort of economics emerges as a science of the highest requirements, both intellectual and moral. The moral tenor of the conclusion to the first chapter helps to overshadow its intellectual radicalism, but freedom in the soul—a freedom won by continence of the most complete sort—is certainly not incompatible with heterodox opinions (cf. *Mem.* 1.2.1–2 and the continent Socrates in Aristophanes' *Clouds*).

Socrates' amusing summary of Critoboulus' financial obligations, which is designed to help wake Critoboulus up to his impending insolvency, may also shed light on his view of the duties of the free citizen. Socrates presents Critoboulus' services to gods, city, foreign guests, fellow citizens, and friends as nothing but burdens (2.5–7). Indeed, he speaks of the Athenians as one might speak of a despotic master, as though those who exercise free political rule are capable of actions not fundamentally different from those of monarchs or despots: the Athenians treat poor Critoboulus as if his property were theirs (2.6). One might try to explain the character of Socrates' litany of responsibilities as the best way of rousing Critoboulus to action, but appealing to the nobility of such actions would be no less effective for this purpose, especially for someone admittedly drawn to it. Socrates had already heard from Ischomachus how the gentleman conceives of public service (11.9; 7.3), but the economy of his life leads Socrates to adopt a different view.

[5] Critoboulus' blithe claim to continence is not even complete: he claims to be continent regarding the "mistresses," not regarding the "masters." He implies greater confidence that he is able to get money than to hold onto it (2.1; cf. 1.20–22).

Socrates' own way of life is an obvious theme of the *Memorabilia* but not of the *Oeconomicus*. It is not Socrates who is the household manager in the usual sense of the term. On the other hand, and in addition to what was argued in the first chapter, his mockery of Critoboulus is reinforced by a summary of his own superior way of solving life's economic problems (2.2, 4, 8). The first chapter implied that only the knower, only the wise man, could be truly wealthy, wealthy in a way that has no obvious connection to the wealth one possesses by law; the second directly presents Critoboulus as very poor and Socrates as rich even in regard to their lawful property, so long at least as their property is measured against the needs of their own particular ways of life. When trying to impress upon Critoboulus the error of his ways and thereby make him eager to learn household management, Socrates does not appeal first to the noble example of Ischomachus; he instead describes his own way of addressing life's economic problems. If the title of the dialogue aptly conveys its subject, it must refer to at least two fundamentally different kinds of household manager, one of which is represented by Socrates. Even in his earlier conversation with Ischomachus, Socrates did not fail to call attention to his own way of life in its differences from that of the gentleman, and especially to his unblushing poverty (11.3–6). Since Socrates is guided by his knowledge of what is truly beneficial, however, his poverty is intimately linked to the rich life he leads.

If Socrates is unwilling or unable to take command of Critoboulus and his household, he softens the blow by implying that he can and will help in other ways to solve Critoboulus' problems. He does so first with three examples that conspire to suggest that these problems will not be hard to solve and that he can be of some help in their solution (2.15). If Critoboulus needed fire or water, Socrates could not be blamed for leading him whence he could get it. And, if he wanted to learn music, he could not justly blame Socrates for showing him others who were more clever at it and who would be grateful for the chance to teach it, if Critoboulus would be their willing student. Perhaps, on second thought, if the third example is closest to the case at hand, Critoboulus' problems will be easy to solve only if he is himself willing and able to learn. This, however, is not so easy as simply hiring a manager or entrusting one's household to Socrates

(1.4; 2.9). Of course this last example also stops short of denying that Socrates possesses some competence in the subject, just as it fails to imply that he would be grateful for the chance to teach it to Critoboulus. Still, if Socrates should show such a teacher to Critoboulus, he could not justly be blamed.

But will Socrates in fact do anything quite like what these examples imply? Once they appear to have buoyed Critoboulus' spirits, Socrates makes this promise: "Then I'll point out to you, Critoboulus, certain others who are much cleverer than I in those things you persist in wanting to learn from me" (2.16). Of course Critoboulus never said he wanted to learn anything, but more striking is Socrates' failure to promise that these potential teachers will be willing to teach Critoboulus, much less that they will be grateful for the opportunity. As he gets himself off the hook, Socrates buoys Critoboulus' hopes for education, but he does not fail to indicate that there exist significant obstacles to its success. Among them is Socrates' own practice of economics, which does not allow him lightly to neglect the supreme good by which he guides his life.

Through the first three chapters, the implicit notion of the work of household management has been to increase the wealth of the household, and the subordinate parts of household management have been looked at from this point of view (1.4; 2.10; 3.8; 6.4). It is important that Socrates expands greatly the meaning of wealth, so that the good of the soul becomes one of the criteria by which to determine it, and important also that he stresses what we might call its moral preconditions (1.15–23); but the emphasis on wealth and profit is striking nonetheless. Not only is the discussion of acquisition not restricted by such themes as justice or nobility, but Socrates makes a pointed reference to war and tyranny as means of increase (1.15). The distinction between household management and money-making is sufficiently blurry that Socrates can hold out the prospect of Critoboulus becoming a "clever money-maker" without any evident lowering of the tenor of the conversation (3.18).[6] The characteristics of Socratic economics are striking in their difference from those of the economics of the gentleman Ischomachus, with whom Socrates had spoken long ago.

[6] For a more expansive and elevated view of household management, see Aristotle *Politics* 1.8–13. The opening lines of chapter 13 form an especially clear contrast with the focus of Socrates' discussion in the *Oeconomicus* (*Pol.* 1259b18–21).

The emphasis on acquisition unqualified by considerations of justice or nobility does not last, however. It is to Critoboulus that we owe this ennobling of the conversation, although it is curious that he ennobles it while also thinking of his ease. Since it is neither easy to acquire workers in all arts nor possible to become experienced in all of them, Critoboulus suggests a more limited focus on "the kinds of knowledge that are reputed to be the noblest and would be especially suitable for my concern" (4.1). The remainder of the conversation, including especially the section recounting Socrates' encounter with Ischomachus, explores the relationship between our need for gain and our attachment to nobility.

Critoboulus' Longings

Chapters 4, 5, and parts of 6 consist primarily of Socrates' sometimes amusing attempts to defend farming on the higher grounds called for by his interlocutor; and, at least by the time it is all over, Critoboulus testifies that these efforts have been successful: "I seem to be quite sufficiently persuaded, Socrates, that farming is indeed the noblest and best and most pleasant way to make a living" (6.11). But since Socrates presents a veritable barrage of arguments that coexist uneasily and are sometimes doubtful for other reasons, it is not easy to know just what it is that persuades Critoboulus. This problem is compounded by the fact that Critoboulus makes only about six short comments in chapter 4 and only one toward the end of chapter 5 (18). Of course Socrates also fell more than a little short of practicing what he preaches here, so we are obliged to wonder what he really thinks of the arguments he presents.

The main division in Socrates' defense of the nobility of farming is that between chapters 4 and 5. The former defends farming by claiming that the king of Persia, exemplar of noble conduct that he was, was concerned with farming as well as with war. The latter defense is linked not to the king but to the free man. It implies that farming is noble by treating it as a livelihood that fosters strength, manliness, cooperation, a readiness to defend the earth, and skill in ruling. Moreover, Socrates now adds the claim that farming is pleasant (5.8–11).

Socrates' main argument in chapter 4 is that farming is the noblest of the arts and that this is demonstrable by the attention paid to it by the king of Persia (4.4–25). Critoboulus doubts on three occasions that the Persian king was much of a farmer, but he never doubts that he is a proper exemplar of nobility. Even when Socrates speaks of the younger Cyrus and thereby implies a defense not only of barbarian monarchy but even of war as a way of securing such rule, Critoboulus does not balk (4.16–25). Socrates has not proven that farming is noble, but he has made it plain that an aspiring Greek gentleman is attracted by such nobility as inheres in ruling as a great monarch, even a monarch who must seize power by force. By so doing, he indicates that the concern for nobility, at least in one of its forms, is a potential threat to republican government as well, of course, as one of its principal supports. Differently put, he explores the question of whether the gentleman would be content under all circumstances to remain a gentleman.[7]

Socrates is shown to be in a better position to resist the allure of such nobility as is represented by the Persian king. Prior to his account of the Persian king, Socrates defends the Greek cities' critical attitude toward the mechanical arts (4.2–3). In so doing he appeals to the effect of these arts on the bodies and souls of those who are diligent in their practice; he mentions as well their effect on friendship and devotion to the city. In the case of the Persian king, there is no such discussion of the effect of his concern with farming on his body, soul, friendships, or—of course—participation in a free city. One may thus be persuaded that the king needs to be concerned with farming without concluding that this concern—or any of his other noble concerns—helps to improve his soul, body, friendships or, more generally, makes him happy. It is true that Lysander pronounces the younger Cyrus to be happy, and even to be happy while also being good (4.25), but Socrates' own defense of the Greek cities suggests other and more demanding criteria by which to evaluate this version of nobility.

After having experimented with Critoboulus' attitude toward the barbarian monarchs, Socrates turns us to a defense of farming that is

[7] Nobility is considered to be a source of strife in another conversation between Socrates and Critoboulus; see *Mem.* 2.6.16–18. See also Aristotle *Politics* 1225a32–41.

more compatible with republican principles. Parts of his argument here are even reminiscent of familiar praises of yeoman farmers as good citizens. There remain multiple reasons to doubt that this chapter is either a candid or an adequate defense of farming, however. One concerns the validity of the claim that the farmer's life is a pleasant one. Socrates moves Critoboulus in part by giving the impression that farming requires a lot of lying around in cool summer breezes, a claim scarcely more credible than what he said of the Persian king (4.9).[8] A second is that several arguments speak in praise of the earth, not farming (5.2–7, 12). And, thanks to the earth, who is identified as a goddess and presented as "nourishing her crops in the open for the strongest to take," this very praise of farming indicates again that farmers are vulnerable to fighters. Socrates' praise of farming in chapter 5 is reminiscent of what he had heard years before from Ischomachus, but neither is it quite the same, even apart from the question of whether both men are candid in their enthusiasm. In particular, and as suggested by the summary and conclusion of his argument, Socrates appears to replace Ischomachus' claim that farming is beloved of the gods with the claim that it is in high repute because it provides good citizens (cf. 6.8–10 with 15.4). Certainly he refrains from saying it is good for the soul (although he does claim that it provides leisure for joining in the concerns of friends and cities). Nor does he echo Ischomachus' claim that the willingness to farm is a good way to determine the quality of someone's soul (20.14–15).

After Critoboulus summons him to complete his account of household management, Socrates proposes that they first go back and agree on what they have already discussed. Needless to say, Socrates' summary of their agreements omits agreements of some importance and adds details that were never agreed upon.

To mention only two points, Socrates fails to refer to the agreements most sought by Critoboulus, those that would pledge Socrates to help his friend. He thus makes no reference to chapter 3, in which he promised to take Critoboulus to learn directly from experts in six different areas of household management. Even if these agreements

[8] As Socrates noted in his earlier conversation with Ischomachus, hoeing is best done in midday in summer, not at the time most pleasing to the hoer (16.14).

were not so important for his teaching about household management, his attitude toward them is certainly related to his own economics, to the economy of his life. Second, Socrates neglects the bulk of chapter 4. Since he also invents points that deepen the republican spirit of chapter 5 (6.6–10), the net effect is to forget the barbarian monarchical defense of farming and overshadow it with the Greek republican one. Since Critoboulus was even more silent in chapter 5 than he was in chapter 4, it is hard to say that Socrates is really summarizing their *agreements*.

Notwithstanding its inexactness, Socrates' summary of the agreements they have reached is warmly received by Critoboulus. He says, "I seem to be quite sufficiently persuaded, Socrates, that farming is indeed the noblest and best and most pleasant way to make a living," and he thus seems more enthusiastic about farming now than he did in the course of the original conversations (6.11). (Critoboulus does not respond to Socrates' reminder of the bad news that one's possessions are limited to those things one knows how to use properly.) If we were sure he would act as he speaks, we could be confident that Critoboulus would now begin to farm in earnest. Now, at least, he says he would be pleased to hear Socrates speak on the subject, and he implies he intends to act on what he learns (6.11).

Socrates here guides the conversation in a different direction, however. Although Critoboulus had asked for the secret of productive farming, Socrates offers instead to recount his encounter with one who really seemed to him to be a gentleman (6.12). Critoboulus' enthusiastic response, however, which includes his only use of a word based on *eros*, suggests that Socrates' offer is not so much a distraction from but a fulfillment of Critoboulus' main interests or longings. This turn is thus not simply contrived by Socrates; it is a consequence of Critoboulus' concern with nobility as expressed first at the outset of chapter 4. Focused in many respects on the problems posed by the mere material conditions of life, the *Oeconomicus* in its own understated way testifies to the great power of the noble longings that are familiar to all and are characteristic of actual and aspiring gentlemen. Although the dialogue is less than one-third complete, Critoboulus' expression of his longing are his last words in it.

Critoboulus' expressed interest is in becoming worthy of the name "gentleman," but Socrates had his own reasons for seeking out a conversation with a gentleman. Socrates did not go to the gentleman with the intention of imitating him but as part of a more general investigation, one that grew out of an attempt to understand such reputed beauty or nobility as could be seen, or at least such visible beauty as is related to human work or action (6.13). Investigating the link between beauty (or nobility) and goodness, Socrates learned that some of those beautiful to look at were not at all good in their souls. He thus lost interest in such nobility (or beauty) as is unaccompanied by what is good, and turned his investigation away from the visibly beautiful and toward those who were called "beautiful and good" (even if they were not at all beautiful to look at). Since a certain Ischomachus was universally acclaimed as one of these, Socrates tried to link up with him. Although this much is discernible, Socrates' jocular account of his famous turn excuses him from saying precisely what he expected to learn from the gentleman or how he expected to learn it. Socrates' comments in the ensuing conversation may help clarify the dim picture sketched by his stated reasons for seeking it.

Ischomachus Section: Overview

A provisional outline of the conversation with Ischomachus is easily supplied. The first four chapters are devoted to Ischomachus' education of his young wife (7–10); a single chapter describes his own daily activities, those of a free man (11); three chapters treat his education of those of his slaves whom he trusts to help him rule his estate (12–14); and in five chapters Ischomachus tries to teach Socrates how to farm (15–19). The penultimate chapter is a hymn to diligence at the expense of knowledge (20); the last chapter corrects the exaggeration of the preceding one by acknowledging the importance of knowledge (and more than knowledge) in ruling. One may simplify this simplification by stressing that Socrates' questioning brings out the extent to which Ischomachus understands himself to be an educator, an educator of his wife and slaves, and especially an educator to diligence. After we hear his educative efforts described, we then see him attempting to educate Socrates, especially in the art of farming, but also in the importance of diligence (20). Though convenient, this outline is merely provisional. Other themes, such as Ischomachus' attitudes toward the gods, his view of the relation between gain and nobility, and the precise difference between his life and that of his servile stewards, rival the nominal subjects in importance and overshadow the distinctions between them. Above all, the nominal subjects of the discrete sections of the dialogue do not bring out the extent to which the abiding subject is a study of Socrates' assessment of the gentleman's life and the opinions on which it rests.

The Ischomachus section as a whole also has a character that is easily summarized. In short, Socrates is here more student than teacher, and he is an uncommonly reserved student as well. Although it may appear unlikely that Socrates had much to learn from Ischomachus, his conduct shows him to have been a patient listener and generally careful not to throw his interlocutor on the defensive. Socrates' conversation with Ischomachus is his longest conversation in all of Xenophon's works, but he speaks only slightly more than 25 percent of the lines in it. Moreover, many of these lines are more or less simple responses to Ischomachus' questions about farming; and he never attacks directly the main content of Ischomachus' remarks. Socrates' reserve is especially striking in the section on Ischomachus' wife. In the about 485 lines in the Oxford text of chapters 7–10, Socrates speaks only about 35, of which 12 are a general introduction to the section. In keeping with this reserve, it is Ischomachus who ends the dialogue with a speech to which Socrates does not respond. If it is important to note the extent to which Socrates tactfully draws Ischomachus out in order to understand him better, the converse is also worth noting: the gentleman makes no effort to learn about the philosopher.

Socrates finds Ischomachus seated in the colonnade of Zeus the Deliverer (or "the Liberator"), the deliverer from the military threat represented by the Persian kings who twice invaded the Greek mainland and, perhaps, the deliverer as well from barbaric notions that fail to support the noble foundations of Greek liberty. Since Ischomachus understands himself to be a good and pious citizen of a free city, this setting is most appropriate. Of course Socrates had earlier stressed his concern with another sort of liberty, the liberty of one's own soul, in whose name political liberty should sometimes be sacrificed (1.17–23). Thus the very setting of the conversation calls attention to a difference between these two men in regard to their ranking of different sorts of liberty and to the kinds of support they may or may not enjoy. Socrates also calls attention to Ischomachus' relative lack of leisure and his fidelity to his promises (7.1–2; cf. 12.1–2).

Ischomachus and His Wife

Of the educations Ischomachus offers, none is more difficult than that of his wife. Only in this case does he pray and sacrifice before beginning the education. His pupil is a fifteen-year-old girl, and great diligence had been shown to ensure that she "see and hear as little as possible and ask the fewest possible questions" (7.5). Ischomachus does imply that she has had an education in one sort of continence, but this looks incomplete when compared with the education of the slave who will be his housekeeper (cf. 7.6 with 9.11). In the case of his wife, then, he faces the challenge of educating almost from scratch his closest partner. Perhaps his sense of his own role in her education and life more generally is among the reasons he never mentions her name.

Notwithstanding these difficulties, in his last words on the subject, Ischomachus proclaims his education of his wife to have been a complete success (10.13). If he really does convey here the secrets of such an education, its usefulness would make it easy to excuse Socrates for not directing the conversation toward such nobler subjects as the gentleman's civic, religious, or military services. At the same time, however, it would be difficult to explain why Socrates neither employed these secrets in his own domestic life (*Symposium* 2.10) nor referred Critoboulus to them. Instead, he deferred to the notorious Aspasia on the question of the educability of wives, not to Ischomachus (3.14). Perhaps Socrates' allusion to a wrestling contest is another sign that he does not take a gentlemanly view of the matter (7.9). Of course Ischomachus does recognize that this is a sensitive problem, and he must be encouraged by the knowledge that he has enlisted the aid of the gods to help solve it.

In contrast to his education of his stewards, which relies heavily on punishments and rewards, praise and blame, Ischomachus' education of his wife employs persuasion. Since its object is to explain to her what her duties are and why she should perform them diligently, it may be called a moral education. Since his views of the gods are its foundation, it is a moral education that invokes and relies upon a theological teaching for its support. Ischomachus does not ask that his wife simply obey him: rather, husband and wife will both obey the gods. Ischomachus' attempt to teach his wife how to act thus turns out to reveal a good deal about his view of the principles by which he himself aspires to act: since he endeavors to teach these principles, he is obliged to explain them as clearly as possible. In some respects at least, Socrates' focus on the wife's education is not at all a bad way to understand the husband as well; certainly it leads to the opinions in which Ischomachus finds the ultimate support for his noble conduct.

Ischomachus' teaching is largely but not entirely a natural theology. It begins from the natural differences between male and female and draws in particular upon the example of bees. Happily, such norms as the gods encourage turn out to be quite like those that gentlemen hold in high esteem. Thus Ischomachus can say to his wife, "And what the god made each to be more capable of by nature, the law [or custom, *nomos*] shows to be noble as well" (7.30; cf. 16). Nature and law or convention are in harmony, and the latter shows the former to be noble as well as natural. In an early formulation he mentioned that he prayed for what was best for the two of them (7.8), but he appears to believe that their conduct will also be noble. The component parts of gentlemanliness ("nobility together with goodness") are as neatly compatible as husband and wife, nature and law.

Neither the gentleman nor his wife is guided by what is immediately pleasant, of course, so it is only at the end of the chapter, after the discussion of divine and natural duties is complete, that pleasure is mentioned (7.41–42). Her life will be pleasant, he insists, but he is careful not to feature pleasure too prominently in its justification. It is not for such reasons that one does what is divinely ordained.

Socrates explores Ischomachus' theological views, which also provide the support for his moral views, only with great circumspection. He has the benefit of an ally in the investigation, however, for Ischomachus' young and sheltered bride is not so timid as to say yes to everything. Of her eight brief remarks in this chapter, three or four require that Ischomachus develop important and sensitive aspects of his teaching (esp. 7.14, 32, 35, 39), and only once does she express enthusiasm about any of the duties he assigns to her (7.37). If Socrates' questions contain the hint of reservations about the adequacy of Ischomachus' education, this need not be explained by envy consequent upon his own dismal record in spousal education: the wife herself shows signs of reservations.[9]

Ischomachus uses an example to illustrate and support his view that the gods have given his wife clear rules of conduct: his wife is like the queen or leading bee, who follows the god's orders and presides over the most important deeds in the hive (7.17, 32–36). His wife is not sure that her tasks are exactly those of the queen bee (7.35), and she suspects that her husband is much more like the leader than she is (7.39). Ischomachus reassures his wife of the importance of her contributions to the household, but he cannot establish that she is really its leader. Nor is he able to respond that his wife's works are really the same as those of the queen bee (cf. 7.35–37 with 33–34). The example of the hive is the most suggestive of the view that the gods must have had an order in mind when they made men and women, but even his wife's questions are able to suggest the limits of the argument that the simple order of the bees is applicable to the case of human beings.

Its misleading account of the wife's works is a sufficient reason to question the bee analogy; so is its preference for queens and its forgetting of kings (7.42; 9.16). But it has the further disadvantage that it leaves no place for noble conduct: bees simply obey the laws of nature's god, but Ischomachus inhabits a world in which there are other laws, laws or conventions whose obedience deserves praise and establishes nobility (7.16, 30), laws whose observance is not compelled and whose violation may be punished. As he says in conclusion, "the noble and good things increase for human beings, not by ripening like the beauties of youth, but through the exercise of the

[9] Historical evidence suggests that Ischomachus' marriage did not end as happily for him as it began: see Strauss, *Xenophon's Socratic Discourse*, 157n. If this historical evidence is sound, it would have to have been known to Socrates' interlocutors, and they could not have failed to see more than a little irony in this aspect of Socrates' account of Ischomachus.

virtues in life" (7.43). Ischomachus himself cannot have been fully satisfied with a metaphor that leaves no place for virtue, for the longings and convictions he feels so strongly.

Helpful though the wife's reservations are as a guide to issues latent in Ischomachus' teaching, there are also other sensitive points in Ischomachus' complicated moral teaching. Ischomachus explains to his wife their reasons for marrying and then explains why the gods established "the pair called male and female." The gods' first concern is the preservation of the species, and they therefore established the pairing of male and female to produce children (7.19). In explaining his own marriage, however, Ischomachus is silent about the species and says that he and his wife have married to be partners in the household and children. The latter are a common good between them and will be their allies and nurses in old age (7.11–12). It is secondary to the gods of nature that, at least in the case of human beings, offspring may assist their parents; the gods' first concern can be satisfied even if Ischomachus and his wife continue to fail to have children and even if their children should neglect them in their old age. Ischomachus' stated concern, on the other hand, is guided by what he will need when he is old; the sense of duty he may feel to preserve the species in general is apparently not primary. He surely enjoys the hope that some god will grant them children, but he is aware that the gods' concerns are not identical to his own, that their general providence does not necessarily provide for all in particular. Although Ischomachus' devotion to noble conduct makes him more vulnerable to danger and imposes great burdens on him, his natural theology stops short of confirming that this conduct will be rewarded. Although he does hope that some god or another will recognize and support his noble course of life, he also betrays the thought that the gods of nature will not. This helps explain the place of prayers and sacrifices in his life: Ischomachus also holds to a belief in gods that is not based directly on his observations of nature (11.7).

A similar difficulty is indicated by the gentleman's pointed reference to the availability of other partners for merely sexual unions (7.11). Presumably because of the gods' concern that the species be continued, they made male and female to be pleasant to one another (7.19; 10.7). This serves their end; but taken by itself, it is a threat to the exclusivity of marriage as well as a reason for it in the first place.

The gods made male and female generally attractive to each other, but individual human beings still try to contrive ways—such as through cosmetics, for example, or by certain kinds of conduct (10)— to strengthen and preserve their particular unions. Ischomachus' gods of nature have ensured that male and female will come together; they have not, however, ensured that particular couples will stay together. Aware of this problem, the gentleman and household manager prays and sacrifices for further assistance in the education of his particular partner for life.

Surely nobility would not be noble if it were immediately pleasant and beneficial, but Ischomachus is not prepared to see his or his wife's conduct as mere self-sacrifice either. Behind his nobility are gods who, albeit darkly, indicate their support for the restraint and aspirations that make Ischomachus' life beautiful to him. In his education of his wife, Ischomachus' sense both of the need for this support and of the uncertainties that surround the actual relation between gods and men is evident, and nowhere is it more evident than when he goes no further than to say that "perhaps" the gods punish violations of their order (7.31). The gentleman needs to see some god as his ally or deliverer, for the gods of nature alone offer insufficient support for his noble conduct. At the same time, however, he worries that these allies are distant or uncertain.[10]

Ischomachus and His Stewards

Chapter 11 is literally the central chapter of the work, and it also has a good claim to being the dramatic center. It is in this chapter that Socrates asks directly about the works of the gentleman and here that he clearly calls attention to himself as someone who has chosen to live a life of a fundamentally different character. It is thus especially in this chapter that the *Oeconomicus* is revealed to culminate in a dramatic confrontation between the philosopher and the gentle-

[10] My account of the gentleman's view of the relationship between what is good and what is noble has benefited from the more thorough and lucid account in Thomas L. Pangle, "Socrates in the Context of Xenophon's Political Writings," in P. A. Vander Waerdt, ed., *The Socratic Movement* (Ithaca: Cornell University Press, 1994).

man. In Xenophon's Socratic writings, of course, dramatic confrontations may be comic, even when serious issues are at stake.

This confrontation is slow to begin, quick to end, and muted while it lasts. It is only here, in the fifth chapter of the Ischomachus section, that Socrates asks directly about the subject for which he ostensibly came to see Ischomachus; and after saying that he wants to hear "fully" about these works (11.1), he announces his readiness to leave after a short conversation (12.1).

The confrontation is muted, of course, by the way Socrates identifies what he stands for. Showing his usual reserve about defending the philosophic life per se, Xenophon's Socrates here shows his comic touch as well and chooses to represent himself as like a horse, poor and possessed of only a good soul (11.4–6). And, on the other side, Socrates does not let Ischomachus enjoy the promised pleasure of an unfettered narration of the things for which he is most highly reputed. Socrates now speaks half the lines in the chapter and directs the conversation not to Ischomachus' most noble deeds but to such subjects as how he exercises for health and good condition, how he practices for war, and how he makes money. Thus their respective lives are rather sketched and hinted at than fully drawn, and we are distracted from the differences between them by Socrates' deference or flattery (11.10–11, 19–20). We are similarly distracted from their seriousness by his levity. Had Xenophon had more of a taste for tragedy, he could have made it plain that Socrates' accusers included gentlemen.[11]

Socrates draws upon Aristophanes' *Clouds* to help establish his posture of inferiority before the perfect gentleman: "I am a man who is reputed to be an idle talker and to measure the air and who is reproached for being poor—which seems to be the most foolish accusation of all" (11.3). Socrates takes up this most foolish accusation (not the less foolish ones) and explains why he is not discouraged by it. He does not deny the truth of this accusation (or of the others); he rather suggests that it is misguided about what is most important in life. Poverty does not prevent one from having a good soul and becoming

[11] Lycon, one of Socrates' accusers, is shown to be an enthusiast for gentlemanship in *Symposium* 2.4–5. If it is really characteristic of gentlemen to look upon their children as the nurses of their old age, it would not be surprising if this should contribute to the friction between them and Socrates, who so attracted the Athenian youth.

good, so Socrates' poverty will not keep him from learning what Ischomachus has to teach. Although Socrates formally retains the modest posture of mere student of gentlemanliness, he does so while affirming with confidence that poverty is no barrier to becoming a good man. This will put in relief Ischomachus' imminent statement of how important money is to him, especially for actions that Socrates calls noble (11.9–10). In expressing his desire to become a good man, Socrates may imply, as his actions also suggest, that he is unconcerned to become a man who is noble in addition to being good, that is, a gentleman. Like the horse's, Socrates' goodness has high natural preconditions and, I presume, enjoys only natural support (cf. *Mem.* 4.1.2).

Ischomachus' summary of his life shows how different he is from Socrates (cf. *Mem.* 1.3.3):

> Since I seem to have learned that the gods do not permit human beings to prosper unless they understand what they ought to do and are diligent in accomplishing it, and that nevertheless they grant only to some of the prudent and diligent to be happy, and not to others, I therefore begin by attending to the gods, and I try to pray to them and act in such a manner that it may be permitted me to acquire health, strength of body, honor in the city, good will among my friends, noble safety in war, and noble increase of riches. (11.8)

The beginning of Ischomachus' statement indicates his natural concern with happiness; the end of it identifies his view of its content. Prudence and diligence are necessary but not sufficient conditions for attaining this happiness, according to Ischomachus; for one needs divine favor as well. Ischomachus thus tries to act piously as well as prudently and diligently,[12] but he refrains from saying that this addition supplies all conditions for his being happy. His knowledge of the gods evidently affords him at least the hope that they will support his noble actions. Perhaps this is what Socrates had in mind when he suggested earlier that free men are in need of good hopes (5.16).

[12] Ischomachus is in fact much more concerned with diligence than he is with prudence. It is true that the very last chapter of the dialogue stresses the importance of knowledge and education, but Ischomachus does not indicate that he has done much to acquire this knowledge (21.5, 11). Surely he considers himself prudent, but his account of his life makes diligence the main theme. Indeed, the wonderful thing about farming is that diligence makes knowledge all but unnecessary.

Again alluding to his own chosen way of life, Socrates asks Ischomachus about the troubles that attend wealth and its acquisition. This is a question of Socratic economics, for it asks whether the noble ends to which his wealth is put are sufficiently rewarding to justify the trouble their pursuit requires. Ischomachus' response shows his finer qualities, for his answer displays the pleasure he takes in using his money unselfishly by honoring the gods magnificently, aiding friends, and adorning the city (11.9). But perhaps his pleasure in these actions is related to his view that by sacrificing magnificently, by adorning the city, and by helping friends, he is likely to win the divine favor, civic honor, and good will from friends he mentioned in the passage quoted above. As he later indicates, even good men become discouraged if their greater contributions do not issue in greater rewards (13.11).

Far from receiving only honor at the hands of the city, it turns out that Ischomachus is a target for sycophants (11.21). Like Socrates, then, he is obliged to defend himself in speech, and he says he practices doing so "constantly" (11.22–23). Unlike Socrates', however, the gentleman's defense is simpler in that it does not begin by investigating what justice is; it is also accompanied by attacks against others for the injustices he knows they commit. Xenophon's Socrates, on the other hand, never punishes or even accuses anyone else of injustice, notwithstanding several good opportunities to do so. This is the case not only because his life is guided by the need to understand before acting, but also because his understanding stresses teaching rather than punishing. In Ischomachus' case, on the other hand, the distinction between punishing and teaching is a blurry one indeed (14.4–5).

The strange conclusion to this central chapter also hearkens back to the *Clouds*, but this time it is Ischomachus who shows that he is familiar with the play. His comment suggests that he might like to possess Socrates' alleged ability to make the weaker argument the stronger, for he does not always find it advantageous to tell the truth. Distinguished by his attention to noble and just conduct, the gentleman is not above a concern with his own advantage, a concern that lives in some tension with his noble unselfishness.

Chapters 12–14 are devoted especially to Ischomachus' education of his stewards. Among the topics taken up under this broad heading are the subjects he tries to teach, the qualities he requires in his students, and the methods he employs when teaching.

It is Socrates who leads Ischomachus to speak of himself as an educator of his stewards, and by so doing he makes it that much easier to observe how different the two men are. It is not that they simply pursue different and unrelated paths in life, but the language of this section leads us to see them as making rival claims to the same activity, that of educating. Indeed, there is also some common ground in the subjects with which they are concerned, for Ischomachus claims to teach at least some of his slaves to feel good will toward him, to be diligent, to be able to teach others how to rule, and to be just. One wonders, in light of such claims, how Socrates could ever have limited himself to but one conversation with this remarkable man.

Apart from his instruction in farming, Ischomachus' education is devoid of intellectual content. It may be loosely described as "motivational" or even more loosely as "moral," and his methods are generally similar in each of the four subjects discussed. Reward, punishment, praise, and blame are the major tools of his education. Ischomachus does mention that speech or reason is useful, but its use is confined to telling his subjects how they can win their rewards of food, drink, or honor (13.9, 12). He never bothers to teach, for example, *why* his slaves should be moved by the honors he offers; nor does he present or rely on a theological education, as he did in the case of his freeborn wife. It is a sign of Socrates' judgment of Ischomachus' education that, in his summary of it, he never uses the words "teach" or "education" (15.1).

Perhaps the superficiality of Ischomachus' educational notions may be excused on the grounds that he has no need of better ones: ruling slaves is simply not that difficult, at least if the master is always on hand and is ready to punish (12.19–20). Even if this were true, a point that Socrates doubts, (13.4; 5.16), Ischomachus is not on hand (12.2). It is because the gentleman is inclined to think of himself more as a beneficent teacher than as a slave master or tyrant that he trusts his stewards to rule well in his absence. What is noteworthy here is not so much how Ischomachus rules but the noble light in which he somehow manages to look upon his rule.

Ischomachus seems at first to see his role as educator as limited to teaching the works of farming (12.3–4). Without much difficulty, however, Socrates leads him to make very bold claims about what he teaches, claims in comparison to which Socrates' own efforts seem rather ordinary (esp. 13.4–5). Ischomachus could have avoided these claims if he were prepared to see himself simply as one who exercises tyrannical rule over unwilling subjects. He is far from blind to the need to use force in ruling a large estate,[13] but as the conclusion of the dialogue confirms, his own self-understanding requires that he see himself and his rule in a nobler light, for tyrannical rule is given to those the gods believe to be "worthy of living like Tantalus in Hades, who is said to spend unending time in fear of a second death" (21.12). It is especially when judged by these high standards, his own, that Ischomachus' actual conduct seems to fall short. Ischomachus' nobility appears to entail some self-deception about its costs to others and its risks to himself. He seeks to increase his wealth only justly and nobly (7.15; 11.8); surely he meets these standards if he can manage his estate securely even when absent, doing so in part by teaching his slaves to be just.

Socrates continues to respect the limits of this friendly conversation, and hence neither asks Ischomachus to explain his understanding of justice nor defends his own view that diligence cannot be taught; but virtually every one of his comments or questions in chapters 12–14 leads Ischomachus to acknowledge that the educational burden he faces is greater than he had implied before.[14] But even though Socrates' questioning is mild by all Socratic standards except those set here in this unique conversation, it appears to have some effect in making Ischomachus more aware of the enormity of the claims he is making and perhaps also in limiting his confidence that he lives up to them fully. In response to Socrates' questions, Ischomachus drops the claim that he succeeds in teaching good will and claims only that his approach is the best there is (12.7); he admits there are many to whom he cannot teach diligence at all (12.8–16); he sees his instruction in how to rule as "very ordinary" and expects

[13] Ischomachus' remarks may betray that he even finds some pleasure in punishing "anyone who looks to be wicked" (7.41).

[14] I see no reason for doubting that Socrates could have reduced the perfect gentleman to the same condition as that to which he reduces Euthydemus, an aspiring gentleman (*Mem.* 4.2.23). Whatever may distinguish the two, it is not that the former scrutinizes his life and its foundations more carefully.

that Socrates will find it ridiculous (13.4). Self-satisfied though he seems, Ischomachus shows at least some awareness of the problems he has not solved adequately and hence of his possible inferiority to the poor man who questions him so delicately (cf. 11.2).

If Ischomachus is wrong in thinking of his rule over his stewards as an education, this mistake also has two possible practical consequences. One is that his enthusiasm for ruling as he does becomes vulnerable in the event that the character of that rule becomes more fully clear to him; the other is that his view of the rule's foundations must tend to keep him from seeing and taking all necessary measures to enforce it. Note, for example, that in Thucydides' presentation of the case of the Athenians in general, even though Diodotus does not agree with Cleon about how best to keep the Athenian empire secure, he stresses even more than his violent rival that vigilance is necessary because the Athenian subjects are not willing subjects and naturally seek to be free (*Peloponnesian War* 3.46). Different though they are, both Cleon and Diodotus agree that the Athenians are not honest with themselves about the oppressive character of their empire (*Peloponnesian War* 3.37; cf. 2.63). Like his fellow citizens with their empire, Ischomachus would need help to see that such "justice" as he practices on his estate may be secured by vigilant enforcement but can never be made secure by teaching. Ischomachus believes that he and his wife are united by a common good (7.7, 12–13); that he does not make this claim in the case of his slaves is a sign of the problem.

The section on the stewards also lends further support to a skeptical reading of the section on the wife. Socrates is not quite so reserved in speaking about the stewards' education as he was in the discussion of the wife's. To the extent that the subject matter is similar, what he says in the latter raises questions that were too sensitive for him to raise directly in the former. In particular, diligence is important to both. Socrates had asked Ischomachus whether he educated his wife "to be capable of being diligent about what's appropriate to her" (7.7), and he followed Ischomachus' long affirmative response by asking, "Did you notice, Ischomachus, that she was stirred to greater diligence by these things?" (8.1). Ischomachus himself acknowledges the importance of this issue in his wife's education when he takes her promise to be diligent to show that he had succeeded (9.1; cf. 14, 17–19). Only later, in the discussion of the stewards, does Socrates say directly that he thought diligence "could *in no way* be taught" (12.10, emphasis added). He must, then, not have been persuaded by Ischomachus' claim to have taught it to his wife.

In keeping with his modest posture as student of his gentlemanly interlocutor, Socrates does not directly explain or defend his view that diligence cannot be taught. The progress of the discussion may begin to indicate his reasons, however. He first secures from Ischomachus the admission that diligence cannot be taught to just anyone: those who lack self-control against the attractions of wine, sleep, and sexual love cannot be taught to be diligent (12.11–13). Self-control against the erotic desire for profit, on the other hand, may actually keep one from learning diligence; at least according to Ischomachus, the desire for profit is one of the chief ways to lead men to be diligent (12.15). A further difficulty is that the teaching of diligence makes demands on the teacher as well: a negligent master should not expect to have diligent servants. The conclusion of Ischomachus' argument to this effect cites favorably a maxim of the barbarian king of Persia: diligence is best secured by keeping one's subjects under constant surveillance. By stressing the need for surveillance to encourage and enforce diligent actions, Ischomachus concedes that he is unable to teach his subjects to be reliably diligent themselves (12.20). Or, differently put, the education of Ischomachus is indistinguishable from his use of rewards and punishments. Surely some household managers will squeeze more work out of their subjects than will others, but Socrates invites Ischomachus and us to note both the high requirements of such successes—requirements on both master and subject—and to inquire whether it is proper to use the word "teaching" in connection with the manager's encouragement of diligence. As it is explained here, Ischomachus' "education" in diligence would not be useful in teaching a free and equal fellow citizen: he would be no more successful in teaching Critoboulus to be diligent than is Socrates.

Finally, Ischomachus' comments on his students shed light on how he judges human beings. He divides the slaves who are his students into two main categories. One group can be led to remarkable accomplishments by way of its bodily desires; this is a bestial education and is useful with slavish types (13.9). The other group is ambitious ("honor loving") and can be led by their desire for praise. Ischomachus does not shrink from saying that he treats these slaves of his as free men and honors them as gentlemen (14.9–10; 13.9). Like Socrates, then, he does not rely only on legal categories when distinguishing between slave and free; unlike Socrates, it is to a man's ambition that he looks in order to make this distinction. Socrates' only words about ambition, on the other hand, refer to "foolish and expensive ambitions," and he sees them as a sign of servitude, not freedom (1.22). Ambition does liberate us from bodily desires and so elevates us above slaves of an obvious sort, but the philosopher is on his guard against other threats to liberty as well (cf. *Mem.* 1.5.6).

Farming

Socrates does not pay Ischomachus' notion of justice the compliment of asking to be instructed in it. Such lessons would be superfluous for a Socrates, and would be painful as well; but Socrates does ask to be taught how to farm. Since Socrates is no more interested in becoming a farmer than in becoming a gentleman, it is not surprising that the discussion of farming is the occasion for exploring indirectly other more pressing issues. Chief among these is the question of what Ischomachus knows in relation to what he thinks he knows. Farming, after all, is what he knows best.

Socrates introduces the discussion of farming by observing that diligence is useless unless one knows its proper object (15.2). Ischomachus naturally takes this to mean that one must know how to farm, but the terms of Socrates' formulation are in fact very broad and may mean more generally that diligence does us no good unless we direct it properly. After all, diligence in some arts is positively harmful to both body and soul (4.2). Socrates does not in fact confirm that farming per se is the object of his question, but he is perfectly clear that he wants to know the art by which people get rich (15.3). Although he pursues the conversation out of an expressed interest in wealth or what is useful, he stops short of confirming that farming is useful (e.g., 15.13: "*if* it happens to be useful," emphasis added). And, when he compliments Ischomachus at the end of his argument in defense of farming, he does not commend him for having established everything he had claimed on farming's behalf. His thesis was that it was the art "most beneficial and pleasant to work at, the noblest and most beloved of gods and human beings, and in addition the easiest to learn" (15.4); but, after all is said and done, Socrates goes no further than to say that it is "easiest to learn" (21.1). Unless farming is also beneficial, pleasant, or most beloved of gods, can Ischomachus know that we should be diligent in its exercise? What will come of this diligence, and where does it fit into the economy of a good human life?

Ischomachus' knowledge of whether to farm is limited by his failure to have considered adequately the proper object of our diligence. In fact his devotion to farming, notwithstanding his encomia to it, may be simply derivative from its profitability in the most ordinary of senses (20.22–29). More surprising, his knowledge of how to farm may also not meet Socrates' standards. Socrates does not object to any of Ischomachus' lessons about how to farm, and in conclusion he professes to have been persuaded that he knows how to do it (19.16). It is nevertheless not entirely clear that Socrates is really persuaded by Ischomachus that he knows the art of farming. At issue is the relative rigor sought by gentlemen and philosophers in their interest in the truth.

Socrates' reluctance to claim that he has learned the art of farming is indicated by the way he responds to Ischomachus' lessons. His responses vary considerably: "it seems to me," "it's likely," "I believe," and "I know with some accuracy" are used in chapter 16, and a similar range is evident throughout the section. Socrates does not consistently profess to know the elements of the art of farming, even though Ischomachus insists that he does (and even though he insists in language that is reminiscent of "the doctrine of recollection"). Ischomachus, on the other hand, proceeds as though agreement between the two of them establishes that Socrates knows the point in question (17.1, 6; 18.3, 5; 19.11–12). Apart from the possibility that Ischomachus may occasionally be wrong even about farming, Socrates' assent to a correct conclusion does not establish that he understands the foundations on which the conclusion rests. Socrates knows that he does not know farming, because his standards for knowledge are higher.[15] And don't parts of the art of farming require practice (17.7)? If so, then perhaps it is not as different from flute playing as Ischomachus had maintained.

Socrates' most open disagreement with Ischomachus is early in the discussion (16.2). After defending some theoreticians of farming who consider it difficult to understand the nature of the earth, Socrates courteously gives in and offers his own evidence suggesting that it is not difficult to distinguish good land from bad. This agreement is limited in two ways, however. One is that the issue was not simply distinguishing good land from bad but also involved knowing what precisely ought to be planted on a particular plot. This is a more complicated question. Hence, for example, Socrates found it necessary to approach different types of people quite differently (*Mem.* 4.1.2ff.). Second, Socrates qualifies his agreement by implying that the evidence in support of it is true only "for the most part" (16.7). Farming will certainly be easier to learn if one seeks to learn it only "for the most part."

The gentleman must be confident that he knows more important matters than farming, as the return of theological issues helps to remind us (15.4; 16.3; 17.2–4). "For the most part," accepted practices will enable Ischomachus' farm to be productive, but one should try to avoid such risks in the more important aspects of life. Ischomachus himself admits that he is vulnerable to such risks, I think, both by stressing that other matters are not so easy to learn as is farming and by his "perhaps" at 7.31. Unless Ischomachus himself endeavors to test his view of nobility and the other central principles of his life, he is exposed to the danger that—when tested either by events or by a Socrates less inclined to listen politely—he will be able to respond only that he is living according to accepted principles, those that are followed or at least admired "for the most part." Although I would not underestimate the devastating potential of a

[15] Could it be to call attention to the looseness of his view of knowledge that Xenophon has Ischomachus speak of beasts of burden as though they are capable of knowledge (19.4)?

cross-examination by Socrates,[16] Xenophon is capable of presenting this problem also in more tragic tones.[17]

Although the forthrightness with which the conventional gentleman describes the principles of his life is not matched by rigor in testing them, Socrates came to understand gentlemanliness to consist precisely in *knowledge* of such principles as nobility, piety, and justice, knowledge gained by constant examination (*Mem.* 1.1.16). And, as we have seen in brief, Socrates' knowledge did not move him to serve the gods or adorn the city in the fashion described by Ischomachus (2.2–8; cf. *Mem.* 1.3.3). Neither did it lead him, of course, to attack Ischomachus in any way. When it came time to defend his own life before a jury much less wise, Socrates was able to claim that he had been diligent over his defense in the noblest way, that is by constant scrutiny of justice and injustice (as well as by acting in accord with the former and abstaining from the latter).[18]

Surely the Socratic discourse recorded in the *Oeconomicus* is part of the larger examination that enabled Socrates to know that he was in the right on these difficult issues and to affirm at his trial the excellence of the unconventional life he led. Although Xenophon manages to establish Socrates' respectability by showing his esteem for Ischomachus and gentlemanliness more generally, the aim of this introductory essay has been to show that and in what respects Socrates rejects the life and opinions of the man to whom he appears to commend his friend Critoboulus. I have stopped short, however, of trying to disclose and test the adequacy of the reasons that must lie behind this rejection.

[16] Consider, for example, the effect on Euthydemus of Socrates' demonstration that he does not know what justice is, for he understands himself to be at least an aspiring gentleman (*Mem.* 4.2.23, 39).

[17] Consider Panthea's reaction to her husband's most noble death, for example: *Cyropaedia* 7.3.8–16.

[18] *Mem.* 4.8.4. Cf. *Apol.* 3. Note also that this most noble defense would not be adequate to protect Socrates against an unjust sentence and that he did not rely on this defense alone. Nor, in fact, did the aspiring gentleman Hermogenes think it sufficient that Socrates was in possession of the noblest defense; he was especially eager that Socrates should seek a defense likely to be effective under the circumstances.

THREE

Symposium

Translated by Robert C. Bartlett

Chapter 1

(1) But[1] in my opinion, not only are the serious deeds of gentlemen[2] worth recalling, but so too are their deeds done in times of play. I wish to make clear those deeds at which I was present and on the basis of which I make this judgment.

(2) It was at the time of the horse race of the Great Panathenian[3] games. Callias the son of Hipponicus happened to be in love with the

I have used the text of François Ollier, *Banquet—Apologie de Socrate* (Paris: Société d'Édition, "Les Belles Lettres," 2d ed., 1972), by permission of Les Belles Lettres, Paris. As will become clear in the notes, I have been somewhat more reluctant than he to accept emendations proposed in the face of a consensus of the mss.

"Symposium" is simply a transliteration of the Greek title *sumposion*; it might be translated as "drinking party" or "banquet." The title appears in one ms. (D, Laurentianus LXXXV–9) as "Symposium of Xenophon the Orator."

[1] The dialogue begins with the word *alla* ("but," "rather") as though in mid-argument or in response to a previous speaker's contrary assertion (see J. D. Denniston, *Greek Particles*, 2d ed., [Oxford: Clarendon Press] *s.v., alla,* 2.8.i [p. 21]). The only other work of Xenophon to begin in this way is the *Constitution of the Lacedaemonians*.

[2] "Gentlemen" will always translate the phrase *kaloikagathoi [andres]*. A more literal translation would be "noble and good [men]"; "gentlemanliness" could thus be translated as "nobility and goodness." *Kalos* by itself refers either to external beauty or to beauty of character; accordingly, it (and only it) will be rendered as "beautiful," "noble," or (in 1.4) "fine." The "beauty contest" in chapter 5 between Socrates and Critoboulus is therefore also a contest in "nobility."

[3] These took place every fourth year and were on a grander scale than the yearly games; they included not only the athletic competitions but sacrifices and a procession (see 8.40).

boy Autolycus and took him to the spectacle on the occasion of the latter's having won the pancratium.[4] When the race ended, he started off for his house in the Piraeus[5] with Autolycus and the boy's father; Niceratus too was accompanying him. (3) But when Callias saw Socrates, Critoboulus, Hermogenes, Antisthenes, and Charmides standing together, he ordered someone to lead those with Autolycus onward, while he himself went over to Socrates and those with him and said, (4) "What a fine thing it is that I've happened upon you! You see, I'm about to give a feast for Autolycus and his father, and I think the setting would appear much more resplendent if the men's quarters were adorned with men whose souls have been purified, like yours, than it would be with generals, cavalry commanders, or those eager for[6] office."

(5) And Socrates said, "You're always making fun of us! You look down on us because, while you've paid a great deal of money to Protagoras for wisdom—and to Gorgias and Prodicus[7] and many others besides—you see that we're just self-taught in philosophy."

(6) And Callias said, "Well up till now, I've kept concealed from you that I can say many wise things. But now, if you come to my house, I'll show you that I am worthy of a very great seriousness."

(7) Now at first, Socrates and those with him thanked him for the invitation, as was fitting, but declined to join in the feasting. But as it became clear that he would become very annoyed should they not come along, they went with him. They then arrived at his house, some having in the meantime exercised and taken a rubdown, others also a bath. (8) Autolycus sat down beside his father, the others reclined as was fitting.

Someone might immediately suppose, in considering what took place, that beauty is something regal by nature, especially if one possesses it together with bashfulness and moderation as was the case with Autolycus then. (9) For in the first place, just as when a light appears in the night and all eyes are led to it, so too was everyone's gaze

[4] An all-out sport combining boxing and wrestling.

[5] The Piraeus is Athens' seaport, some five miles from the city.

[6] Literally, "serious about (political) office." It is related to the word translated in Xenophon's introductory remark as "seriousness" (*spoudēs*).

[7] Three well-known Sophists or rhetoricians, all of whom are portrayed in Plato's dialogues, above all in the *Protagoras* and the *Gorgias*; see also 4.62 and *Memorabilia* 2.1.21ff.

then drawn toward Autolycus' beauty. Moreover, there was not an onlooker whose soul was unaffected by the boy in some way: some, at any rate, grew quiet, others also took on a sort of dignified pose. (10) Everyone under the sway of one of the gods is held to be worth beholding; but whereas those influenced by other gods are fiercer in appearance, more frightening in utterance, and carry themselves more vehemently, those inspired by the moderate Eros have eyes of a more kindly disposition, a gentler voice, and a mien more becoming liberality.[8] Such indeed characterized Callias at that time on account of Eros, making him worthy to be beheld by the initiates of this god.

(11) So they were feasting in silence, as though ordered to do so by some superior.[9] But Philippus the jester then knocked at the door and told the porter to announce who he was and why he wished to be led in. He said that he'd come having made the appropriate preparations—so as to dine at another's expense. And he said that his slave-boy was very weary from what he was carrying—nothing—and from having missed his breakfast. (12) When Callias heard this, he said, "Well surely it's shameful, men, to begrudge him our hospitality. So let him in." And as he said this he looked toward Autolycus, evidently to ascertain what he thought of his quip.

(13) But Philippus, standing now in the room where the feast was taking place, said, "You all know that I am a jester. And I've come here eagerly, believing that it is funnier to come to a feast uninvited than invited."

"So recline," Callias said, "for those present, as you see, are full of seriousness and are perhaps rather in need of laughter."

(14) While they were dining, Philippus immediately tried to say something funny so that he might accomplish that for the sake of which he was always invited to feasts. But when he didn't incite anyone to laugh, he clearly grew annoyed. A little while later, he wanted to say something else funny, but when they didn't laugh at him then either, he stopped in the middle of the feast, covered himself up, and

[8] Liberality (*eleutherios*) generally speaking is behavior appropriate to a free man (*eleutheros*) and came to signify more narrowly the freedom from an undue attachment to wealth, i.e., generosity (see, e.g., 4.43 below and Aristotle *Nicomachean Ethics* 4.1).

[9] The adjective (*kreittōn*) can mean "better" because "stronger," an ambiguity the translation attempts to preserve. "Most excellent" will always be used to render the word in the superlative degree (*kratistos*), as in, e.g., 8.38–39.

laid down. (15) And Callias said, "What's this, Philippus? Are you in the grip of some pain?"

Groaning aloud he said, "Yes by Zeus, Callias! A great one! For since laughter has perished among human beings, my business has come to ruin. You see, before now, I was invited to feasts so that the guests[10] would be delighted by my making them laugh. But now, what reason is there to invite me, and who will do so? For I, at least, could no more be serious than become immortal. And nobody will invite me with the intention of being invited in return, since everyone knows there is no precedent[11] for having a feast at my house." And while he was saying this, he was wiping his nose and crying, as was clear from his voice. (16) Everyone was trying to reassure him that they would laugh next time, and were bidding him to feast, when Critoboulus burst out laughing at Philippus' lamentation. As soon as Philippus perceived Critoboulus' laughter, he uncovered himself, exhorted his soul to be confident, since there would be future engagements[12], and began to feast again.

Chapter 2

(1) When the tables had been taken away and they had poured a libation and sung a paean, a certain fellow[13] from Syracuse arrived for their entertainment. He had with him a good flute[14]-girl, a dancing girl—one of those capable of doing wondrous things—and a boy very much in the bloom of his youth able to play the harp[15] and dance very beautifully. The Syracusan made money by showing these off in performance. (2) When the flute-girl had played her flute

[10] Literally, "those who are together" (see n. 20 below).

[11] Literally, "principle" or "starting point" (*archēn*).

[12] Philippus uses a term that can refer to the contributions to a festival or common meal, to the meals themselves, or to encounters or "engagements" (in the hostile sense).

[13] Literally, "human being."

[14] The usual translation of the Greek, *aulos*. The aulos was in fact a double-reeded wind instrument more akin to the modern oboe than the flute.

[15] The word translated as "harp" (*cithara*) was an instrument somewhat akin to the modern harp, with eight to ten strings on a U-shaped frame backed by a tortoise shell sounding board.

for them and the boy his harp, and both were held to delight very competently, Socrates said, "By Zeus, Callias, you are putting on a perfect dinner! For not only have you provided a faultless feast, you are also furnishing the most pleasant sights and sounds."

(3) And the other said, "What then if someone brings us some perfume so that we may enjoy ourselves amidst pleasant odors as well?"

"No no!" said Socrates, "for you see, just as one kind of dress is beautiful for a woman and another for a man,[16] so too one fragrance is proper for a man and another for a woman. For doubtless no man anoints himself with perfume for the sake of a man. And indeed women—especially if they are brides, like Niceratus' here and Critoboulus'—what need do they have of additional perfume? (4) For they smell of it themselves. And the fragrance of the olive in the gymnasia is more pleasant to a woman when it is present than is perfume, and when absent she longs for it all the more. Indeed, everyone who is anointed with perfume, both slave and freeman, immediately smells alike. And the fragrances of the labors and practices characteristic of liberality require in the first place much time if they are to be pleasant and characteristic of liberality."[17]

And Lycon said, "Now these things might hold for the young, but for those of us who no longer exercise in the gymnasium, of what ought we to smell?"

"Of gentlemanliness, by Zeus!" said Socrates.

"And where might one lay hold of this scent?"

"Not, by Zeus," he said, "from the perfume peddlers!"

"But from where then?"

"Theognis said,

> For from the good you will be taught good things.
> But if you mingle with evil men,
> You will destroy even the intelligence you had."[18]

[16] The word (*anēr*) connotes a manly man, a "real man."

[17] The reading of the mss. Ollier's text, following Athenaeus, reads: "And the fragrances of the labors characteristic of liberality require in the first place upright practices over much time if they are to be pleasant and characteristic of liberality."

[18] See Theognis *Elegies* 35–36. The text as it has come down to us reads *mathēseai* ("you will learn"), although both Xenophon (see also *Memorabilia* 1.2.20) and Plato (*Meno* 95d 6) read *didakseai* ("you will be taught"). See J. Mitscherling, "Xenophon and Plato," *Classical Quarterly*, n.s. 32 (1982): 468–69.

(5) And Lycon said, "Do you hear this, son?"

"Yes, by Zeus," Socrates said, "and he makes use of it too! When, that is, he wished to carry off the prize for the pancratium, he considered with you [who would be able to teach him those things, and he associated with that man. Similarly, if he wishes to carry off the prize for virtue, he will consult with you][19] in turn as to who is in his opinion most capable in the practice of these things, and he'll associate[20] with him."

(6) At this point, many spoke out. Someone among them said, "Where then will he find a teacher of this?" Someone else said that this is not even teachable, another that this must be learned[21] above all else.

(7) And Socrates said, "Since this is disputable, let's put it off for another time and for now, let's finish off what is at hand. For I, at least, see that this dancing girl has taken her place and that some hoops have been brought to her."

(8) After this, the other girl began to play the flute for the dancer and someone standing beside her passed twelve hoops over to her. As she took them she danced and threw them spinning into the air, calculating how high she would have to throw them in order to catch them on the beat.

(9) And Socrates said, "It is clear, men, that in many other things as well as in what this girl is doing, the feminine nature is not at all inferior to the man's, but it lacks judgment[22] and strength. As a result, if someone among you has a wife, let him be confident in teaching her whatever he might want her to know in dealing with[23] her."

[19] There appears to be a lacuna in the text. I supply what I take to be missing.

[20] The verb (*suneinai*) has a range of meanings, from simply "being with" to "associating with" to "having sexual intercourse with" (for this latter, see, e.g., 4.57, 8.23). It will be translated as "associate with," but the extended meaning should be kept in mind.

[21] Reading *mathēteon* with the mss. rather than *mathēton* ("can be learned") with Ollier.

[22] Reading *gnōmēs* with the mss. instead of *rhōmēs* ("force" or "strength") with C. J. W. Mosche (*Oekonomikus, Apologie des Sokrates, Symposium und Hiero* [Frankfurt: Osterrieth, 1799]).

[23] The verb Socrates here uses (*chraomai*) has a wide range of meanings, including "to use" or "to make use of," "to deal with or treat," and even "to have sexual intercourse."

(10) And Antisthenes said, "How is it, then, Socrates, that while recognizing this, you too do not educate Xanthippe,[24] but deal with one who is the most difficult of present-day women and, I suppose, of those past and future too?"

"Because I see," he said, "that those who wish to become skilled horsemen acquire not the horses that readily obey, but high-spirited ones. For they believe that if they are able to subdue such horses, they will easily deal with[25] the rest. And I too, in my desire to deal and associate with human beings, have acquired her, knowing full well that if I can endure her, I'll easily associate with all other human beings."

And indeed this speech was held to have been spoken not wide of the mark.

(11) After this, a hoop was brought in, studded all-round with straight daggers. The dancing girl tumbled head first into and then through this in such a way that the onlookers were frightened lest she be hurt, but she performed this confidently and safely.

(12) And Socrates, calling to Antisthenes, said, "I suppose that at least those who see this will no longer dispute that even courage[26] is teachable, when she, though a woman, throws herself so daringly into the swords."

(13) And Antisthenes said, "Then wouldn't it be most excellent for the Syracusan here to show the city his dancing girl and to say that if the Athenians give him money, he'll make all Athenians dare to face the spear head-on?"

(14) And Philippus said, "Yes by Zeus! And I for my part would gladly watch Peisander the demagogue[27] learn how to tumble through daggers! As it is, he's not even willing to join the army on account of his inability to stare spears in the face!"

(15) After this, the boy danced, and Socrates said, "Did you see that although the boy is beautiful, nonetheless he seems still more beautiful with the dance routines than he does at rest?"

[24] Xanthippe was the wife of Socrates, renowned for her difficult behavior: see *Memorabilia* 2.2 and Diogenes Laertius *Lives of the Famous Philosophers* 2.36–37.

[25] See n. 23 above.

[26] Or, "manliness."

[27] Peisander was a leader of the Four Hundred, apparently notorious for his cowardice: see Aristophanes *Birds* 1555ff.

And Charmides said, "You seem to be praising the dance teacher."

(16) "Yes by Zeus!" said Socrates, "and I thought of something else in addition, that no part of his body was idle during the dance, but his neck, legs, and arms were exercised at the same time, just as one who intends to maintain his body in a good condition should dance. And I," he said, "would very gladly learn the routines from you, Syracusan."

And he said, "So what use will you make of them?"

(17) "I'll dance, by Zeus!"

At this everyone laughed. Socrates' face became very serious, and he said, "Are you laughing at me? Is it because I wish to exercise for better health, or for more pleasure in eating and sleeping, or because I am eager for such exercises—not like the long-distance runners who build up their legs but have scrawny shoulders, nor like the boxers who build up their shoulders but have scrawny legs—but by working every part of my body to create a complete equilibrium? (18) Or are you laughing because it won't be necessary for me to seek out an exercise partner, or to get undressed in a crowd—I'm an old man[28]—but a house big enough for seven couches will be sufficient for me, just as, even now, this room was sufficient for the boy here to work up a sweat? Is it because in winter I'll exercise inside and in shade when it is scorchingly hot? (19) Or are you laughing at this, that I have a bit of a paunch and wish to make it less? Or don't you know that just recently Charmides here caught me dancing at daybreak?"

"Yes by Zeus!" Charmides said. "And at first, at any rate, I was dumbstruck and feared that you were mad. But when I heard from you things similar to what you are saying now, I myself went home and, not danced—for I've never learned how—but did calisthenics, for this I knew how to do."

(20) "By Zeus," said Philippus, "and your legs and your shoulders are so equal in strength that, in my opinion, if you were to weigh your upper and lower halves for the Market Regulators, like loaves of bread, you'd get off scot-free!"[29]

And Callias said, "Socrates, summon me when you intend to learn how to dance so that I may be your partner and learn along with you."

[28] Or, "elder." The word "man" does not appear in the Greek (cf. n. 16 above).

[29] The Market Regulators weighed imported grain to insure against fraudulent dealings; see Plato *Laws* 760b, Aristotle *Politics* 1321b30 and context.

(21) "Come now," Philippus said, "let the flute be played for me as well so I too may dance!" And when he stood up, he went through the dances of the boy and girl and parodied them. (22) To begin with, since they had praised the way the boy seemed to be still more beautiful with his dance movements, Philippus replied in turn by making every part of his body that was in motion more laughable than it is by nature. And just as the girl had bent over backward in imitation of a wheel, so Philippus tried to do the same by bending over forward. Finally, as they had praised the boy because he exercised his whole body in his dance, Philippus bid the flute-girl to pick up the tempo and he let loose everything—legs, arms, and head. (23) When he was worn out, he reclined and said, "Here's proof, men, that my dance steps too supply exercise nobly. I'm thirsty, at any rate! Let the slave-boy fill a big drinking bowl for me!"

"By Zeus," Callias said, "and one for us, since we too are thirsty from laughing at you!"

(24) And Socrates in turn said, "Well, men, in my opinion it is very much the best thing to drink, for it really is the case that wine, by watering souls, puts pains to rest for some, just as mandragola does human beings, and it awakens affection in other souls, just as oil does the flame. (25) And yet it is my opinion too that men's[30] bodies[31] undergo the same things as do plants growing in the earth. For when the god waters them too much all at once, they also are unable to stand up straight or to breathe the morning air. But when they drink only so much as is pleasing, they will grow very straight, flourish, and arrive at the fruit-bearing stage.

(26) "Thus, if we too pour the drink all at once, our bodies and our minds will soon stagger, and we'll be unable to catch our breath, let alone say anything of substance. But if the slave-boys besprinkle our small cups with frequent little drops—to speak in Gorgian[32] phrases—in this way we won't be overpowered by the

[30] One ms. (E Laurentianus LXXX–13) and Athenaeus read "human beings' " rather than "men's."

[31] "Bodies" (*sōmata*) is the reading of Ollier's text, following Athenaeus (see also S. L. Radt, "Zu Xenophons *Symposion*" *Mnemosyne* 43 [1990]: 1–2, 24–5). The mss. (and Stobaeus *Florilegium*) read "banquets" (*sumposia*).

[32] The rhetorician Gorgias is meant (see n. 7 above). The form of the verb Socrates here uses (*epipsakadzōsin* instead of *epipsekadzōsin*) is found only in old Attic and is therefore somewhat affected, as the translation "besprinkle" attempts to suggest.

wine and get drunk, but rather we'll be coaxed into a greater playfulness."

(27) These things indeed seemed best to everyone.[33] But Philippus set it down in addition that the wine-servers ought to imitate the good charioteers by having the drinking cups go around faster. Indeed, this the wine-servers did.

Chapter 3

(1) After this the boy tuned his lyre to the flute and began to play and sing. At this everyone applauded, and Charmides said, "Well in my opinion, men, what Socrates said regarding the wine applies also to this mixing of youths in their bloom with music: on the one hand it lays pains to rest, and it awakens erotic passion[34] on the other."

(2) After this Socrates again spoke: "These people seem capable of pleasing us, men. But I know that we suppose we are very much better than they. Isn't it shameful, then, if we won't even try, when we are together[35], in some way to benefit or delight one another?"

Here many spoke: "Well then, you show us the way to the kinds of speeches that we might avail ourselves of and so best do this."

(3) He said, "I would most gladly have Callias fulfill his promise. For doubtless he said that if we should dine together, he would display his wisdom."

"And display it I will," he said, "if all of you too bring forward whatever good thing each one of you knows."

"Well no one opposes you in this," he said, "namely, our saying whatever it is each one of us believes to be the most valuable thing he knows."

(4) "I, then, " he[36] said, "say to you what it is I most pride myself on: I think that I am capable of making human beings better."

[33] Or, "These things were passed by everyone." Xenophon here speaks in legislative terms, beginning this sentence with the same formula used in the laws passed by the Athenian assembly ("It seems best to the people that . . ."). In the immediate sequel, Philippus makes an "amendment" to the "decree" just passed.

[34] Literally, "Aphrodite." Socrates had in fact not spoken of Aphrodite but rather of "affection" (see 2.24).

[35] See n. 20 above.

[36] The speaker is evidently Callias.

And Antisthenes said, "By teaching some vulgar art or gentlemanliness?"

"Gentlemanliness, if justice is this."

"By Zeus" said Antisthenes, "it, at least, is so most indisputably! For you see, there are times when courage and wisdom are held to be harmful to both friends and the city, but justice isn't intermingled with injustice in even a single respect."

(5) "When each of you has said what he has that is beneficial, then I too will unbegrudgingly[37] name that art through which I'm able to bring this about. But you say next, Niceratus," he said, "what sort of knowledge it is that you pride yourself on."

And he said, "My father[38] was concerned that I become a good man and so compelled me to learn all the lines of Homer. And now I could recite the whole *Iliad* and *Odyssey* by heart."

(6) "Has it escaped you," Antisthenes said, "that all the rhapsodes too know these verses?"

"How could it escape one who listens to them almost every day?"

"Do you know, then," he said, "of any tribe stupider than the rhapsodes?"

"No by Zeus," said Niceratus, "not in my opinion at least!"

"For it is clear," Socrates said, "that they do not know the hidden meanings. But you've paid a great deal of money to Stesimbrotus and Anaximander[39] and many others so that nothing of what is most worthwhile has escaped you. (7) Now what do you, Critoboulus, most pride yourself on?"

"On my beauty," he said.

"Then you too," Socrates said, "will be able to say that you are capable of making us better with your beauty?"

"If not, it's at any rate clear that I appear to be a good-for-nothing."

(8) "Now what about you," Socrates said, "what do you pride yourself on, Antisthenes?"

[37] That is, gladly or unrestrainedly. It is related to the verb "to bear a grudge" that appears at 3.14, 4.43, and 6.6.

[38] Niceratus is the son of the famed Athenian general, Nicias.

[39] Stesimbrotus was a biographer and Homeric scholar, fragments of whose writings survive. The Anaximander mentioned here is not the famous pre-Socratic philosopher but a Homeric critic; cf. Felix Buffière, *Les Mythes d'Homère et la Pensée Grecque* (Paris: Société d'Édition , "Les Belles Lettres," 1956), 132–33 and n. 30.

"On my wealth," he said. Hermogenes then asked whether he had a lot of money, and he swore that he had not even an obol.[40]

"Well do you possess a lot of land then?"

"Perhaps it might be enough for Autolycus here to dust himself with."[41]

(9) "We must listen to you too. And what about you, Charmides, what do you pride yourself on?" he said.

"I in turn pride myself on my poverty," he said.

"By Zeus," said Socrates, "that's a charming thing! For this indeed is least of all envied, least of all fought over, and is preserved when unguarded and strengthened when neglected!"

(10) "And you," said Callias, "what do you pride yourself on, Socrates?"

And Socrates, drawing up his face in a very solemn manner, said, "On pimping." When they laughed at him, he said, "You laugh, but I know that I would make a great deal of money should I wish to make use of this art."

(11) "As for you, Philippus," said Lycon, "it's clear that you pride yourself on making people laugh."

"More justly, I suppose, than does Callippides[42] the actor, who is overly pompous because he can make a packed house weep."

(12) "Surely you too, Lycon," said Antisthenes, "will say what it is you pride yourself on?"

"Why, don't you all know that it is on my son here?"

Someone said, "Well, it's clear that he, at least, prides himself on being the victor!"

Autolycus blushed and said, "No by Zeus, I don't!"

(13) Everyone then looked toward him, pleased at his having spoken. Someone asked him, "Well then, on what, Autolycus?"

He said, "On my father," and as he did so he nestled against him.

When Callias saw this he said, "Do you know, Lycon, that you are the wealthiest of human beings?"

"By Zeus," he said, "indeed I do not know this!"

[40] A small unit of Athenian currency, one-sixth of a drachma.

[41] It was the custom for athletes to rub down with oil and then fine sand or powder; see, e.g., H. A. Harris, *Greek Athletes and Athletics* (Westwood, Conn.: Greenwood Press, 1979), 102–3.

[42] Callipides was a famous tragic actor.

"Well does it escape you that you wouldn't take the King's[43] money in place of your son?"

"I've been caught red-handed," he said, "being the wealthiest of human beings, as it seems!"

(14) "And you, Hermogenes," said Niceratus, "what do you exult in[44] most of all?"

And he said, "The virtue and power of my friends and that, being of this sort, they are concerned with me."

At this point everyone turned toward him, and many asked in unison whether he would make clear to them who these were. He said that he would not begrudge[45] doing so.

CHAPTER 4

(1) After this Socrates said, "Well then, it remains for us to demonstrate that the things each of us claimed really are worth a great deal."

"I'd like you to listen to me first," said Callias. "For all the while I hear you[46] being at a loss as to what the just is, I'm actually making human beings more just."

"How, best one?" he said.

"By giving them money, by Zeus!"

(2) And Antisthenes stood up and in a very refutative manner asked, "Callias, in your opinion, do human beings possess justice in their souls or in their wallets?"

"In their souls," he said.

"And so do you make their souls more just by putting money in their wallets?"

"Absolutely."

"How?"

"Since they know they'll have something with which to purchase the necessities, they don't wish to run the risk of committing crimes."

[43] The King of Persia is meant. The expression is proverbial (see also 4.11).

[44] The word Niceratus uses often has religious overtones. It appears only here in the *Symposium*.

[45] See n. 37 above.

[46] Callias here uses the plural "you."

(3) "And do they pay you back the money they receive?"

"By Zeus," he said, "no indeed!"

"What then, instead of the money, do they give you gratitude?"

"No by Zeus," he said, "not even this! Rather, some are even more hostile than before!"

"It's amazing!" Antisthenes said, looking at Callias as though he'd refuted him. "You're able to make them just toward others, but not toward you yourself?"

(4) "And why is this amazing?" Callias said. "Don't you see many carpenters and house-builders who construct houses for many others but are unable to build them for themselves and live instead in rented houses? So own up, you Sophist, that you've been refuted!"

(5) "By Zeus," said Socrates, "let him own up to it. For even the prophets are doubtless said to foretell the future for others, but not to foresee what will come for themselves."

(6) Here this speech came to a close.

After this Niceratus said, "I'd like you to hear from me too in what respects you'll be better if you associate with me. For doubtless you know that the most wise Homer has written about almost all human affairs. Whoever among you, then, wishes to become an expert household manager, public speaker, or general, or to become like Achilles, Ajax, Nestor, or Odysseus, let him pay court to me. For I understand all these things."

"Surely then you understand how to rule as a king," said Antisthenes, "since you know that he praised Agamemnon as a 'good king and strong spearman'?"[47]

"Yes by Zeus!" he said, "and I for my part know that one driving a chariot must turn close to the post,

> And he himself must lean from the well-polished chariot board
> Gently to the left, and the horse on the right
> He must spur on and urge along, and slacken his hands to yield
> the reins.[48]

[47] *Iliad* 3.179.

[48] *Iliad* 23.335–37. The text as it has come down to us differs slightly from Niceratus' recitation. The humor of this citation apparently stems from the fact that chariot racing had become completely obsolete by this time.

(7) "I know something else in addition to this, and it is possible for you to test it immediately. For Homer says somewhere, 'an onion as a relish for the drink.'[49] Now if someone brings an onion, you will immediately be benefited very much in this, for you'll drink more pleasantly."

(8) And Charmides said, "Men, Niceratus wants to come home smelling of onions so his wife may believe that it didn't even enter anyone's head to kiss him!"

"By Zeus!" said Socrates, "but we run the risk of acquiring, I suppose, a ridiculous reputation as well. For the onion really does seem to be a relish, since it not only enhances the pleasure of food but that of drink too. Yet if we are going to nibble on this after dinner also, see to it that someone will not say we went to Callias' to overindulge."

(9) "Not at all, Socrates," he said. "For it is noble for one setting off to battle to nibble on an onion, just as some feed their cocks garlic before putting them together to fight. But perhaps we are deliberating as to how we'll kiss someone rather than do battle with him." (10) And at about this point, this speech came to a close.

Critoboulus said, "I then will speak next about the reasons why I pride myself on my beauty."

"Speak," they said.

"Well, if on the one hand I am not beautiful, as I suppose I am, then you would justly pay the penalty for the deception. For although no one administers an oath to you, you always swear and affirm that I am beautiful—and I trust in it, for I believe you are gentlemen. (11) Now if on the other hand I really *am* beautiful and you suffer the same things in regard to me as I do in regard to the one who is beautiful in my opinion, then I swear by all the gods that I wouldn't choose the King's empire in place of being beautiful. (12) For now I gaze at Cleinias[50] with more pleasure than at all the other things that are beautiful among human beings; I would accept being

[49] *Iliad* 11.630.

[50] Cleinias is either the son or the cousin of Alcibiades and is evidently the object of Critoboulus' affections as related in *Mem.* 1.3.8–10. In Plato's *Euthydemus*, Cleinias is said to have a great many lovers or admirers (273a).

blind to all the rest before I would accept being blind only to Cleinias. I am burdened by the night and by sleep because I do not see him then, and I know the greatest gratitude to the day and to the sun because they reveal Cleinias to me.

(13) "It's a worthy thing indeed for us beautiful ones to pride ourselves on this too, that while the strong one must acquire good things by toiling, and the brave by running risks, and the wise by talking, the beautiful one can accomplish everything while being at leisure. (14) Now although I know that money is a pleasant possession, I, at least, would with greater pleasure give my property to Cleinias than I would receive more from another. I would with greater pleasure be a slave than a free man were Cleinias willing to rule me, for I would toil for him more easily than be at rest, and I would with greater pleasure run risks for him than live risk-free. (15) As a result, Callias, if you pride yourself on being able to make human beings more just, then I, in leading them to every virtue, am more just than you. For on account of what we instill in the lovers, we beautiful ones make them more liberal as regards money, fonder of hard work and noble action in dangers, and especially more bashful and continent, for they are abashed at the things that they want most of all. (16) Indeed, those who do not elect the beautiful as generals are mad. I, at least, would even go through fire with Cleinias, and I know that you would with me as well. So do not be at a loss any longer, Socrates, as to whether my beauty will benefit human beings.

(17) "And beauty ought not to be dishonored because it fades quickly, since just as a boy becomes beautiful, so too does a lad, a man, and an old man. There is proof of this: the beautiful elders are selected as Athena's olive-branch bearers, on the grounds that there is a beauty accompanying every age. (18) And if it is pleasant to have one's wants fulfilled by those who are willing, I know well that at this very moment I could, without saying a word, persuade this boy and the girl to kiss me more quickly than you could, Socrates, even if you were to say many wise things."

(19) "What's this?" said Socrates. "Do you make such boasts on the grounds that you are more beautiful even than I?"

"Yes by Zeus" said Critoboulus, "otherwise I would be the ugliest of all the Silenuses[51] in the satyr plays!" (Socrates did bear a resemblance to them.)[52]

(20) "Well then," said Socrates, "see to it that you remember the beauty contest when the speeches proposed have gone around. Let us be judged, not by Alexander[53] son of Priam, but by these very ones who, as you suppose, desire to kiss you."

(21) "Socrates," he said, "couldn't you entrust the matter to Cleinias?"

And he said, "Won't you stop bringing Cleinias to mind?"

"If I don't mention his name, do you suppose that I call him to mind any less? Don't you know that I have so clear an image of him in my soul that, if I were a sculptor or painter, I could produce a likeness of him no less from this image than from actually looking upon him?"

(22) And Socrates replied, "Why then, if you have so lifelike an image, do you burden me with these matters and drag me around to where you will see him?"

"Because, Socrates, while the sight of him is capable of delighting me, seeing his image does not supply pleasure but rather instills longing in me."

(23) And Hermogenes said, "Well I, Socrates, do not think it at all appropriate for you to overlook Critoboulus' being so dumbstruck by love."

"Is it your opinion that it is after his associating with me that he is so disposed?"

"Well when, then?"

"Don't you see that the down of his beard is just now descending alongside his ears, but that Cleinias already has hair creeping along the nape of his neck? It was when he went to the same school as Cleinias that Critoboulus became so vehemently inflamed with de-

[51] Silenuses were creatures, half-horse (or goat) and half-man, usually old, and given to mischief. They were apparently portrayed also as old drunkards, though not without intellectual talents: the education of Dionysus was entrusted to them.

[52] Xenophon's comment here is considered suspect by some editors but is present in the mss.

[53] Alexander, or Paris, was called on to judge the beauty of Hera, Athena, and Aphrodite (cf. *Iliad* 24.28–30; Euripides *Helen* 23–30).

sire. (24) Because his father perceived this, he entrusted him to me, hoping I might be able to benefit him in some way.

"He is in any case much better already. For before, like those who gaze upon the Gorgons,[54] Critoboulus stared at him with a stony gaze and, like a stone,[55] did not leave him for any reason. (25) But now I've already seen him blink! And yet, by the gods, men, it is my opinion at least," he said, "that—just between ourselves[56]—he has even kissed Cleinias. There is no more fearsome a spark of love than this, for it is insatiable and supplies certain sweet hopes. (26) Perhaps it is overly honored because, of all acts, only touching one another with the lips[57] has the same name as the love belonging to souls.[58] This is why I assert it is necessary for one who will be capable of moderation to abstain from the kisses of those in their bloom."

(27) And Charmides said, "But why in the world, Socrates, do you spook us, your friends, away from the beautiful ones in this way, when I saw you yourself—yes, by Apollo!—when both you and Critoboulus were searching for something in the same book at the gymnasium, your head against his head, your bare shoulder against his bare shoulder?"

(28) "Ah hah!" he said. "So that's why, like someone who'd been bitten by a wild beast, I felt a pain in my shoulder for more than five days and why I thought there was something like a sting in my heart! But now, Critoboulus, I proclaim before all these witnesses that you are not to lay hold of me until your beard is as long as the hair on your head!"

(29) And in this way they mixed the playful and serious.

[54] Gorgons were mythical creatures the sight of which turned men to stone: *Odyssey* 11.634–35.

[55] The adverb this phrase translates (*lithinōs*) is omitted by Ollier but is present in the mss.

[56] Reading, with Ollier, the *hēmin autois* ("ourselves") of Leonclavius (*Xenophontis Opera* [Frankfurt, 1569]).

[57] Reading, with Ollier, the emendation *stomasi* instead of *sōmasi* ("bodies") with the mss.

[58] The same verb (*philein*) means both to kiss and to love unerotically or as a friend. The sentence is omitted by Ollier, following Dindorf (*Xenophontis Opera* [Leipzig: B. G. Teubner, 1852–54]), but is present in the mss. Cf. Pierre Gorisson, "Notes sur le *Banquet* de Xénophon," in *Recueil commemoratif du xe anniversaire de la Faculté de Philosophie et Lettres* (Louvain: Editions Nauwaerts, 1968), 171–82.

Then Callias said, "It's your turn, Charmides, to say why you pride yourself on poverty."

"Surely it's agreed to," he said, "that it is better[59] to be bold than fearful, to be free rather than a slave, to be tended to rather than to tend to another, and to be trusted by the fatherland rather than distrusted by it. (30) Now when I was a wealthy man in this city, in the first place I used to fear that someone would break into my house, steal my money, and do some evil to my very person. Second, I used to tend to the sycophants,[60] knowing that I was more capable of suffering at their hands than making them do so at mine. Moreover, some expense was always assigned to me by the city, and I wasn't able to travel abroad. (31) But now, as I am deprived of my properties abroad and do not reap the benefits from those at home, and my household goods have been sold, I stretch out and sleep pleasantly, I have become trusted by the city, and no longer am I threatened but rather I now threaten others; I am also permitted as a free man both to travel abroad and to return home. And now the wealthy rise out of their seats and make way for me in the streets; (32) now I am akin to a tyrant, but then I clearly was a slave. Then too I used to pay taxes to the people, but now the city supports me at its expense. And when I was wealthy, they used to reproach me because I associated with Socrates, but now that I have become poor, it's no longer of any concern to anyone. Further, when I had a lot, I always used to lose something, either on account of the city or through chance. But now I lose nothing, for I have nothing to lose, and I always hope that I'll lay hold of something."

(33) "Well then," said Callias, "do you pray never to become wealthy, and if you see some good vision in your sleep, do you sacrifice to the gods that avert evil?"

"By Zeus no!" he said. "*This* I do not do, but I bear up with a real love of danger if I expect to lay hold of something from somewhere or other."

(34) "But come now," Socrates said, "you tell us in turn, Antisthenes, how it is that, having so little, you pride yourself on wealth."

[59] Or "superior," "stronger" (*kreittōn*); see n. 9 above.

[60] Or, "extortioners." Strictly speaking, sycophants were those who threatened to bring formal judicial actions against (wealthy) citizens unless they received a payoff (see *Memorabilia* 2.9, and *Oeconomicus* 11.21).

"Because I believe, men, that human beings do not have wealth and poverty in their household but in their souls. (35) For I see many private persons who, although they have a great deal of wealth, believe they are so poor that they take on every toil and every danger to possess more. I also know brothers each of whom received an equal inheritance, but the one now has enough, and even more than enough, for his expenses, while the other is in need of everything. (36) I perceive also that some tyrants are so hungry for money that they do things far more terrible than the destitute. Doubtless it is because of want that some of these latter steal, others burgle houses, and that still others ply the slave trade. But there are some tyrants who do away with whole households, slaughter masses, and often sell even entire cities into slavery for the sake of money. (37) Now I for my part feel great pity for them because of their extremely harsh sickness. For in my opinion they suffer the same things as someone who could never be satiated although he had and ate a great deal. But I have so much that I myself can scarcely find it all.[61] Nevertheless, I can eat to the point that I'm not hungry and can drink until I'm not thirsty and be dressed in such a way that I'm no colder when outside than the fabulously wealthy Callias here. (38) When I am indoors, the walls are in my opinion very warm cloaks, the ceilings very thick mantles. The bedding I have is so adequate that it is a great task just to wake up. If my body ever requires sexual pleasure,[62] whatever is near to hand is so satisfactory to me that those women whom I visit welcome me most warmly because no one else is willing to go to them. (39) Now all these things are so pleasant in my opinion that in doing each of them I would not pray to be more pleased, but less—some of them being in my opinion more pleasant than is beneficial.

(40) "The most valuable possession in my wealth I reckon to be this, that if someone were to take from me all that I now have, I see no task so base that it would not be sufficient to provide my sustenance. (41) For whenever I wish to experience pleasure, I do not buy precious things from the marketplace—for they are expensive—but I dispense things from my soul. And it makes a much greater differ-

[61] Reading *aneuriskō* as suggested by G. L. Cooper, "A Better Solution for the Text of Xenophon, *Symp.* 4.37" *Classical Quarterly* 21 (1971): 62–63.

[62] Literally, "the things (or pleasures) belonging to Aphrodite"; cf. 3.1, end.

ence in regard to pleasure when I lay before me what was lacking after I've endured a wait than when I consume some precious thing, just as now I drink this Thasian wine that I've happened upon, although I'm not thirsty. (42) And indeed it is likely that those who look to cheap things are more just, at least, than those who seek out expensive things, for those who are satisfied by what is near to hand least covet what belongs to others. (43) It is also worthwhile to consider that such wealth makes people liberal. For Socrates here, from whom I acquired this wealth, did not come to my aid calculating the number or weight of the goods involved, but gave over to me so much as I could carry. Now I too begrudge no one, but make a display to all my friends of my unbegrudging plenty[63] and share the wealth of my soul with anyone who so desires. (44) Moreover, you see that the most exquisite possession, leisure, is always available to me so that I can behold the worthiest sights, listen to the worthiest sounds and, what I value most, spend the day at leisure with Socrates. He too does not marvel at[64] those who rack up the most gold, but he rather spends his days associating with those who are pleasing to him."

Thus did he speak.

(45) Callias said, "By Hera! Among the reasons why I envy your wealth is that the city doesn't command you and treat you like a slave, and that human beings don't become angry if you don't loan them money."

"But by Zeus," said Niceratus, "don't envy him! For I'm going to visit him with the intention of borrowing this capacity to be self-sufficient. Having been taught by Homer to count,

> Seven unfired tripods, ten talents of gold
> Twenty blazing cauldrons, and twelve horses[65]

by weight and number, I never stop desiring the greatest wealth possible. On the basis of this, perhaps I am too fond of money in the opinion of some."

[63] See n. 37 above.
[64] Or, "admire."
[65] *Iliad* 11.122f., 264f.

At this everyone laughed, believing that he had said what was indeed the case.[66]

(46) After this someone said, "It's your task, Hermogenes, to say who your friends are and to show both that they are capable of great things and that they care for you; in this way you may be held to take pride in them justly."

(47) "Well now, it is quite clear that both Greeks and barbarians believe the gods know everything, both what is[67] and what will be. All cities, at any rate, and all nations ask the gods, by means of divination, what they ought to do and what not. And indeed, that we believe they are capable of doing good and bad is clear as well. At any rate all ask the gods to avert wretched things and grant the good. (48) So you see, these gods who know all things and are able to do all things are my friends in such a way that, through their care for me, I have never yet escaped their notice, night or day, wherever I may be setting off or in whatever I may be about to do. Through their foreknowledge of what will result from every action, they signify to me whatever I must do and what I ought not by sending me voices, dreams, and birds of omen as messengers. Whenever I obey them, I have never yet repented of it; but now and again when I failed to believe them, I was punished."

(49) And Socrates said, "Well there is nothing unbelievable in these things. Yet I for my part would gladly learn how it is that you tend to them and thus have them as friends."

"By Zeus," said Hermogenes, "very inexpensively! For I praise them but spend no money; I always offer up something from what they give me; I speak as piously[68] as I can; and I never wittingly lie when I have invoked them as witnesses."

"By Zeus," said Socrates, "if you, being of this sort, have them as friends, the gods too, it seems, are pleased by gentlemanliness!"

(50) This speech was thus delivered seriously.

When they came to Philippus, they asked him what he saw in jesting that he prided himself on. "Isn't it a worthwhile thing?" he said.

[66] Literally, "the things that exist," "the beings" (*ta onta*).

[67] Literally, "the things that exist," "the beings" (see the preceding note).

[68] Radt, "Zu Xenophons *Symposion*," 27, argues that the verb Hermogenes here uses (*euphēmeō*) has its idiomatic meaning, "to hush up," "to keep quiet" (see, e.g., Plato *Euthydemus* 301a7; *Symposium* 214d5) and would accordingly shed some light on Hermogenes' subsequent reluctance to speak (6.1–4).

"Everyone knows that I am a jester, and they eagerly invite me to these affairs when they are in a good way, but take to their heels and never look back when they're dealt something bad, afraid that they may laugh unwittingly."

(51) And Niceratus said, "By Zeus, you do justly pride yourself! For some of my friends, in turn, keep out of my path when they are faring well, but others, if they are dealt something bad, trace their family roots to me and never leave my side!"

(52) "Well now. What about you, Syracusan," said Charmides, "what do you pride yourself on? Or is it clear that it is on your boy?"

"No by Zeus," he said, "no indeed! But I am very much afraid for him: I sense that certain persons are plotting to corrupt[69] him."

(53) When Socrates heard this, he said, "Heracles! How great an injustice do they suppose has been done by your boy such that they want to kill him?"

"They don't want to kill him," he said, "but to persuade him to sleep with them."

"You, as it seems, believe that if this should happen, he would be corrupted?"

"Yes by Zeus," he said, "in every respect!"

(54) "Then you yourself don't sleep with him?"

"Yes by Zeus—all night every night!"

"By Hera," said Socrates, "what great good fortune for you that your skin is of such a nature that it alone doesn't corrupt those with whom you sleep! It's a worthy thing, as a result, for you to pride yourself on your skin, if nothing else!"

(55) "But by Zeus I don't pride myself on that!" he said.

"But on what, then?"

"By Zeus, on fools! For they support me by coming to see my puppet shows."

"So that's why," Philippus said, "I heard you praying yesterday to the gods for them to give you, wherever you may be, an abundant harvest, but a dearth of the sensible."

[69] Or, "destroy," as Socrates seems to suppose in the immediate sequel. The same verb was used in the formal charge against Socrates of having "corrupted" the young: see *Memorabilia* 1.1.1; cf. also *Symp.* 5.10, end.

(56) "Well now," said Callias. "As for you, Socrates, what do you have to say that makes it a worthy thing for you to pride yourself on such an ill-reputed art as the one you mentioned?"

And he said, "Let us agree in the first place what sorts of things the pimp's tasks are. And don't shrink from answering all that I ask, so we may know how much we agree on. Does this seem best to you all?" he said.

"Certainly," they said. And when once they had began to say, "Certainly," they all said this in reply to what followed.

(57) "In your opinion," he said, "isn't it the task of the good pimp to display the woman or the man being pimped in a way pleasing to those with whom he or she may be together?"

"Certainly," they said.

"Surely one way to please is the appropriate arrangement of hair and clothing?"

"Certainly," they said.

(58) "And surely we know this too, that it is possible for a human being to look at someone in both a friendly and a hateful way using the same eyes?"

"Certainly," they said.

"What then? Is it possible also to speak bashfully and boldly using the same voice?"

"Certainly," they said.

"What then? Don't some speeches cause hatred, but some lead to friendship?"

"Certainly."

(59) "Surely, then, of these things, the good pimp would teach what is advantageous with a view to pleasing?"

"Certainly," they said.

"Who would be better," he said, "the pimp able to make them pleasing to one person or the pimp who could make them pleasing to many?"

At this point, however, they were divided: some said, "Clearly whoever could make them pleasing to the most"; others simply said, "Certainly."

(60) Saying that this too was agreed on, Socrates continued: "If someone were able to show them off in a manner pleasing to the entire city, would he not then be an altogether good pimp?"

"Clearly so, by Zeus!" they all said.

"Then if such a one were able to bring this about from among those he manages, wouldn't he justly pride himself on his art and justly receive a great deal of money?"

(61) When all agreed to this, he said, "And indeed in my opinion, Antisthenes is such a one."

And Antisthenes said, "Is it to me, Socrates, that you are handing over your art?"

"Yes by Zeus!" he said. "For I see that you have also practiced well the art attendant upon mine."

"What's that?"

"The art of the go-between[70]," he said.

(62) Becoming very angry, Antisthenes asked, "And what do you know, Socrates, of my having done such a thing?"

"I know," he said, "that you have acted as a go-between for Callias here and the wise Prodicus, when you saw the former in love with philosophy and the latter in need of money. And I know that you brought him together also with Hippias the Elean[71] from whom he learned his skill in memorization. It is indeed on account of this that Callias has become more skilled in erotic matters, for he never forgets anything beautiful he sees.

(63) "And doubtless it was just recently that, by praising the Heraclean stranger[72] to me, you made me desire him and introduced him to me. I certainly am grateful to you, for he is in my opinion very much the gentleman. And by praising Aeschylus the Phliasian[73] to me, and me to him, didn't you arrange it in such a way that, being in love because of your speeches, we sought out one another like dogs on a hunt? (64) Having seen that you are capable of doing these things well, then, I believe you are a good go-between. For one who is capable of recognizing those who are beneficial to one another[74] and can make these desire one another, this man would in my opinion be capable also of making cities friends and of bringing together suitable

[70] Or, "procurer." As Antisthenes' reaction makes clear, the connotations of this word are altogether disreputable.

[71] A Sophist, after whom Plato named two dialogues. See also *Memorabilia* 4.4.5ff.

[72] It is not known to whom Socrates here refers.

[73] Nothing is known of this figure.

[74] Reading, with Ollier, *hautois* as proposed by Leonclavius (*Xenophontis Opera* [Frankfurt, 1569]) instead of *autōi* ("to himself") of the mss.

spouses, and would be a very worthy possession to cities, friends, and allies.[75] But you got angry, as though you had heard yourself spoken of badly when I said that you are a good go-between."

"But by Zeus," he said, "I'm not so now. For if I can do these things, my soul shall be overloaded with riches in every respect." And this round of the speeches came to a close.

Chapter 5

(1) Callias said, "Now you, Critoboulus, aren't you holding out on the beauty contest against Socrates?"

"Yes, by Zeus, he is," said Socrates, "for perhaps he now sees that the pimp is well thought of by the judges!"

(2) "Even so," said Critoboulus, "I'm not backing out. So instruct us, if you have something wise to say, as to how you are more beautiful than I. Just let someone bring the lamp up close," he said.

"Well then," Socrates said, "first I summon you to the examination[76] of the court. So answer."

"Just ask."

(3) "Do you believe that the beautiful exists only in a human being, or in something else as well?"

"By Zeus," he said, "I say that it is also in a horse, an ox, and many inanimate things. I know, at any rate, that a shield is beautiful, as well as a sword and a spear."

(4) "And how is it that although none of these is similar to the other, they are all beautiful?"

"If, by Zeus," he said, "they've been well wrought with a view to the tasks for which we acquire them, or if they've been well adapted by nature with a view to the things we need, then these," Critoboulus said, "are beautiful."

[75] The phrase "and allies" (*kai summachois*) is suspected by many and is deleted by Ollier, following Sauppe (*Xenophontis Opera* [Leipzig: B. Tauchnitz, 1865–66]). Gorissen, "Notes sur le *Banquet*," 184–85, suggests "spouses" (*suggamois*).

[76] This is a technical legal term referring to the magistrates' examination of persons involved in a suit prior to their coming to trial.

(5) "Do you know for the sake of what we need eyes?"

"That's clear," he said, "in order to see."

"So then already my eyes would be more beautiful than yours."

"How so?"

"Because yours only see straight ahead, but mine, because they bulge out, see to the sides as well."

"Do you mean," he said, "that the crab has the best eyes of all the animals?"

"Doubtless in every respect," he said, "since he has by nature the best eyes also with a view to strength."

(6) "Well," he said, "which nose is more beautiful, yours or mine?"

"I think mine is," he said, "if in fact the gods made our nostrils for the sake of smelling. For yours look down to the ground, but mine flare upwards so they can receive smells from everywhere."

"How is the flat nose more beautiful than the straight?"

"Because," he said, "it doesn't block the eyes, but rather allows them immediately to see whatever they wish. A high nose, as if in insolent opposition, builds a wall between the eyes."

(7) "As for the mouth," Critoboulus said, "I concede the point. For if it has been made for the sake of biting, you could bite off something much bigger than I could. And because of the thickness of your lips, don't you suppose that your kiss would be the softer?"

"It seems," Socrates said, "that, according to your argument, I have an uglier mouth than that of an ass! But do you reckon it to be no proof of my being more beautiful than you that the River Nymphs, being goddesses, give birth to the Silenuses who bear a greater resemblance to me than to you?"

(8) And Critoboulus said, "I'm no longer able to speak against you. Let them distribute the ballots so that I may know as quickly as possible what I must either suffer or pay. Just let them vote in secret," he said, "for I'm afraid that the wealth you and Antisthenes have may overpower me."

(9) The girl and the boy cast their votes in secret. Meanwhile Socrates saw to it both that the lamp was brought around in turn to Critoboulus, in order for the judges not to be deceived, and that the victor's wreath would not be a fillet but kisses from the judges. (10) When the votes had been turned out and all were in Critoboulus' favor, Socrates said, "Ah well! It seems that your money, Crito-

boulus, isn't similar to Callias'. For his makes people more just, but yours, like most, is capable of corrupting both jurors and judges."

Chapter 6

(1) After this, some bade Critoboulus to take his victory kisses, some bade him to ask for the permission of[77] the youths'[78] master, and others made other jokes. But here too Hermogenes was silent. Socrates called him by name and said, "Could you tell us, Hermogenes, what 'convivial misbehavior' is?"

And he replied, "If you are asking what it is, I don't know. Yet I might be able to say what it seems to me to be."

"Well, state what it seems to be," he said.

(2) " 'To give pain, under the influence of wine, to one's companions,' this is what I judge 'convivial misbehavior' to be."

"Then don't you know," he said, "that you are now giving pain to us by being silent?"

"Do you mean when you are talking?"

"No, but when we leave gaps in our talking."

"What? Has it escaped your attention that someone could not get even a hair in edgewise, let alone a word?"

(3) And Socrates said, "Callias, could you come to the aid of a man being refuted?"

"Indeed I can," he said. "For whenever the flute is sounded, we are altogether silent."

And Hermogenes said, "Do you wish, then, that, just as Nicostratus the actor used to recite tetrameters along with the flute, so I too should converse with you all accompanied by the flute?"

(4) And Socrates said, "In the name of the gods, Hermogenes, do so. For I suppose that, just as the song is more pleasant with the flute, so too your speeches would be made pleasant in some way by the sounds, especially if you should gesticulate, like the flute-girl, while you speak."

77 Literally, "to persuade."

78 Only the word "master" appears in the Greek and probably refers, as the translation suggests, to the Syracusan.

(5) And Callias said, "Whenever Antisthenes here refutes someone at the banquet, what will be the tune?"

And Antisthenes said, "I think that hissing[79] would be fitting for the one being refuted."

(6) Such were the speeches being given when the Syracusan saw that they were neglecting his shows and taking pleasure in one another. Being envious of[80] Socrates, he said, "Are you, Socrates, the one nicknamed the 'Thinker'?"[81]

"Surely that would be nobler than if I were called the 'Thoughtless.'"

"Unless, that is, you were held to be a thinker of the things aloft."

(7) "Do you know anything loftier than the gods?"

"But by Zeus," he said, "they say that you do not care about them, but about the least beneficial things."

"Surely in this way too," he said, "I would care about the gods: just existing[82] they do benefit from on high, and from on high they furnish light.[83] And if what I say falls flat, you are to blame," he said, "for giving me these troubles."

(8) "Well then, let it be. But tell me how many flea's feet you are from me. For they say you measure these things."[84]

And Antisthenes said, "You are clever, Philippus, at doing caricatures.[85] Doesn't this man in your opinion take after one wanting to be abusive?"

"Yes by Zeus, he does," Philippus said, "and after many others too!"

(9) "But nevertheless," Socrates said, "don't do a caricature of him, lest you too take after someone wanting to be abusive."

[79] This refers also to the sound of a shepherd's pipe.

[80] Or, "Bearing a grudge against . . ."

[81] The Syracusan here alludes to Aristophanes' *Clouds* (see lines 266 and 414; also 94), first performed in 423 B.C. (see n. 9 to the interpretive essay, this work).

[82] Reading *ontes* with the mss. instead of the conjecture, *huontes* ("raining") accepted by Ollier. For a defense of the mss., see L. Parmentier, "Xénophon, *Banquet*, 6.7," *Revue de l'instruction publique en Belgique* 1 (1900): 244.

[83] Socrates' reply contains an untranslatable pun, made up of the components of the word used by the Syracusan to charge that Socrates is concerned with the least beneficial things: *tōn anōphelestatōn*. Socrates replies that the gods benefit (*ōphelousin*) from on high (*anōthen*).

[84] See Aristophanes *Clouds* 144ff.

[85] Comic imitations of others was a customary form of entertainment at banquets.

"But if in fact I compare him in my caricature to all the finest gentlemen,[86] someone would justly compare me to one who praises rather than abuses."

"Even now you seem to take after one who abuses, if you say that everyone is better than he."[87]

(10) "But do you want me to liken him to those who are more wretched?"

"Not to those who are more wretched either."

"But to nobody?"

"Don't liken him to a nobody either."[88]

"But if I keep quiet, I don't know how I'll make myself deserving of the dinner!"

"That's easy," he said, "if you keep quiet about the things one ought not say."

Thus this convivial misbehavior was quenched.

Chapter 7

(1) After this, some of the others continued to bid Philippus to do a caricature, but others continued to prevent him. Amidst this uproar, Socrates again spoke: "Since we all wish to speak, wouldn't it be best now for us to sing together?" As soon as he said this, he began a song. (2) After he[89] had sung, a potter's wheel was brought in for the dancing girl, on which she was to perform some wondrous feats. At this point Socrates said, "Syracusan, it is likely[90], just as you say, that I really am a thinker. Right now, at any rate, I'm considering how your boy here and this girl may spend their time as easily as possible, and

[86] Literally, "the noble and best," a slight variation on the customary formula (see n. 2 above).

[87] Reading *beltiō* rather than *beltiōn* with the mss. ("if you say that you are better than he in all respects"). Ollier reproduces Marchant's suggestion (itself inspired in part by an earlier emendation of Leonclavius) which would read as follows: "if you say that all things are better than he."

[88] Following the reading of the mss. and the translation suggested by Gorissen, "Notes sur le *Banquet*," 185–86.

[89] Reading *ēsen* with the mss. instead of Mosche's *ēsan* ("they had sung").

[90] Literally, "I run the risk of being" (*kinduneuō*).

how we may be especially delighted in watching them—what I know well you too want. (3) In my opinion, leaping into daggers is an exhibition of danger, something not at all appropriate to a banquet. Moreover, reading and writing on a spinning wheel may be something of a wonder, but I can't understand what pleasure even these things would supply. Nor is watching those who are beautiful and in bloom twisting around their bodies and imitating wheels more pleasant than watching them at rest. (4) For indeed, it is nothing very rare to happen upon wondrous things, if someone is wanting in these. It is possible to wonder very much and without delay at what is near to hand: why in the world does the lamp supply light by having a brilliant flame, while brass, which is brilliant as well, does not produce light but reflects off itself images of other things? And how is it that oil, while being wet, increases the flame, but water, because it is wet, extinguishes the fire? But these things too do not urge one on to the same thing as does wine. (5) If they were to dance routines depicting the Graces, the Seasons, and the Nymphs to the accompaniment of the flute, I think they would spend their time more easily and the banquet would be much more agreeable."

The Syracusan then said, "But by Zeus, Socrates, you speak nobly, and I'll bring in performances that will please you all!"

CHAPTER 8

(1) The Syracusan withdrew to prepare himself,[91] and Socrates in turn began a new speech. "Well, men," he said, "when a great daimon is present, one that is equal in age to the everlasting gods but youngest in appearance, one that extends over all things in its magnitude but is equivalent to[92] the human soul—I mean Eros—isn't it

[91] Radt ("Zu Xenophons *Symposion*," 28) argues that the verb usually translated as "was applauded" should be taken in the middle rather than the passive voice and that it accordingly means to practice or prepare oneself. This accords with the Latin translation of Leonclavius (1569) as well as the German of G. P. Landmann (*Das Gastmahl* [Hamburg: Rowohlt, 1957]).

[92] Reading *isoumenou* with the mss. instead of the conjecture *hidroumenou* ("seated" or "dwelling in") accepted by Ollier. H. Richards, "Notes on the *Symposium* of Xenophon," *Classical Review* 16 (1902): 294, suggests *eisduomenou* ("enters into").

fitting for us not to forget Him, especially when we are all fellow-worshippers[93] of this god? (2) For I cannot mention a time in my life when I wasn't in love with someone,[94] and I know that Charmides here possesses many lovers and that there are some whom he himself has desired. Critoboulus, who is at present still a beloved, already desires others. (3) Moreover, Niceratus too, as I hear, loves his wife and is loved in return. And as for Hermogenes, who among us doesn't know that he is melting away with love of gentlemanliness, whatever in the world it may be? Don't you see how serious are his brows, how steady his eye, how measured his speeches, how gentle his voice, how cheerful his character? And although he associates with the most august[95] gods as friends, don't you see that he doesn't feel contempt for us human beings? Are only you, Antisthenes, not in love with anyone?"

(4) "By the gods," he said, "I am very much so—with you!"

Socrates said, jokingly and coyly, "Don't bother me right now; (5) you see I've other things to do."

And Antisthenes said, "How clear it is that you are always doing such things, you pimp of yourself! At one time you fail to converse with me, using your *daimonion*[96] as an excuse, at another time you claim that you're seeking out someone[97] else."

(6) And Socrates said, "In the name of the gods, Antisthenes, just don't thrash me! The rest of your harshness I bear and will continue to bear in a friendly way. But let us cover over your love since it is not of my soul but of my nice form.

(7) "That you, Callias, love Autolycus the whole city knows, as do, I think, many foreigners too. The reason for this is that both of your fathers are renowned, and you yourselves are well known. (8) I for my part always used to admire your nature, but I do so now much more, since I see that you are in love with one who is not delicate through luxuriousness or effeminate through softness, but with one

[93] Strictly speaking, the "worshippers" here (*thiasōtai*) are those who belong to a *thiasos*, a religious association devoted to the worship of a particular divinity or divinities.

[94] Or, "something."

[95] Or, "solemn."

[96] Socrates' "daimon" or divine voice: see n. 5 to the translation of the *Apology of Socrates to the Jury*, this work.

[97] Or, "something."

who displays to all his strength, endurance, courage, and moderation. Desiring such things is a sure sign of the nature of the beloved.[98]

(9) "Now whether Aphrodite is single or dual, Heavenly and Vulgar, I don't know. For even Zeus, who is held to be the same, has many names. But I do know, at least, that there are separate altars and temples for each, as well as separate sacrifices—the Vulgar Aphrodite's being the more impure, the Heavenly's the more chaste. (10) You might conjecture that the Vulgar Aphrodite sends the loves of the bodies, the Heavenly one the loves of the soul, of friendship, and of noble deeds. Indeed, Callias, it is by this latter sort of Eros that you are in my opinion restrained. (11) I offer as evidence of this the gentlemanliness of your beloved and that I see you invite his father to your get-togethers[99] with the boy. For none of these is concealed from the father by the lover who is a gentleman."

(12) And Hermogenes said, "By Hera, Socrates! I admire, among many other things about you, that you are now gratifying Callias even as you are teaching him the sort of person he ought to be."

"Yes by Zeus," he said, "and so that he may be delighted still more, I wish to bear witness to him that the love of the soul is much superior to that of the body. (13) For we all know that there is no association with[100] another worthy of any account in the absence of friendship. The friendly love, at any rate, of those who admire the character is called a private[101] and voluntary compulsion,[102] but many of those who desire the body blame and despise the ways of the beloved. (14) Even if both[103] feel affection, doubtless the bloom of youth soon fades, and when this is absent, the friendship necessarily fades and dies along with it. But for so long as the soul approaches greater prudence, it also becomes worthier of love. (15)

[98] Reading *erōmenou* ("of the beloved") with the mss. rather than Mosche's *erastou* ("of the lover"). A papyrus fragment, apparently from the 2d century A.D. (Ollier, *Banquet-Apologie de Socrate*, 36), reads "*erōtos*" ("of Eros"). According to the reading of some mss., the phrase might also be rendered, "Desiring such things is a sure sign also of the nature of the beloved."

[99] See n. 20 above.

[100] See n. 20 above.

[101] Reading *idia* ("private") with the mss. instead of the conjecture *hēdeia* ("pleasant") accepted by Ollier.

[102] Literally, "necessity." The word can also refer to the bonds of kinship.

[103] The reading of the mss., defended by Radt, "Zu Xenophons *Symposion*," 29–30. Ollier's text reads: "Even if they feel affection for both [the body and the soul], . . ."

Moreover, there is in the use of the bodily form a certain satiety, the result of which is that one necessarily suffers in regard to one's beloved what one suffers in regard to food, through having more than one's fill. The friendship of the soul, because of being chaste, is also less likely to be sated, although it is not thereby, as someone might suppose, also less graced by Aphrodite.[104] Rather, the prayer in which we beseech the goddess to grant her grace to our words and deeds is clearly fulfilled. (16) The soul that blossoms with a liberal bodily appearance and a bashful, well-born character and that, from the outset, is capable of leading its peers while being at the same time of a friendly disposition—that such a soul cherishes and has a friendly love of the beloved requires no further argument. And that it is likely for such a lover to be loved in return by the boy I shall now teach.

(17) "Who could hate that person by whom, in the first place, he knows he is thought to be a gentleman; when, second, he sees that the person is more serious about the noble beauties of the boy than his own pleasure; when, in addition, he trusts that the friendship would not diminish, whether he were to lose his youthful bloom or, through illness, to become less attractive in bodily form? (18) To those, indeed, for whom friendly love is something shared, how could it not of necessity be the case that they look upon one another with pleasure, that they converse together benevolently, that they trust and are trusted, that they take thought for one another, that they rejoice together at noble actions and become vexed together if some misfortune should cross their path? How could it not be that they live their lives contentedly whenever they are together in good health and are together all the more if one or the other of them takes ill, and care for one another when absent still more than when present? Are not all these the things graced by Aphrodite? It is, at any rate, through such deeds that they live out their lives to old age being lovers of the friendship and making use of it.

(19) "But why would the boy return the love of one attached only to the body? Would it be because the lover allots to himself the things that he desires and to the boy the most disgraceful things? Or is it that, on account of what he is eager to do with the boy, he keeps the

[104] Cf. nn. 34 and 62 above.

beloved's relatives from him most of all? (20) The lover, moreover, who does not use force but persuasion is for this reason to be hated all the more, since by resorting to force he displays his own wretchedness, but by persuading he corrupts the soul of the one who is seduced. (21) And does the one who sells his youthful bloom for money love the buyer any more than does the seller who hawks his wares in the marketplace? Indeed, the boy will not feel a friendly affection for the lover because he, in his bloom, associates with one who is not, nor because he is beautiful and the lover is no longer so, nor because he, who is not in love, associates with one who is. For the boy doesn't even share in the gratifications of sex[105] as does a woman with a man, but watches, stone-cold sober, the one intoxicated by sexual gratification. (22) It would be no wonder if, as a result, he comes to feel contempt for his lover. And one might discover, in examining this, that while nothing harsh has arisen from those loved for their character, already many impious things have been done as a result of this shameless association.

(23) "I'll now make clear that the association is illiberal for the one loving the body rather than for the one loving the soul. For he who teaches what ought to be said and done would justly be honored as Cheiron and Phoenix were by Achilles. But he who yearns for the body would fittingly be treated as a beggar: he is always shadowing the boy, pleading for and needing still another kiss or some other caress. (24) If I speak rather bluntly, don't be amazed, for the wine is urging me on, and the Eros that always dwells with me goads me into speaking freely regarding the Eros that is its opponent. (25) For in my opinion, the person who applies his mind to the form[106] is akin to one who has rented land: he does not tend to it so that it may become more valuable, but so that he may harvest as many blooms as possible. But the person who seeks out friendship is more akin to one who possesses the family fields: he brings, that is, whatever he can from everywhere and makes the beloved more valuable. (26) Among the beloveds, moreover, he who knows that, by offering up his bodily form, he'll rule the lover, will in all likelihood act corruptly in other respects. But the beloved who recognizes that he will not retain

[105] Literally, "the things belonging to (or characteristic of) Aphrodite" (see nn. 34 and 62).

[106] The word is *eidos* ("form," "class," or "kind").

the friendship unless he is a gentleman is likely to care more for virtue. (27) But the greatest good for one yearning to make of his beloved a good friend is that he himself must practice virtue, for one who does wretched things himself cannot make the one he is with good, nor can one exhibiting shamelessness and incontinence make the beloved continent and bashful.

(28) "And I desire, Callias, to tell you a tale that shows that not only human beings but gods and heroes as well value more the friendship of the soul than the use of the body. (29) For all the mortal women whose bodily form Zeus loved, these he left as mortals after having associated with[107] them. But all the men whose good souls he might cherish, these he made immortal, among whom are Heracles and the Dioscuroi,[108] and there are said to be others. (30) And I assert that even Ganymede[109] was borne up to Olympus by Zeus not for the sake of his body but of his soul. Even his name offers evidence of this. For there is, I think, in Homer,

> and he rejoices in hearing.[110]

This means, 'he takes pleasure in hearing.' There is also somewhere else,

> knowing shrewd schemes in his mind.[111]

This in turn means, 'knowing wise deliberations in his mind.' So on the basis of these two together, the one called 'Ganymede' was honored among the gods not for the pleasure of his body but for that of his judgment.[112] (31) Furthermore, Niceratus, Homer has portrayed Achilles as avenging in a most outstanding way the death of Patrocles—presented as his comrade, not his beloved. And Orestes, Py-

[107] See n. 20 above.

[108] "Dioscuroi" literally means "the sons (or youths) of Zeus," namely Castor and Polydeuces.

[109] A very young boy, renowned for his beauty, taken by Zeus to be his cupbearer and beloved. See, e.g., *Iliad* 20.231ff.; Theognis 1345ff.; Plato *Phaedrus* 255c; *Laws* 636c–d.

[110] The phrase does not appear in the extant writings of Homer.

[111] The line as quoted does not appear in Homer (cf., e.g., *Iliad* 17.325).

[112] Socrates' etymology is untranslatable. He suggests that "Gany-" means "rejoice" or "takes pleasure in" and "-mede" means "schemes" or "deliberations." Thus the boy's very name suggests "taking pleasure in deliberations," a cerebral activity to be sure.

lades, Theseus, Peirithous, and many other of the best demigods are praised in song as having accomplished in common the greatest and noblest things, not on account of having slept together but rather of their admiration for one another.

(32) "What then? Might not someone discover that all present-day noble deeds are done by those willing to toil and run risks for the sake of commendation rather than by those accustomed to choose pleasure before good repute? And yet Pausanias[113], the lover of Agathon the poet, in making a defense on behalf of those who wallow together in incontinence, said that the stoutest army could be made up of beloveds and their lovers. (33) For he said that he supposes these especially would be ashamed to abandon one another. What amazing things he says, if in fact those who are accustomed to paying no heed to reproach and who act shamelessly with one another would be especially ashamed at doing something shameful! (34) He adduced as evidence the Thebans and the Eleans as ones who've recognized these things. He said that although they sleep with their beloveds, they nevertheless arrange them alongside themselves in battle. But there is nothing relevant in what he said, for while these things are customs among them, among us they are subject to the greatest reproach. In my opinion, at least, those who make these arrangements seem to doubt whether, once left alone, their beloveds will carry out the deeds of noble men. (35) But by believing that if someone has even longed for the body, he'll no longer attain anything noble and good, the Lacedaemonians make their beloveds so completely good that they are ashamed to leave those around them, whether they are with foreigners or even if they are not stationed in the same city[114] as their lover. For they believe that not Shamelessness but Shame[115] is a goddess.

(36) "Now in my opinion, we would all be in agreement as to what I'm saying if we were to examine the following question: to a boy loved in which of the two ways would someone be more inclined to entrust for safe keeping his money, children, or a debt of gratitude? I think that even the person who uses the beloved's form would entrust all these things more to one with a comely soul. (37)

[113] In Plato's *Symposium*, it is Phaedrus who makes the argument indicated (see 178a6ff.).

[114] Reading *polei* with the mss. instead of Ollier's *taksei* ("line of battle").

[115] Or, "Bashfulness."

Indeed, Callias, it is in my opinion a worthy thing for you to feel gratitude to the gods because they have instilled in you a love of Autolycus. For that he is a lover of honor[116] is quite clear, he who endured many toils and much pain for the sake of being proclaimed the victor in the pancratium. (38) If he should suppose that he will adorn not only himself and his father, but also that he will become capable, through manly goodness, of doing good to his friends and of augmenting the fatherland by erecting trophies against its enemies—and that through these things his face and his name will be known among both Greeks and barbarians—how can you not suppose that he would treat with the greatest honors anyone he considered to be the most excellent helpmate in such things? (39) So if you wish to be pleasing to him, you must consider the sorts of things Themistocles knew so as to be capable of liberating Greece; you must consider whatever in the world were the sorts of things Pericles knew so as to be held to be a most excellent counselor to the fatherland, and to examine how in the world Solon had philosophized before he laid down most excellent laws for the city; you must also search out the sorts of things the Lacedaemonians practice such that they are held to be most excellent leaders—the most excellent among them are always brought to your home as ambassadors. (40) Know well, then, that the city would quickly entrust itself to you, if you so wish. For the greatest things belong to you: you are of a good family,[117] a priest of the gods descended from Erechtheus[118], gods who led the army under Iacchus[119] against the Barbarian. And now in the festival you make an appearance as priest that is more impressive than your ancestors. Your body too is the worthiest in the city to behold and is capable of bearing up under hardship.

(41) "If in the opinion of you all I am speaking more seriously than is appropriate with a view to drinking, don't marvel at it. For I spend my days as one who is always, together with the city, a fellow lover

[116] Or, "ambitious."

[117] Literally, "you are a Eupatrides," the name of the Athenians of the first class.

[118] A legendary king of Athens reared by Athena (*Iliad* 2.547ff.). Cf. *Memorabilia* 3.5.10.

[119] In this context, the name may refer to Dionysus himself; see Walter Burkert, *Griechische Religion der archaischen und Klassichen Epoche* (Mainz: W. Kohlhammer, 1977), 127.

of those who are by nature good and who seek out virtue ambitiously."

(42) Now as the others were discussing what had been said, Autolycus was observing Callias. And Callias, while watching the boy out of the corner of his eye, said, "Surely, then, Socrates, you'll act as a pimp for me in regard to the city so that I may tend to its affairs and always be pleasing to it?"

(43) "Yes, by Zeus!" he said. "If, that is, they see that you really do care for virtue and not merely seem to.[120] For false reputation is soon refuted by the test of experience, but true manly goodness, unless a god hinders it, always supplies a more brilliant fame when put into practice."

CHAPTER 9

(1) Here this speech came to a close. Autolycus got up from his seat to go for a walk, as it was then his time to do so. His father Lycon, leaving with him, turned and said, "By Hera, Socrates, you are in my opinion a noble and good human being."[121]

(2) After this, a sort of throne was set down in the room, and the Syracusan then came in. He said, "Men, Ariadne will enter the chamber she shares with Dionysus. After this, Dionysus will enter, having drunk a little with the gods, and he will come to her. They will then be playful with one another."

(3) After this, Ariadne entered, adorned as a bride, and sat down on the throne. While Dionysus had not yet appeared, a Bacchic rhythm was played on the flute. It was at this point that they admired the dance instructor, for as soon as Ariadne heard this, she acted in such a way that all could see she listened with pleasure. She did not go to meet him, nor even get up, but it was clear that she was still only with difficulty. (4) When Dionysus espied her, he danced

[120] The verb translated as "to seem" (*dokein*) is related to the word translated as "reputation" (*doxa*) in the next sentence.

[121] Or, "gentleperson"; Lycon substitutes "human being" (*anthrōpos*) for "man" (*anēr*) in the customary formula elsewhere translated as "gentleman" (see nn. 2 and 16 above).

over to her, sat down on her lap as one would in the most affectionate[122] way, took her in his arms, and kissed her. And although she seemed bashful, she nevertheless affectionately embraced him in return. When the banqueters saw this, they clapped as they shouted, "Encore!" (5) Then, when Dionysus had stood up and helped Ariadne rise alongside him, one could behold them assuming the poses of those kissing and embracing one another. When the onlookers saw that Dionysus really was noble and that Ariadne was in her bloom, and that the two were not playing at kissing one another but were genuinely kissing with their mouths, all were carried away. (6) For they heard Dionysus ask her if she loved[123] him, and she vowed that she did in such a way that not only Dionysus[124] but all those present too would have sworn an oath that the boy and the girl were loved by one another. For they appeared not to have learned their poses as a routine, but rather to have been permitted to do what they had long been desiring. (7) Finally, when the banqueters saw that they had embraced one another and were off to their marriage bed, those who were unmarried swore that they would marry, and those who were married mounted their horses and rode off to their wives so as to obtain these things. Socrates and the others who remained went off with Callias to walk with Lycon and his son.

Such was the conclusion of this banquet.

[122] *Philikōtata*": an adverb related to the word for "friend" and hence also to the verb meaning "to kiss" which appears at the end of the sentence (see also n. 58 above).

[123] Here and again at the end of this sentence, the verb is *philein* (see n. 58 above).

[124] Ollier, following Shenkl (*Xenophontis Opera*, [Berlin: Weidman, 1869]) suggests a lacuna at this point.

On the *Symposium*

Robert C. Bartlett

The *Symposium* (*Banquet*) of Xenophon details a single evening spent by Socrates and a number of his students and acquaintances. In it we see something of the various types of human beings who were attracted to Socrates and the differing motivations or hopes they had in seeking out his company. Xenophon thus brings to light, with his customary good humor and light touch, the character of Socrates' circle. At the same time, the *Symposium* presents questions central to Socratic philosophy with remarkable brevity and—again—humor. To come to see those questions, however, readers must first be willing to immerse themselves in the details, even the seemingly frivolous details, of this the most lighthearted of Xenophon's Socratic writings, for only a combination of lightheartedness and seriousness will reveal Xenophon's aim. What follows is intended to be merely an introductory outline of some of the most striking features of the dialogue.

Xenophon's Introductory Statement and the Opening Scenes

The *Symposium* begins rather abruptly with a concise statement of purpose: "But in my opinion, not only are the serious deeds of gentlemen worth recalling, but so too are their deeds done in times of

This essay has benefited from the analysis of the *Symposium* in Leo Strauss, *Xenophon's Socrates* (Ithaca: Cornell University Press, 1972).

play. I wish to make clear those deeds at which I was present and on the basis of which I make this judgment" (1.1).[1] In the first place, then, Xenophon aims at a certain elevation or rehabilitation of the playful, and this implies that such a rehabilitation is both necessary and worthwhile. The very word for "play" in Greek (*paidia*) indicates its relation to "child" (*pais*); it runs the risk of being identified with a kind of childishness and as such is not obviously a worthwhile object of concern for gentlemen. Xenophon's very attempt to elevate the playful may even suggest something of a break from the gentlemanly point of view: "But in my opinion, . . ." Why, then, might such a recollection of and, presumably, a further reflection on playful deeds be worthwhile? With a view to what end or aim is Xenophon concerned to recount this evening's doings and sayings?

One may begin from the observation that the *Symposium* is a kind of companion or counterpart to Xenophon's *Hellenica,* a book concerned with the very serious deeds of gentlemen, above all in times of war.[2] And in that serious book, Socrates appears only once, "Socrates the son of Sophroniscus," as he is called, and he there comes to sight as a dutiful and law-abiding citizen. About his thought we learn nothing. When gentlemen are at their most serious, when they are called upon to act as political men, Socrates appears only at the margins. In the *Symposium,* by contrast, Socrates is so to speak everywhere: he dominates the dialogue.

To see somewhat more clearly the possible antagonism between the playful gentlemanliness of Socrates and its serious counterpart, it may be helpful to consider an extreme statement of the gentlemanly contempt for what is playful, given in the *Cyropaedia* by a certain Aglaïtadas—a "most serious man" (*Cyr.* 2.2.16)—on the occasion, as it happens, of a dinner party (*Cyr.* 2.1.30ff.). Aglaïtadas there states his preference for crying over laughing on the grounds that what may be called moral education depends on crying, that is, on punishment; it is by means of tears that fathers instill or contrive moderation in sons, teachers the good objects of study in children, and the laws justice in citizens. The austere gentleman Aglaïtadas thus identifies as the core of his opposition to the playful the demands of moral education or of that education to justice and moderation whose efficacy would seem

[1] Except where noted, references are to the *Symposium* by chapter and section.
[2] See Leo Strauss, *Xenophon's Socrates* (Ithaca: Cornell University Press, 1972), 143.

to depend on the prospect of punishment. This must be contrasted with the education evident throughout Xenophon's Socratic writings: Socratic education seems to have more in common with laughter than with tears, as is clear not least in the *Symposium* itself; whereas according to Aglaïtadas, "the one who instills laughter in his friends acts much less worthily than does the one who makes his friends cry" (*Cyr.* 2.2.14), according to Xenophon, Socrates "profited those who spent time with him no less when he was playful than when serious" (*Mem.* 4.1.1; cf. also 1.3.8). This suggests that there could be an education that depends on something other than the threat of punishment—on, for example, the promise of the pleasures of understanding—and that is therefore education in a deeper sense. The moral education of the gentleman, then, may not be the whole or even the highest part of Socratic instruction. To put this another way, Socrates spent the entirety of his adult life in pursuit of education (*paideia*) or of that which is, according to the gentleman, the activity proper only to the young (cf. Plato *Gorgias* 485a4–e2). Since Socrates seems never to have ceased wondering "whatever in the world gentlemanliness may be" (8.3), the whole of his life is in a sense playful or lacking in seriousness: Socrates' life seems to have been devoted to the serious *inquiry* into what virtue (gentlemanliness) is, and as a result he had neither the time nor the capacity to *act* seriously. Moreover, just as Socrates' serious thought or inquiry seems lacking in seriousness from the gentlemanly point of view, so too the serious deeds of gentlemen, in the absence of an adequate reflection on gentlemanliness, would seem deficient in seriousness to Socrates. If, then, Socrates at his most serious is nonetheless playful in the eyes of a gentleman, and vice versa, perhaps the playful is a point of contact between the gentleman and the philosopher: by recollecting the playful deeds in question, Xenophon may earn for himself a freedom or license to present the serious playfulness of Socrates in an atmosphere not altogether inimical to it.

As the dialogue opens, the magnificent Great Panathenaic Games are underway, and Callias is just returning from a horse race with his young beloved, Autolycus, who is a recent victor in no less than the pancratium, an all-out sport combining wrestling and boxing. They, along with the boy's father, Lycon, and Niceratus, son of the most prominent general of Athens, are heading off to one of Callias' homes, in the Athenian port of the Piraeus. Among those out and about is Socrates, together with four of his associates (Critoboulus,

Hermogenes, Antisthenes, and Charmides), although we do not learn what they are doing or are about to do. Presumably they have no firm commitments, for, despite an initial reluctance, they agree to join Callias in the feast planned for Autolycus and his father.

In what is one of his longest editorial comments, Xenophon describes the scene once inside Callias' home: all eyes are riveted on the young Autolycus on account of his beauty, accompanied as it was at that time by bashfulness and moderation (1.8–11, beg.). One might well think, on the basis of what takes place, that beauty is something regal or kingly, for it rules those present with a firm hand. Callias' party in fact begins in somber silence (1.11, beg; 13, end). We do not know whether Xenophon's own silence at this point is due to the effects on him of Autolycus' beauty or whether it has a different cause, for Xenophon remained silent the entire evening. Whether or not seeing such beauty reduced Xenophon to silence, it clearly induced him to reflect on the power of beauty over the human soul and in particular the soul under the sway of eros; Xenophon himself, in other words, was not simply overcome by the sight of the boy's beauty (1.8–10). This initial description of Autolycus does serve to establish beauty and eros as important themes for the evening, themes to which Socrates and his companions return.

The spell cast by Autolycus is not broken by Philippus the jester, much as he attempts to do so, and only his failure provides a modicum of levity (1.16). Philippus remarks in passing that since laughter has perished among human beings, his services are no longer desired. The arrival of the uninvited but named jester is soon complemented by that of the unnamed but invited entertainer from Syracuse who brings with him two girls, one a flute-player, the other an acrobatic dancer, as well as a boy who both dances and plays the harp (*cithara*). The stage is thus set for the drinking party to begin.

Virtue, Knowledge, and Pride

After the necessary preliminaries, the flutist and the boy perform (2.1). Socrates then sets the action of the dialogue in motion by complimenting Callias on the perfect dinner they are enjoying, enhanced as it is by the most pleasant sights and sounds. Perhaps Socrates is about to have Callias fulfill his promise to say many wise things (1.6; cf. 3.3); Socrates at any rate furnishes his host with the opportunity to add to this list of pleasures one that has been altogether lacking so far, the pleasure of good conversation. To say the least, Callias does not avail himself of that opportunity: "What then if someone brings us some perfume so that we may enjoy ourselves amidst pleasant odors as well?" (2.3) (Earlier Xenophon had remarked that, before coming to Callias' house, some had exercised and taken a rubdown, others also a bath; presumably some had exercised but not bathed [1.7].) Socrates nevertheless refuses to let go the possibility of elevating the proceedings. He simply speaks of what interests him most within the limits imposed on him by his host: the virtue of one's soul is discussed from the point of view of how one's body smells.

According to Socrates, perfume is improper for a real man, the oil of the gymnasium being the proper scent, because once perfume is applied, every free man and slave immediately smells alike. The ease with which the line between slave and free may be blurred is surprising, and Lycon the father is understandably concerned to know of what those who no longer frequent the gymnasiums—the mature men—ought to smell. Socrates replies, "Of gentlemanliness, by Zeus!" This amounts to saying that gentlemen ought to smell of gentlemanliness, and Lycon accordingly asks where this scent may be obtained. In his reply, Socrates has recourse to a poet (Theognis) who says that "from the good you will be taught good things." Lycon is apparently pleased by this, since he asks his son whether he hears what has been said. Before Autolycus can respond, however, Socrates speaks for the boy and proves that indeed he has not only listened to this advice but acts on it as well. For when Autolycus wished to carry off the prize at the Games, he in consultation with his father decided who was best at this and trained with that man. Autolycus will do the same, Socrates says, when he decides to carry off the prize in virtue. Despite difficulties in the text, Socrates here seems to imply that Autolycus has yet to pay sufficient attention to virtue (see also 8.38) and that his father, who should be consulted in choosing a teacher of virtue, is presumably not adequate as a teacher of virtue himself. Being a champion athlete, however, Autolycus surely smells of the oil of the gymnasium, the smell appropriate to virtuous men. Is Autolycus closer to the slave who conceals his slavishness by means of the scents of the gymnasia than to the true gentleman who smells as he does on account of his exertions over a long period of time? However absurd or laughable the standard may be with a view to which the education of the young to virtue is here discussed, the issues connected with that education are in no way laughable; the figure at the center of this discussion is the father, Lycon, one of Socrates' three official accusers (Plato *Apol.* 36a9), the presence of whom is sufficient to remind us that Socrates was put to death on a charge of corrupting the young, that is, of leading them to vice rather than to virtue.

The mention of "virtue" causes something of a controversy to erupt concerning its teachability. Socrates is nevertheless reluctant to pounce on this typically Socratic question, and he suggests instead that they pay attention to the performance at hand, namely to that of the acrobatic dancer. Socrates concludes on the basis of the girl's routine that, with some qualifications, the feminine nature is not inferior to a man's and that "if someone among you has a wife, let him be confident in teaching her whatever he might want her to know in dealing with her" (2.9). Socrates thus returns, in a manner suitable to the proceedings, to the question of virtue: it would indeed seem to be teachable. And yet as the heavy-handed Antisthenes points out, Socrates himself has been singularly unsuccessful in teaching his own wife, Xanthippe. If arguably the greatest teacher known to mankind could not teach his spouse, is virtue really teachable? The acrobatic dancer next performs a feat so daring—a leap through a dagger-studded hoop—that Socrates is compelled to conclude that "even courage [manliness] is teachable" (2.12). The virtue which the acrobatic performer thus displays—and which would seem to be a product of habituation or constant practice—does seem teachable, and the Syracusan here seems to be a better teacher of virtue so understood than is Socrates. It remains a question, however, whether virtue can be taught by more elevated means, above all by reason (*logos*); the answer to this question would at the same time be an answer to the question of the rationality of moral virtue (cf. *Mem.* 1.2.19–23). It is safest to conclude, on the basis of these playful passages, only that the question of the teachability and hence of the rationality of virtue is of concern to Socrates. It seems clear too that, even if virtue is itself teachable, it does not follow that all can be taught it: Socrates' attempts to teach Xanthippe perhaps show the limits to the power of reasonable instruction (consider also 2.24–26 in the light of 27; 7.1–2).

Despite the availability of these pleasant diversions, the guests decide, largely at the urging of Socrates, to entertain as well as to benefit themselves by stating "whatever good thing each knows," or "what each believes is the most valuable thing he knows" (3.3), a proposal that undergoes a final alteration, at the hands of Callias, to become simply what each prides himself on, knowledge or not (3.4). All take their turn doing so (chapter 3), and then each in turn explains or justifies himself (chapter 4).

Callias begins by stating that he is most proud of his capacity "to make human beings better" (3.4). This proves to mean that by giving people money he relieves them of the need to commit injustice so as to obtain "the necessities" (4.2). As becomes clear in his exchange with Antisthenes, this capacity to make others better is of no manifest benefit to Callias himself. Indeed, he often incurs the enmity rather than the gratitude of those he has helped (4.2–4). We hear next from Niceratus, who prides himself on his capacity to recite from memory the whole of the *Iliad* and the *Odyssey* (3.5–6). According to Niceratus, thorough knowledge of Homer supplies knowledge of human affairs, for "wisest Homer wrote about pretty much all human things." And like Callias, Niceratus believes that he can benefit others: "I would like you to hear from me too in what respects you'll become better if you associate with me" (4.6).

The case of Critoboulus, who speaks next (3.7), is somewhat more complicated. Although under questioning from Socrates he claims that the beauty on which he prides himself is indeed capable of improving those present, we see in the elaboration of his contention that his beauty permits him easily to acquire "good things" for himself while it at the same time leads those who fall under its sway to care about "every virtue" (4.10–28). Critoboulus' point of pride, then, is good both for himself and for others.

Antisthenes (3.8) claims to pride himself on his "wealth," for although he is in fact very poor—he has very little money and no land—he is "wealthy" insofar as he has learned to maximize the pleasure he receives from the least expensive sources. The "wealth" of his soul is such that his body receives no less pleasure from cheap wine, inexpensive clothing, and easy gratification as do others from their more costly goods or pursuits. Antisthenes is thus the sole beneficiary of the "wealth" on which he prides himself, although he is willing to share his understanding with anyone, just as Socrates had done with him.[3] Charmides, the next speaker, complements Antisthenes insofar as he prides himself on his poverty, although his poverty is in no way metaphorical (3.9). He explains that when he was a wealthy man in Athens, he was burdened by many fears and concerns, but now that he has been deprived of his properties abroad and does not reap the benefits of those at home, he is carefree and at leisure. Among other things, Charmides feels like a tyrant in democratic Athens now that he is at least a nominal member of the *demos*, whereas previously he was compelled to obey the powers that be in the manner of a slave (4.29–33). And not least, Charmides notes that, "they used to reproach me when I was wealthy because I associated with Socrates, but now that I have become poor, it's no longer of any concern to anyone."

After the mention of Socrates by Antisthenes and Charmides, the only ones to have done so, we hear from Socrates himself. Asked what it is he prides himself on, Socrates drew up his face "in a very solemn manner [and] said, 'On pimping' " (3.10). As Xenophon reports, those present laughed. Socrates goes on to explain that he does not in fact practice the art in question, but this explanation requires some qualification, for in the course of his long speech in chapter 8 Socrates explicitly acts as a "pimp" between Callias and the city of Athens (8.39–43). The long speech in question culminates, that is, in Socrates' attempt to supply to Callias' weak or at any rate ambiguous attachment to moral virtue a new, more secure foundation by channeling Callias' extremely erotic nature into political endeavors meant to win him the respect not only of his fellow citizens but above all of his young beloved, Autolycus (consider 8.42). This exhortation to take virtue more seriously and to tend to the affairs of the city is greeted enthusiastically by Callias, and he indeed became

[3] For all of Antisthenes' crudity, he has nonetheless seen *something* of the character of Socratic continence: cf. 4.37–38, 41, 44 with, e.g., *Apol.* 18 and *Mem.* 4.5.9. It goes almost without saying that the end with a view to which Socrates makes these calculations differs from Antisthenes': cf. 4.38, end and 41 beg. with *Mem.* 4.5.6, beg.

a statesman and military commander, as Xenophon tells us in the *Hellenica* (4.5.13, 14; 5.4.22; 6.3.2ff.; cf. *Symp.* 1.4, end). Unfortunately, Callias was incompetent (*Hellenica* 6.3.2ff.), and the sole instance of Socrates' pimping is therefore a failure. This accords with the fact that it is one of the "playful deeds" presented in the *Symposium*.

Although Socrates is himself uninterested in practicing the art of the pimp, the man to whom he hands over his art, Antisthenes, is pleased to do so, despite an initial hesitation (4.61–64). Socrates is certain that Antisthenes will practice this art well because he has already shown that he is an able practitioner of the attendant art of the "go-between," having brought Socrates together, not with the city or even with fellow citizens, but with certain interesting foreigners (the Heraclean stranger and Aeschylus the Phliasian) who have been beneficial to Socrates and he to them. Socrates refuses to practice the art of the pimp seriously because he is already the beneficiary of the art akin to it; he is more interested in being brought together with certain individuals than he is in performing any comparable service for others or for the city.[4] At most, Socrates acts as a "pimp" only for himself, as Antisthenes later points out (8.5). One may draw this conclusion: both Antisthenes and Charmides pride themselves on something of which they are the main beneficiaries, and however beneficial and even public-spirited Socrates' art may be, he prefers either to practice it only for himself or to be benefited by an art akin to his own.

The conversation subsequently turns from Socrates to Philippus the jester (3.11), who prides himself on his capacity to make people laugh, that is, to benefit them in a manner. We hear next from Lycon and Autolycus, who pride themselves on one another (3.12–13), but since it would be inappropriate to ask them to explain or justify their point of pride, neither delivers a long speech in chapter 4.[5] We hear finally from Hermogenes who prides himself on the power and

[4] Consider here the possibility mentioned but not taken up at 4.59 according to which the best "pimp" would be one capable of making a person pleasing to one rather than to many. If Socrates is indeed "always, together with the city, a fellow lover of those who are by nature good and who seek out virtue ambitiously" (8.41), one must wonder whether he is not in competition with the city for those most promising souls.

[5] They are replaced in chapter 4 by the Syracusan, who prides himself on "fools," i.e., those who come to see his "puppet shows" and thus support him.

virtue of his friends and that, being of the sort they are, they care for him. If one leaves aside for the time being the complicated case of what proves to be Hermogenes' divine friendship—we will return to him later—one detects a change in the character of the pride of each of the speakers as one approaches and then departs from Socrates: from the selflessness of Callias and Niceratus, to the "in-between" case of Critoboulus, to its opposite in Charmides, and then again from the pleasantries of Philippus to the noble pride of father for son and son for father.

Eros

Since our aim is to come to understand something of the nature of Socrates in and through the *Symposium,* we must try to see Socrates in his relation to *eros* or love, arguably *the* theme of the work. Socrates' main speech in chapter 8 begins as a praise of the god or "daimon" *Eros,* and he explicitly affirms there that he is himself a lover: "I can't mention a time when I wasn't in love with someone" (8.2). In the *Memorabilia,* however, Xenophon tells us that Socrates "often said that he was in love with someone," this being an example of one of Socrates' instructive jokes (cf. *Mem.* 4.1.2, beg., with 1.1, end; cf. also Plato *Gorgias* 481d1–4 with *Symposium* 216d2–4, 217b7–218d5). And Socrates' long speech on *eros* is singularly unerotic in any ordinary sense; he castigates the love that includes love of the body and praises the chaste love of friends because only it leads one to be concerned with the virtue of one's own soul: "the greatest good for one yearning to make of his beloved a good friend is that he himself must practice virtue" (8.27). Thus not a love affair but the concern for excellence to which one is led by it is the crucial consideration according to Socrates. The speech that begins as a praise of *eros* culminates in a praise of the health of one's own soul.

We also learn that Charmides came across Socrates at home early one morning, alone, dancing (2.19). So strange did this appear to Charmides that he feared for Socrates' sanity, but Socrates allayed that fear by explaining that dancing is preferable to gymnastics with a view to maintaining a sound physical condition because (among other reasons) one need not find a partner to practice it (2.17–19). Socrates is a radically solitary figure, so much so that he might at first sight appear mad to any average observer. Callias, for example, wonders whether he couldn't come along and partner Socrates should the latter receive dance lessons from the Syracusan. Callias assumes that Socrates is as in need of a partner as he himself is, but this request receives no reply; it is quietly dropped because, to repeat, Socrates requires no partner (2.20, end).

Since Socrates' long speech in chapter 8 appears to be critical only of pederasty, one might suppose that Socrates takes a much kindlier view of other manifestations of *eros* (consider, however, 8.29); Socrates is, after all, a married man (2.10). And yet as we have already had occasion to see, after Socrates exhorts the married men among them to be confident in teaching their wives whatever they might wish them to know, Antisthenes asks his indelicate question: "How is it, Socrates, that while recognizing this, you too do not teach Xanthippe, but deal with the most difficult of present-day women, and, I suppose, of those past and future too?" Socrates accounts for his marriage, in a suitably lighthearted way, by explaining its utility: if he could learn to deal with Xanthippe, he could deal with anybody (2.10). That his marriage is not a union of two lovers is clearly implied at the end of the *Symposium*, for after the married men among those present rode off to be with their wives, spurred on by the display of genuine love between the two young performers, Xenophon remarks as follows: "Socrates and the others who remained went off with Callias to join Lycon and his son for a walk" (9.7, end). The husband Socrates really belongs among the unmarried men; he is a de facto bachelor.[6]

In order to understand Socrates better insofar as he is not a lover ordinarily understood, it may be helpful to sketch the state of soul of his opposite, the lover Critoboulus, who is head over heels in love with a certain Cleinias (4.10ff.). Critoboulus longs to look upon

[6] This view of Socrates as a nonlover is confirmed in the strongest terms by Friedrich Nietzsche: "I imagine that a married philosopher belongs in comedy, and as for that great exception, Socrates, it would almost seem that the malicious Socrates got married in a spirit of irony, precisely in order to prove that contention" (*Genealogy of Morals*, 3.7; cf. also *Human, All Too Human* §433). See also Leo Strauss, *On Tyranny*, rev. and expanded ed. (New York: Free Press, 1991), 196.

and always to be with his love; he is burdened by the night and by sleep because he does not see Cleinias then, and he knows the greatest gratitude to the day and to the sun because they reveal Cleinias to him. He would walk through fire with his love and would prefer to risk his life for him than to live risk-free without him. Critoboulus thus longs to be with his love and would rather risk dying than be without him (4.12, 14, 16). Socrates claims in the sequel to have moderated Critoboulus' infatuation ("I've already seen him blink!"), despite the fact that, as he fears, Critoboulus has gone so far as to kiss Cleinias: "there is no more fearsome a spark of love than this, for it is insatiable and supplies certain sweet hopes" (4.24). Now it would be wrong to suppose that the "hopes" in question are only or even primarily those of bodily gratification, for such desire, although an aspect of *eros*, is by no means the whole of *eros*. What, then, are the hopes characteristic of *eros*, hopes that would as such be present in Critoboulus and, presumably, absent from Socrates?

In the opening scenes, Callias welcomes the arrival of Philippus the jester amid the hushed dining of the guests: "Take a couch, . . . for those present, as you see, are full of seriousness and are perhaps rather in need of laughter" (1.13). After two failed attempts to make the guests laugh, Philippus laments that, since laughter has perished among human beings, his business has come to ruin. Who will want a jester under such circumstances? And he is incapable of taking up another line of work: "For I, at least, could no more be serious than become immortal" (1.15). Seriousness is as far from Philippus as immortality, and as this passing remark suggests (unwittingly to be sure), seriousness and immortality seem to belong together. For as was to some extent evident already in the remarks of Critoboulus, *eros* would seem to be or to include the longing for a kind of "wholeness" or completion, the desire to know the contentment found only in the transcending of our merely fragmentary, needy, and defective selves, in the self-forgetting union with another that, being true happiness, we hope will last forever. Thus Critoboulus longs to be with Cleinias night and day, for only then is he free of longing and truly happy, and he is willing to run any risks for Cleinias without fear of the consequences for himself; Critoboulus the lover believes that he could walk unscathed through fire with his beloved (4.16). The love he feels for Cleinias, that is, fosters in Critoboulus the "sweet hope" of an everlasting or immortal happiness.

Xenophon presents this character of *eros* in a beautiful manner by means of the final performance of the Syracusan's troupe (9.2ff.). The handsome young boy, playing the part of Dionysus, courts the young girl, dressed as the bride Ariadne, but it soon becomes clear that the love they are portraying between these two is genuinely and deeply felt by the performers for one another; their portrayal permits the young lovers to kiss and thus "to do what they had long been desiring" (9.6). Might it be that, at the very moment when the spectators realize that the performers are genuinely in love with one another, or when the performers cease to be the divine "Dionysus" and his beloved "Ariadne" in the eyes of the spectators, they in fact become, or at any rate approach, immortals? Xenophon refers to them both by the names of those they represent (9.2–6), and at that moment, they would seem to be participating in immortality to the extent possible for human beings. Let us recall that Socrates himself identifies *eros* as a "daimon," that is, as that which is the bond or link between mortals and immortals, between "Ariadne" and "Dionysus" (8.1).

Nobility and Beauty

None of this is meant to deny the fact, of which there is ample evidence, that Socrates is concerned with and moved by (physical) beauty. If Socrates is not a lover in any ordinary sense, neither is he a cold fish (cf. *Cyr.* 7.4.22; cf. also *Mem.* 3.11.1 with *Cyr.* 5.1.4–18). In fact, after Socrates warns those present that "it is necessary for one who will be capable of moderation to abstain from the kisses of those in their bloom" (4.26), Charmides blows the whistle: "But why in the world, Socrates, do you spook us, your friends, away from the beautiful ones in this way, when I saw you yourself—yes, by Apollo!—when both you and Critoboulus were searching for something in the same book at the gymnasium, your head against his head, your bare shoulder against his bare shoulder?" (4.27; consider also Plato, *Charmides* 155d3–4). To this rather embarrassing query, Socrates replies as follows: "Ah hah! So that's why, like someone who'd been bitten by a wild beast, I felt a pain in my shoulder for more than five days and why I thought there was something like a sting in my heart! But now, Critoboulus, I proclaim before all these witnesses that you are not to lay hold of me until your beard is as full as the hair on your head!" (4.28). Although attracted to and pleased by the presence of beauty, then, Socrates is himself so moderate or continent as regards the pleasures of Aphrodite (*Mem.* 1.2.1) that he runs no risk of being diverted from his principal interest or activity by indulging his taste for beauty; such continence evidently renders Socrates capable of withstanding the charms of those in their bloom: after all, Socrates is capable of reading even while touching the bare shoulder of the handsome Critoboulus.

Socrates' peculiarities in these regards cannot be understood apart from a consideration of the beauty of the soul, that is, of nobility.[7] With this in mind, let us turn first to the "beauty contest" between Socrates and Critoboulus that takes up the whole of the fifth and central chapter of the *Symposium*. Critoboulus initially proposes it in the course of his long speech: "I know well that right now I could more quickly persuade this boy here and the girl to kiss me while remaining silent than you could even if you were to say many wise things." "What's this?" Socrates replies, "are you making these boasts on the grounds that you are more beautiful [noble] than I?" (4.18–19). Socrates thus transforms what was at the outset to be a contest between his wisdom and Critoboulus' beauty into one concerning beauty (nobility) alone. Socrates evidently prefers to conceal his wisdom and to reveal his "beauty"—what is in fact his ugliness, as the lamp that Socrates has brought up close makes clear and as no less than Xenophon himself confirms (5.9; 4.19, end). At the same time, one cannot dismiss out of hand the possibility that Socrates does indeed reveal something of his wisdom by drawing attention to his ugliness, or that there may be something ugly (ignoble) about Socrates' wisdom.

As the beauty contest proper proceeds, Socratic wisdom is not in fact wholly absent, for when Socrates asks Critoboulus how it is that

[7] The Greek (*to kalon*) may be translated as beauty, fineness, or nobility, an ambiguity that must be kept in mind throughout.

many different things (e.g., human beings, oxen, shields, spears) can all nonetheless be beautiful (noble), Critoboulus gives a Socratic answer. Things are beautiful or noble if "they are well wrought with a view to the tasks for which we acquire them, or if they are well adapted by nature with a view to the things we need" (5.4; cf. *Mem.* 3.8.4–7; 4.6.8). What is beautiful is thus inseparable from considerations of what is good and, according to Socrates, there is nothing good that is not as such good for some need (*Mem.* 3.8.1–3). The beautiful or noble is, in short, indistinguishable from the useful. It follows that even a dung basket is noble or beautiful if it is well made with a view to its tasks. As in the *Memorabilia*, then, Socrates here (together with Critoboulus) seems to deny that there is a class of noble things that are such apart from considerations of their utility.

As soon as this contest has concluded, Socrates draws attention to the fact that the unusually pious Hermogenes is displeased with the proceedings (6.1). The playful contest or quarrel between Critoboulus and Socrates concerning nobility, a contest Socrates loses by unanimous decision, is thus followed immediately by a somewhat less playful contest or quarrel between Hermogenes and Socrates. And Socrates loses this contest too: he is compelled to admit that he has been "refuted" by Hermogenes (6.3).[8] Hermogenes' silence cannot be

[8] Of all the figures presented in the *Symposium*, Hermogenes seems to occupy a peculiarly important place in Xenophon's works. The bulk of the *Apology of Socrates to the Jury* is seen through his eyes, and the exchange between Socrates and Hermogenes in the *Symposium* (at 4.50 and context) is the only one Xenophon identifies as having been entirely serious (cf. 4.29). Hermogenes is mentioned three separate times in the *Memorabilia*, more than any other figure in the *Symposium*, and he is the only one of these who is listed in the *Memorabilia* also as being an "associate" or "student" of Socrates (1.2.48; 2.10.3ff.; 4.8.4). In this list as well as in that with which the *Symposium* begins (1.3), Hermogenes occupies literally the central place, and, as we have just seen, only Hermogenes has the honor of having Socrates admit that he has been refuted by him. Still, if Hermogenes' prominence is easy to discern, its basis is not. There is little rapport, let alone intimacy, evident in the *Symposium* between Hermogenes and the Socratic circle: Hermogenes is the last to be asked what it is he prides himself on—even Philippus is asked before him—and when he replies that it is on his friends and their care for him, without having yet mentioned the gods, Xenophon says that "all" looked at Hermogenes and "many" asked who these friends might be (3.14); those present do not consider themselves, at any rate, to be among his caring friends. Even the evidence supplied by the *Memorabilia* is more ambiguous than would first seem, for to be an "associate" of Socrates may be very far from being a "friend" or "companion" (cf. *Mem.* 1.4.1, end). The context in which Xenophon makes this list requires that he emphasize those of Socrates' associates who never had any political ambition and who never got into any trouble. Further, after Socrates has taken Her-

taken for acquiescence, and Socrates, so far from being satisfied with that silence, knows that the failure to come to terms with Hermogenes constitutes his own refutation. The mere assertion of the identity of the noble things with the good or useful things, in the absence of any argument as to the soundness of that identification (5), leads rightly and necessarily to the refutation of Socrates at the hands of a Hermogenes (6.3). Xenophon in the *Symposium* (and *Memorabilia*) is evidently willing to present Socrates' "utilitarian" view of nobility while being at the same time unwilling to present the arguments Socrates must have seen in order to find his way to that view and therefore also reasonably to reject any competing views of beauty or nobility.

Socrates' subsequent exchanges with the Syracusan entertainer (6.6–7.5) may shed some light on this difficulty for, in contrast to the rather muted quarrel between Socrates and Hermogenes, the criticisms leveled by the Syracusan are bluntness itself (6.6). Although he merely repeats the slander first presented publicly by Aristophanes in his *Clouds*,[9] that slander would seem to touch on the most fundamental questions. The Syracusan, being envious of Socrates, asks him whether he isn't the so-called Thinker, and in particular the Thinker "of the things aloft." This is tantamount to an accusation of atheism, for the scientific or philosophic inquiry into the heavens was held to be impious because it implied a denial of the divinity of the heavenly bodies (e.g., Plato *Apol.* 18b6–c2; 19c2–d7; 26d1–e4). Socrates himself makes the thrust of the charge explicit: "Do you know anything loftier than the gods?" Socrates thus implies that his own inquiries are altogether pious because they are concerned precisely with the gods, the "loftiest" things (cf. *Mem.* 4.7.6)—this in

mogenes to task for being overly silent amid the festivities, he suggests that if Hermogenes were to speak while gesticulating like the flute-girl, to the accompaniment of her music, his speeches or arguments would then be pleasant. Apparently Socrates finds them unpleasant when not so adorned.

[9] Aristophanes *Clouds* 144ff.; see also *Oeconomicus*, 11.3. The *Clouds* was first presented in 423 B.C., about two years before the dramatic date of the *Symposium* (421 B.C.). A more or less precise dating of the latter is possible because of Autolycus' victory in the Games, thought to have been held in 421. The comic poet Eupolis produced his *Autolycus*, apparently mocking the boy's victory, his parents, and his relationship with Callias, in 420 (see Athenaeus 216d and Ian C. Storey, "Dating and Re-dating Eupolis," *Phoenix* 44 [1990]: 28ff., as well as J. K. Davies, *Athenian Propertied Families* [Oxford: Clarendon Press, 1971], 331 [but cf. 260], and O. J. Todd's introductory essay to the *Banquet* in the Loeb Library edition [531]).

contrast to the idle talk, which the Syracusan repeats as well, that Socrates does not in fact care about the gods at all (6.7). However much the pious, Socratic Hermogenes may frown on Socrates' playfulness (4.23), he surely would not go so far as to charge him with atheism, and the kinship between Hermogenes and the Syracusan as critics or "accusers" of Socrates in chapter 6 is only superficial.[10] Socrates' principal defense against the charge of atheism is to make what he admits is a bad pun, although he does thereby succeed in changing the focus of the Syracusan's attack from Socrates' being a "Thinker" of the things excessively great for human beings to his being concerned with the things beneath human concern: "Tell me how many flea's feet you are from me, for they say you measure these things" (6.8; cf. Aristophanes *Clouds* 144–47).

Socrates is prevented from replying because he must stave off the counterattacks attempted by Antisthenes and Philippus; only in the next chapter, after Socrates has restored order not by means of any speech (*logos*) but by means of a song, does he have the opportunity to address the Syracusan: "Syracusan, it's likely, just as you say, that I really am a 'Thinker' " (7.2). Socrates proceeds first to offer a critique of the performances thus far,[11] then to suggest a new program that would be both less taxing on the performers and more delightful to the audience. In the course of doing so, Socrates admits not only that he is a "Thinker" but that his thoughts include the "wonders" of natural science: "why in the world does the lamp supply light by having a brilliant flame, while brass, which is brilliant as well, does not produce light but reflects off itself images of other things? And how is it that oil, while being wet, increases the flame, but water, because it is wet, extinguishes the fire?" (cf. the theological importance of "light" at 6.7 with its scientific counterpart at 7.4).[12] And Socrates' boldness is rewarded. The Syracusan not only

[10] Both are in fact accusers only half-seriously: Lycon is the true accuser.

[11] Among other things, Socrates in effect retracts his earlier compliment of the boy's dance (cf. 7.3, end, with 2.15), thus confirming Charmides' suspicion that Socrates was really more interested in the dance teacher than the dance (2.15, end).

[12] Consider also Xenophon's as-it-were parenthetical admissions concerning Socrates' interest in and knowledge of natural science at *Mem.* 1.1.11, middle; 4.6.1; 4.7.5, 7 (also Plato *Phaedo* 95dff.). As for Xenophon's most conspicuous denial of Socrates' interest in natural science (*Mem.* 1.1.10–16), it must suffice to note that these passages are explicitly devoted to a defense of Socrates and simply contradict the pas-

ceases to be annoyed with Socrates, he is in fact reconciled with him; he gladly hears Socrates' criticisms and profits from them (cf. 7.5 with 9.2ff.).

If the exchanges between Socrates and Hermogenes highlight a possible difficulty with, or at any rate challenge to, Socrates' understanding of the world, those between Socrates and the Syracusan would seem to bring out a certain strength or skill on Socrates' part. For although the Syracusan's objections are apparently moral ones—principally that the studies in which Socrates is engaged are indecent because premised on the denial of the existence of the gods—the Syracusan is strangely unperturbed when Socrates admits that, to repeat, he is indeed a "Thinker" whose concerns include natural science. What seems to be decisive in the eyes of the Syracusan is Socrates' skillful advice on how best to please those present. Perhaps the quarrel between the two, then, concerns not so much matters of morality as of rhetoric; it may concern above all the proper presentation of their respective "wonders"—a term that is applied both to the objects of contemplation and to the Syracusan's performances (e.g., 2.1, 7.3–4). Socrates in his exchanges with the Syracusan shows that he understands the art of "performance," that is, that he knows, with a view to one's audience, how best to present "wonders" to be looked upon (contemplated). In contrast to the preceding exchanges with Hermogenes, Socrates here proves to be a deft rhetorician; he understands that a song is sometimes more effective than an argument (*logos*). The Syracusan thus no longer has any ground of complaint: "But by Zeus, Socrates, you speak nobly, and I'll bring in performances that will please you all!"[13]

One might suppose that the Socrates who appears unconcerned with nobility apart from utility and who is accordingly refuted by

---

sages referred to above. Even in the argument in question, Xenophon admits that Socrates had private thoughts or judgments that as such could not be known publicly (cf. 1.1.10, beg., with 1.1.17, beg.).

[13] Leo Strauss has suggested that the Syracusan is in fact "Themistogenes of Syracuse," i.e., Xenophon himself: see Strauss's *Xenophon's Socrates*, 178; and "Xenophon's *Anabasis*," in *Studies in Platonic Political Philosophy* (Chicago: University of Chicago Press, 1983), 106. As for the identification of Themistogenes with Xenophon, see, e.g., Plutarch *De Gloria Atheniensium* 345e and Malcolm Maclaren, Jr., "Xenophon and Themistogenes," *Transactions and Proceedings of the Philological Association of America* 65 (1934): 240–47.

Hermogenes (5–6.5) is the "pre-Socratic" Socrates, the "Thinker" parodied by Aristophanes who may know the heavenly things but is woefully lacking in the comprehension of the human things, lacking in particular any adequate response to that understanding of the world according to which heaven and earth form an ordered whole because of the rule of benevolent gods (consider also Plato *Phaedo* 96aff.). On the other hand, it might well seem that the Socrates who rebuffs precisely the Aristophanic accusations of the Syracusan by showing that he has in fact given thought to "the loftiest things" as well as to the human things, and in particular to the necessity of adapting the presentation of "wonders" with a view to one's audience, is very much the (as-it-were) "post-Socratic" Socrates, that is, Socrates *after* his turn to moral and political investigations.

It would probably be more precise to say that, because Xenophon refuses to permit us to see directly the chain of reasoning Socrates followed in confronting the most impressive gentlemanly understanding of the world, he thereby suppresses also the turn in question: much more than in the *Memorabilia*, we see the continuity of Socrates' life; we see not only the persistence in it of a recalcitrance to an understanding of nobility apart from utility but also the true end with a view to which Socrates practiced his "utilitarian" calculations, namely his continued interest in natural science or in "what *each* of the beings is" and not, for example, the resolution of family squabbles (*Mem*. 4.6.1, emphasis added). To put this another way, we see in the *Symposium* both the position or predicament that led to Hermogenes' refutation and to Aristophanes' criticisms on the one hand (5)—"Socrates" abstracting from reflection on the noble things held to be irreducible to utility—and at least intimations of the position that is immune to that criticism on the other—"Socrates" for whom the noble things so understood (including and above all "the loftiest things") are or have been an object of reflection (6.6–7.5). And going together with this reflection on the loftiest things is a new interest in rhetoric, in the proper presentation of one's thought or wisdom.

Xenophon points to the importance of such reflection by presenting the reduction of nobility (beauty) to utility in such a way that the reader cannot help but doubt its adequacy. According to it, the lips of an ass would be most beautiful with a view to kissing because they are biggest and softest, Socrates' being next most beautiful, and those of the handsome young Critoboulus being the ugliest. The reader cannot help but wonder, in other words, whether there is not a category of the beautiful separable from the good (useful). This could mean a number of things, for example that beauty in at least some cases is not good but harmful either to those who behold it or to those who possess it: Socrates claims, after losing the beauty contest by unanimous decision, that Critoboulus' beauty is sufficient to "corrupt" judge and jury alike, just as the Syracusan fears that the beauty of his young boy has led some to wish to "corrupt" the lad (5.10, 4.52–53). But the reluctance to reduce nobility to considerations of utility is surely also, and more important, characteristic of those who maintain that there is a nobility that is higher or grander than what is good because useful, or who maintain, in other words, that nobility is choiceworthy apart from any calculation as to its possible utility. Callias' art of making human beings better, for example, is a worthwhile activity because of the good it bestows on others, despite the fact that it is harmful to himself. And in the *Memorabilia,* Socrates advises Pericles the son of the great Pericles on certain practical political measures and urges him to carry them out, for if he does so, "it will be noble for you and good for the city" (3.5.25–28). The service to one's city, then, is good for the city and noble for the individual; the noble and the good are here separate considerations, just as they are by implication in the very title "gentleman" (literally, "noble and good man"). As Aristotle says, the gentleman acts for the sake of what is noble, that is, not with a view to some further reward or recompense apart from the beauty of the actions themselves (e.g., *Eth. Nic.* 1120a23–24).

In the *Symposium,* Hermogenes is by far the most impressive spokesman of this view; he is according to Socrates a man who "melts away with love of gentlemanliness [nobility and goodness]." This serious concern for gentlemanliness proves to be inseparable from Hermogenes' friendship with the gods, and it therefore becomes necessary to try to understand the link between Hermogenes' serious love of nobility and that which he "exults in" most, the power and virtue of his friends the gods.

Nobility and Piety

Hermogenes begins his most comprehensive statement concerning his belief in the gods (4.46ff.) by making two observations: that all human beings, Greeks as well as barbarians, make use of prophecy to ask the gods what they ought to do and what not; and that all human beings ask the gods to avert wretched things and grant the good. On the basis of these observations he concludes: that Greeks and barbarians believe the gods know all things, present and future; and that all believe the gods can do good and evil. Hermogenes sums up the point by stating that the gods "know all things and are capable of all things" (4.48, beg.), and it is precisely these gods who are his friends and who look after him (4.48).

To begin with, there are a couple of peculiarities in Hermogenes' procedure. For from the fact (if such it be) that all believe *x*, Hermogenes concludes that *x* is so; one could compare this with Socrates' own, more cautious procedure at the beginning of his long speech in chapter 8, where he refuses to make any conclusions about the true Aphrodite and even about the true Zeus on the basis of conventional belief or practice (8.9). Second, it does not follow that all people believe the gods to be omnipotent (nor, again, that the gods are so in fact) from the observation that all human beings ask gods to grant good things and avert the evil: perhaps the gods can grant some goods but not all, just as they may be able to avert some evils but not all. The conclusion that the gods are omnipotent is Hermogenes' own: omnipotence presupposes omniscience, and most human beings "believe that the gods know some things but not others" (*Mem.* 1.1.19). And yet it is surely not an arbitrary conclusion, for Hermogenes believes also that the gods watch over him in everything he is about to do or wherever he may be about to set off, that they offer him signs as to what he should do, and that they reward and punish him in perfect accordance with his obedience to those signs. It would seem that only all-knowing and all-powerful gods could know the heart and mind of every individual at every moment and always assign to him in the proper manner his just due. As for the facts to which Hermogenes appeals and that are obviously so powerful to him, namely that the gods have made known to him their extraordinary care for him, Xenophon permits us to wonder whether, in one crucial case at least, the providence Hermogenes attributes to the gods is not due in fact to the calculations of Socrates. For in the *Memorabilia* we learn that Hermogenes is extremely poor, so much so that he is on the brink of utter ruin (2.10.2). Seeing this, Socrates went to a certain Diodorus and convinced him that it would be worth Diodorus' while to spend a little money and thus acquire an able and loyal servant in the person of Hermogenes: as Socrates says, in bad times good friends are cheap to acquire. Convinced of the shrewdness of this plan, Diodorus urged Socrates to approach Hermogenes, but Socrates understandably insisted that Diodorus do so himself. Thus Diodorus—whose name means "gift of Zeus"—appeared to Hermogenes out of the blue with an offer of desperately needed sustenance (for other doubts concerning the providence of the gods, consider 2.25; cf. also 5.6 [Socrates' divinely crafted nostrils that catch odors from all sides] in the light of *Mem.* 1.4.6, mid.).

However this may be, one can surely say of Hermogenes that, within the limits imposed by his poverty, he practices perfect gentlemanliness and, again within those limits, he serves the gods irreproachably (4.49; cf. *Mem.* 1.3.3). As Socrates says, "If, being of this sort, Hermogenes, you have them as friends, the gods too, it seems, are pleased by gentlemanliness [nobility and goodness]" (4.49, end). The nobility that transcends calculations of utility turns out to be supplemented and supported by gods who, in their perfect knowledge and capacity, see to it that the good of each is provided for. Hermogenes assures his well-being with the greatest imaginable security precisely by acting for the sake of what is noble in the spirit of perfect gentlemanliness, or by forgetting considerations of his own well-being. If the gods are pleased by nobility and goodness, it is sensible to be noble and good and hence to please providential gods (see also *Mem.* 4.3.17). There is a kinship between this understanding of the world and that characteristic of the lover Critoboulus who, in his very willingness to "forget" himself, to run any risk for the sake of his beloved, is nonetheless sustained by the sweet hope of attaining thereby his own everlasting happiness (consider also, e.g., Aristotle *Nic. Eth.* 1155b23–26; 1159a10–12; 1166a14–18). The sight of Cleinias' beauty inspires in Critoboulus hopes that are much the same as those Hermogenes entertains as a result of his confidence in his own nobility.

* * *

Not least among the merits of Xenophon's *Symposium* is that it encourages reflection on Socrates and the Socratic life beginning from and in the light of questions of immediate relevance and importance—of beauty, nobility, and love. Not least among its charms, moreover, is the graceful, lively humor that accompanies that reflection. This humor or lightheartedness can be appreciated fully, however, only in view of the fate, known to Xenophon, of the majority of the dialogue's participants.

Despite the apparent festivity in Athens and the jocularity of much of the banquet, these are on the whole hard times. The Peloponnesian War is now in its tenth year, and even if the Peace of Nicias is about to be or has just been concluded (Thucydides 5.20),[14] whatever hopes that truce may have engendered were soon struck down. Callias in time loses much of the fortune that makes possible the evening's splendor—he is called a "begging priest" in Aristotle's *Rhetoric* (1405a19–21)—and there are indications that he lost even his priesthood.[15] Both Niceratus and Autolycus are killed by order of the Thirty, a brutal oligarchy installed in Athens by Sparta at the end of the war, and it is reported that Niceratus' bride (2.3, 8.3) commits suicide upon hearing of her husband's death.[16] Charmides, on the other hand, becomes an active member of the similarly brutal Ten, ruling in the very place where the evening's festivities take place, the Piraeus (consider 4.32–33). Xenophon tells us of his subsequent death in battle (*Hellen.* 2.4.19). Finally, Socrates is put to death by Athens after having been accused, by Meletus, Anytus, and the Lycon here present, of impiety and of corrupting the young. Whether or not Lycon in turn suffered at the hands of Antisthenes in the backlash that followed Socrates' death, as Meletus and Anytus apparently did, is unknown (cf. Diogenes Laertius 6.9–10).

None of these facts prevented Xenophon the Socratic from writing a dialogue that is as far from tragedy as possible. The Socratic understanding of the world that issues in the apparent strangeness and even madness of Socrates seems to issue also in the most remarkable com-

[14] See also A. Rapaport, "Ad Xenophontis *Convivium* 1.1," *Eos* (1925): 134.

[15] See Davies, *Athenian Propertied Families*, 269.

[16] Hieronymus *adv. Jovinianum* 1.310 = *Patrologiae Cursus Completus, series Latina*, ed. J.-P. Migne, (Paris: Garnier, 1844), 23: 286b.

bination of toughness and delicacy, of seriousness and humor. That understanding appears to be a kind of inoculation against despair to the extent possible for human beings (consider Plutarch *Consolatio ad Apollonium* 33.11ff.), not despite but because of its willingness to see the world as it is. The example of Socrates suggests that, in order eventually so to see the world, one must begin with an examination of one's passionate longings and noble hopes, not in the spirit of a debunker but as one who wishes to do full justice to true nobility and goodness. The noble or beautiful things of most concern to Socrates are attractive as they are without addition or support, for merely beholding the objects of contemplation seems to be good in and of itself for the one who does so. Having no additional expectations from beauty, or making no additional demands on the world, Socrates is to a remarkable degree free of the reliance on the extraordinary means otherwise needed to fulfill them. And Xenophon therein permits us to begin to see for ourselves the true nobility of Socrates, for clarity of mind or freedom from self-contradiction, although perhaps rendering one immune to "certain sweet hopes," is surely not without a beauty or goodness of its own.

Contributors

Wayne Ambler is Associate Professor of Political Science at the University of Dallas.

Robert C. Bartlett is the Andrew W. Mellon Postdoctoral Fellow in the Departments of Political Science and Classics at Emory University.

Carnes Lord is Professor of Political Science at Adelphi University.

Thomas L. Pangle is Professor of Political Science at the University of Toronto.

Andrew Patch is a doctoral candidate in the Department of Political Science at the University of Toronto.

Index of Names